Divided Minds

DIVIDED MINDS

Twin Sisters and Their Journey Through Schizophrenia

PAMELA SPIRO WAGNER AND
CAROLYN S. SPIRO, M.D.

ST MARTINS GRIFFIN
New York

www.stmartins.com

Book Design by Mary A. Wirth

LIBRARY OF CONGRESS CATALOGING-IN-PUBLICATION DATA

Wagner, Pamela Spiro.
    Divided minds : twin sisters and their journey through schizophrenia / Pamela Spiro Wagner and Carolyn Spiro.
        p. cm.
    ISBN-13: 978-0-312-32065-2
    ISBN-10: 0-312-32065-5
    1. Wagner, Pamela Spiro—Mental health. 2. Spiro, Carolyn. 3. Schizophrenics—Connecticut—Biography. 4. Psychiatrists—Connecticut—Biography. 5. Twins—Connecticut—Biography. I. Spiro, Carolyn. II. Title.

RC514.W165 2005
362.196'898'00922746—dc22   2005002212

First St. Martin's Griffin Edition: August 2006

10 9 8 7 6 5 4 3 2 1

*For our parents,
our siblings, Philip and Martha,
and all families struggling with schizophrenia
and other brain diseases*

$\mathcal{A}$UTHORS' $\mathcal{N}$OTE

Other than our own names and the names of our immediate family members, most of the names of the people, hospitals, hospital units, and businesses included in this book have been changed. Some identifying details have also been changed and certain people, including some of the doctors and patients, are amalgamations. Conversations recounted from memory are expressed as dialogue.

"Dum Spiro, Spero."

WHILE I BREATHE, I HOPE.

DIVIDED MINDS

$\mathcal{P}$ROLOGUE

DECEMBER 29, 1999–Y2K MELTDOWN

Pamela

I barely remember the day the world ended.
Even now it replays like a grade-B movie.

> *Early morning shot, the sun is barely rising over tired-looking city streets. Cut to a small apartment bedroom on the top floor of a high-rise. Cigarettes overflow in half a dozen ashtrays; coffee cups, clothing, and books are strewn about. A middle-aged woman, distraught, smoking frantically, is half yelling half whispering on the phone to someone she calls Nina but doesn't seem to know well. There's a sudden hammering at the door. She puts down the phone, yells hoarsely, "Who's there? Go away!" More pounding, followed by sounds from the phone. She fumbles, brings the receiver back to her ear. "What are you talking about? Nina! You told me you wouldn't . . ." She's still protesting when the door is forced open. Paramedics and police quickly take over . . . FADE.*

Nina—whoever she is at the other end of the hotline—must have secretly called the police. "Get out of here!" I yell, trying to push them back, still on the phone.

"I hate you, Nina!" I scream. "I told you I didn't want the goon squad. Why did you do this?"

The female officer takes the phone from me, murmurs something into the receiver. She hangs up. I back up against the wall, trying to get as far away from the intruders as I can.

"Now, what's going on here, Miss Wagner?"

"It's Pam, just Pam. And I don't *need* to jump. It'll all be over in a couple of days."

"What'll be over?" one of them asks.

But I can't explain. How can I condense into a sentence or two something that has been building up for more than a year? That the world is ending, that I can't stop it, that it's my fault because I didn't try hard enough to warn people. Tears start coming down my cheeks. But instead I insist I'm safe. I won't do anything to hurt myself. A good night's sleep is all I need.

I'm not lying, exactly, just not telling the whole truth. I don't tell them that Dr. Riordan, the psychiatrist who saved my life, is retiring unexpectedly, *after* taking a vacation starting in January, or that my best friend and I had a terrible fight right after Christmas that ended our twenty-year relationship. I can't tell them I really believe the Y2K bug will bring an end to civilization, should a biblical Armageddon fail to materialize. Nor if it did, how I would most certainly not be going to heaven. Nor can I tell them how the voices, silent for three months on a new medication, have returned with a vengeance, bringing hell to my nights and days. With scathing criticism and a constant scornful commentary on everything I do, they sometimes order me to do things I shouldn't. So far, I've stopped myself, but I might not always be able to. Or that I barricade the door each night for fear of beings from the higher dimensions coming to spirit me away, useless as any physical barrier would be against them. I don't mention the NSA, DIA, or Interpol surveillance I've detected in my walls or how intercepted conversations among these agencies have intruded into TV shows.

Oh, I want to tell them all this, I really do. But I know too well what would happen, and I don't want them to take me away. Still the tears keep coming. A paramedic reaches out to put an arm around my shoulders.

"Don't touch me!" I shriek, shrinking from contact. "Go away! Leave me alone! Get out of my apartment. *Now!* Who the hell do you think you are?"

They look stunned. Meanwhile my hands are doing weird things up near my face. I can't help it. It takes too much concentration to still them and keep my brain under control at the same time.

One of the policemen looks through my room. Pawing through my things, he picks up one of my pill bottles, gestures to one of his buddies. They confer in low voices.

Together they collect all my medications and ask me if I have been taking them.

"Of course!" This is the truth. One cop shakes his head. I don't like him; he hasn't been on my side from the start. I realize he's connected to the Five People who monitor my movements wherever I go, their true identities always disguised. He has something to do with the other dimensions, the Supermetal Canister and, most important of all, Gray Crinkled Paper. I'm not sure how deep it goes. But something tells me to keep as far from him as I can.

In the end, it's no dice. All they can see is the mess, the pill bottles, the ashtrays, the way my hands keep moving, my tearfulness. And the inescapable fact that I live on the twelfth floor. To them it suggests too much trouble, more than they can leave behind. They're going to take me to the hospital, just to make sure I'm all right. They tell me if the doctor okays it, I can come right back home. But I know they're only sweetening an offer I can't refuse.

I know this. I *know* this. But I start yelling anyway. "I'm all right," I scream. "I'm not going anywhere. I don't need a doctor. I'm *fine, goddamn it!*"

That's when they harden. I don't look at people, but I should have, then I would have sensed it coming. They huddle around a crackling walkie-talkie. Then one of them tells me in kindergarten words that I have two choices: I can go with the EMTs the easy way or with the cops the hard way.

"Take your pick, Pamela, we don't have all day."

"Shit," I mutter. I know they mean it. I've been through this business before. I give up, but it's hard to swallow when they start crowding me, watching my every move. Do they think I'm going to slit my throat with a sharpened sock?

"Can I at least put on my clothes without all of you watching?"

The female medic motions the men out of the bedroom. I struggle into a dirty black sweater, add dark sunglasses on top of my regular ones, then, wrapping a hooded black muffler around my face— protection—I shuffle out into the living room in my coat. Clinging to what shreds of dignity still fall to me, I keep my body rigid, making them lift me onto the stretcher like a plank of wood. Then they start tightening the straps around my wrists. This time I do resist.

"Please, no! I'm not gonna do anything. I'll be good, I promise." Panic has turned my voice to a whisper. They sigh, looking at each other, eyes rolling. I know what they're thinking: *Oh, no, not again.* Amazingly, though, they concede, deciding to risk it rather than face another fight. But I feel useless and despised, a worn-out left shoe, something they want to dump as soon as possible.

Finally, the procession—guards, handmaidens, heavy artillery— begins down the hall to the elevator. I don't know who's out there watching, but even with my eyes screwed shut I sense the old ladies peeking through their doors. I can feel the stares, I can hear the rumor mill start to grind.

"You old hens," I mutter. "Chickenshit begock-begocks!" My hands fly up to my mouth to muffle the curses because I know my swearing always gets me in trouble. But it's some protection, and what else do I have to defend myself with?

You know how people say only sticks and stones can break your bones? Well, that's a damn lie. Even bullets are nothing compared to the ax murderers in people's eyes. And ain't it strange how it's the same people murdering you who just moments before were murmuring, "Don't be frightened. We're going to help you"?

A new problem. They want to take me to City Hospital, the biggest and nearest. No way, José—I refuse point-blank. The ER nurses there have tried to kill me one too many times, not to mention the Five People who once secretly irradiated me in the nuclear physics lab. They'll take me to the University Hospital in Farmington or I'm not going anywhere. That's my right and they'd better do as I say, or else. A mostly empty threat, perhaps, but they know I'm right. And they agree, though it's a much longer drive and it's obvious they can't wait to get rid of me.

The ride uses up all my resources. When we finally arrive, I'm sweating, trembling, at the end of my rope. The paramedics roll the gurney inside the ER, sign me over, then disgorge me into a small cubicle. The smell of the place hits me like a shock wave—rubbing alcohol, disinfectant, and something so sweetly acidic it makes me retch. Before I can say anything, a nurse and an aide hurry in, wrestle my bag and coat away from me. Without a blink, they order me to take off my clothes. I hit the roof, yelling and cursing. "I'm not fucking undressing! There's nothing the fuck wrong with me!"

"You should be ashamed of yourself," one of them scolds. "This is a family hospital."

"Oh, sure," I scoff. "Those asshole rugrats out there spitting up on their parents hear worse every day on TV!"

"That's enough, Pamela," she warns.

"Bullshit! I don't give a fuck!"

If I don't calm down, they'll give me a needle, the other threatens.

"I *am* calm!" I scream, and I counterthreaten even louder. I'm thinking, *Stay calm? I'm fighting for my life here!*

Then it's a blur. As if on signal, people suddenly crowd into the small room. Men in surgical scrubs grab me while the nurses, still telling me no one is going to hurt me, hold me down, and I'm yelling and struggling against all of them and somehow my clothes are taken away and somebody comes at me with a syringe full of something the aides smirkingly call "vitamin H"—Haldol—and it hurts like hell when they jam it in my rear end.

That's where the struggle ends. They've won and they know it. The room clears like a bad fart, but I let the entire ER know I intend to sue: I have a right to refuse medication and it was given to me against my will, violating my constitutional rights and—

Loud enough for everyone to hear, one of the aides mutters, "So fine, sue the whole damn hospital. Meanwhile, shut up and go to sleep."

Then I'm left alone on the narrow hospital bed, side rails up, in nothing but my underwear and two flimsy hospital gowns, one open to the back, one over it, open to the front. I can only seethe at the injustice. Rocking, muttering, sobbing, I rage and rage at the aide guarding the doorway, but she only ignores me, yawning with deliberation and exaggerated boredom, telling me in no uncertain terms: *You're nothing new. I've seen it all before.*

"They can't drug me up without a fight," I keep yelling, continuing my harangue. "I'll see you all in court, just watch me!"

But after a while I get woozy. I can't sit up straight anymore. I have to hold on to the side rails. My words get mushier and mushier. My brain fogs up, my eyes cross. I'm getting confused; I can't remember the beginnings of my sentences by the time I get to the end of them. Against every inch of my will, my jaw sags, my eyelids droop, and I slump back against the pillow. I think, *Maybe I'll close my eyes for just a moment.* Though I promise myself I won't give in to sleep, my mind keeps drifting away no matter how I try to bring myself back to consciousness. No use. It may not be voluntary, only the drug that makes me compliant, but either way, before I know it, I'm out like a light.

I awake in the psychiatric ward, on a bare mattress on the floor of an empty room. Alone.

Those are angry feet.

The on-call doctor who owns them doesn't introduce himself when he pushes through the door, just demands that I answer his questions. This is before I've had coffee or breakfast or been given medicine for the abnormal sleepiness of narcolepsy, a condition that has plagued me for decades. Looking up from the mattress on the floor, I see a baobab tree—massive, rooted, menacing—his balled fists soldered inside the pockets of his white coat. Dark hair, heavy features—these are more sensed than seen. I know from the moment he commandeers the room that I'm in trouble.

I sit up and try to mumble coherently, don't manage it very well, still stuporous from the Haldol the night before. He asks me to repeat myself time after time, but his feet keep distracting me.

I hate everybody. I hate my patients, they whine. Then angry: *They bore me to death! I wish they'd all kill themselves!*

Through the din I manage to make out the question: "Can you tell me what worries you the most right now?"

Honestly? Does he really mean it? Will he help? "My cats," I answer without hesitation. "No one's taking care of them. I'm afraid they'll starve."

Baobab harrumphs. "That should be the least of your worries." His feet chime in: *I hate you, moron. Do the world a favor, why don't you. Go out and get hit by a bus.*

"You fucking Nazi!" I can feel the veins popping out on my neck. "The 'least of my worries'? People like you are the worst of my worries!"

Seething, I answer his next questions with a stony silence. Finally, I order him to leave, threatening that if he so much as sets foot in my room again, I'll . . .

But I have to leave this unfinished because a phalanx of nurses rushes in to assist him. He waves them off. I'm no threat to *him.*

Dismissing me, he turns on the leather of his self-satisfied, smirking shoes and goose-steps out the door.

"Hey, fuck you too!" I yell after him, but he pays no attention.

I need to tell my identical twin sister, Lynnie, or Carolyn as she now calls herself, where I am, what is going on, what they are doing to me. But to get to the phone means dodging the dogs and Christmas trees that keep popping up in front of me, throwing me off balance as I swerve to avoid them. I screw up my courage and dash around the nurses' station, setting off a flurry of alarm as aides rush to block the exit. I can tell they are relieved when I head instead toward the phone. They have no idea I am making my way through a flickering cloud of gnatlike "red strychnines," which swarm about me like those tiny insects that gather around streetlamps on a summer night.

"I'm scared, Lynnie, they're doing things to me. I can't stay here," I whisper. But she doesn't take the danger seriously. She talks to me in the controlled, overly patient tones of a parent calming a distraught child. You'll be okay, she promises. She will visit me soon, but meanwhile there isn't any danger. I'm in the right place.

"Argh!"

Someone has tapped me on the shoulder.

"What do you want!"

The nurse holds out a little cup. More pills. "Please take them now. I need to make sure you swallow them."

"Lynnie, I gotta go—" I cup my hand around the receiver, hoping the nurse won't know whom I am talking to. "I'll call you back—when it's safer."

I down the pills. *If they're poison, well, then, I'm dead. Who gives a shit?* Then it's back through the same obstacle course to my room, where I lie down, cold and shivering under a single blanket. My watch reads barely eight P.M. How can I sleep when they can do anything to me without my knowing it? Better force myself to stay awake. *Yeah, ha, ha, ha,* I laugh to myself without humor. It has been years since I've gone a full day without several naps, and now I'm going to keep myself up all night?

A screech of electronic feedback splinters the hush, someone adjusting a microphone. Then, resounding throughout the ward, replayed for everyone to hear, is the conversation I've just had on the phone with Lynnie, only this time with nurses' threats added: *So, she's upset, is she? Just let her wait till she's alone with us!* My heart races. A sudden sweat moistens my palms. What can I do? Where can I go? These people listened in to my phone call and taped it. Now they're going to get revenge . . . and I'm locked in the ward alone with them?

There's no way out. Lynnie can't help me now. No one can. I realize no one will ever know what really happened to me. Oh, excuses will be proffered, there'll be talk of accidents and statistics, of regrettable mistakes. But no one will be told the truth. And of course that is the point: to murder me and get away with it.

But I still can't go down without a fight.

I zigzag back to the phone, dodging bullets, and mash at numbers blindly. I know they are watching. If they hear me, God only knows what will happen. Lynnie has to come and get me. *Now*.

"They're gonna kill me!" I whisper as soon as she answers. "Lynnie, *please*, I'll do anything, I *promise*. I'll take any medication, go to any other hospital, see any doctor, but I can't stay here—" By this time I'm yelling so loud that no one needs to record anything. "What?! You want a reason? Okay, listen to this!"

I hold the phone out in the air. The recording of our call is still playing.

"Is that enough? They taped us! Now they're going to get back at me. You heard those threats!"

The line is quiet.

"Well? Answer me! You've got to come get me. Obviously I can't stay here."

"Pammy?" She clears her throat. "Please don't hang up or get angry. You want the truth? I didn't hear a thing. Nobody taped us, no one's talking about hurting you. You're hallucinating."

"What's wrong with you? They just said they were going to teach me a lesson!"

"They're not real, Pam, those are just your voices. They're in your mind. Try to believe me."

"Lynnie, please, *please*! If you don't get me out of here they're going to kill me!" I start crying.

"Listen to me, Pammy. Listen." She sighs. "Let me talk to someone there, okay? Isn't there anyone on the staff you trust? Will you go find someone?"

I'm shaking too hard to keep the phone to my ear.

"Pammy—"

Then someone pries the phone from me and pushes me gently in the direction of the seclusion room they've put me in. As I stumble away, I hear the lilt of her voice saying, "Hello, this is Stacy. I'm one of the nurses on duty tonight." Murmuring follows. "Yes, yes, I understand, and that's what we're trying . . ." Stacy has a British accent, I note. *A Brit! Oh, so MI-6 is after me too?* But from my room I can no longer make out her words.

I check my watch again. Nine-thirty P.M. One night before New Year's Eve, 1999. With space-time poised on the brink, Armageddon has arrived.

Book One

Pamela

I know where Mrs. Jardin keeps the crowns, we all do. They are locked in a cabinet high above the utility sink in which we wash our paintbrushes and the yellow sponge erasers used for clearing the blackboard at the end of each day. Only on very special occasions, like a birthday, does she take a crown out of the cabinet and with great dignity crown the lucky king or queen of the day, a royal blue velvet coronet trimmed with silver foil for girls, a glowing red and gold one for boys.

This day is *my* day, my birthday, and I've been waiting all semester for the chance to feel the sweet pressure of that blue crown on my head. In the morning, Mrs. Jardin mentions something "extra special" for me that afternoon, and I hope our class mother, responsible for party refreshments, is bringing chocolate cupcakes with fudge icing, mine with six pink-candy-striped candles, one for each year.

Poor Lynnie, I think generously. Her teacher, Mrs. Connelly, who is young and pretty, unlike old Mrs. Jardin with the sticky, prickly porcupine gray hair, doesn't make much of birthdays, not even for first graders.

A published author, Mrs. Jardin is considered the best of the three first-grade teachers. Every year at the spring Book Fair, she sets up a table where she sells autographed copies of her books, which are wildly if locally popular, even though they were printed at her own expense. I know that even though she's scary and *old,* I'm supposed to be proud to be in her class. But my secret, kept from everyone like a picked scab, is that I wish I had Mrs. Connelly, even without the crowns, because her room is neat and clean and calm, not bubbling over with clamor and rickety excitement all the time.

Along with writing, reading, and arithmetic, Mrs. Jardin teaches us "etickette." Which means manners. The girls have learned to tuck needed Kleenex up our sleeves instead of stuffing our pockets with them. "Gentlemen" always open the door for "ladies" and slide out their chairs behind them at the table, slipping them back underneath their fannies just in time. That "patience is a virtue" and it is "better to give than receive" are maxims repeated like the eleventh and twelfth commandments several times a week, as occasions demand.

The morning yawns on through reading groups and arithmetic lessons into lunch, then recess, then art class. Finally, Mrs. Jardin teases me with a stern smile. "Well, this is someone's special day, isn't it?" She draws a footstool over to the utility sink, climbs on, and reaches up with a key to unlock the cabinet. Spellbound, I close my eyes, opening them again only after I hear the clunk of her footsteps back on the floor. She holds the red crown in one hand and the blue crown in the other. Why two crowns? Is there a boy with a November 17 birthday? Then there's a knock at the door, followed by Mrs. Connelly, holding Lynnie by the hand.

"Be good, Lynnie," Mrs. Connelly urges her, after nodding at Mrs. Jardin as if it has been prearranged. "Remember, you're a guest." Then she heads back out the door, leaving Lynnie standing up front, next to the teacher's desk.

"Since you and Lynnie are identical twins," Mrs. Jardin says, "do you two know what identical means?"

"I know! I know!" I wave my hand and jump up and down.

"That's good, Pammy. What about you, Lynnie?"

As usual Lynnie just bites her lower lip and looks at me.

"Lynnie, it means we look just the same, like our dresses!" I match my blue print dress to hers.

"That's right, Pammy." Mrs. Jardin smiles down at me. "We thought it would be nice for you to have your sister join us for the party."

That's when the terrible realization comes to me: The two crowns are for *us,* for Lynnie and me. But there is only one blue one, only one to crown a girl. Lynnie is already fingering it, tipping it on its side, preparing to pick it up and put it on her head.

I leap forward. "That's my crown!" I cry. "I've got dibs on the girls' crown!"

Swiftly, almost without moving, Lynnie ducks her head and eases the crown on top.

"No!" I wail. "This is my party! That's *my* crown. Tell her, Mrs. Jardin. *She* has to wear the boys' crown. She doesn't even belong here, she's just a visitor!"

"Now, hush, Pammy," Mrs. Jardin scolds. "She's your sister and a guest. A good hostess offers her guest the choice of crowns, doesn't she?"

Lynnie is smiling now, with a look of open triumph, her eyes sneering "nyah, nyah, nyah!" The beautiful blue crown matches the blue pattern in her dress so perfectly it almost seems she's planned it.

I lose my fight to keep my tears at bay.

"Come, come, Pammy. Have you forgotten your manners? You have a perfectly good crown right here. What's wrong with red? Now, be a big girl. What's gotten into you?" Mrs. Jardin's words cut into my heart like broken glass. I sniffle miserably and shake my head.

"Good, then put on your crown and let's have no more of this. Sometimes we learn from our disappointments."

I obey, my face pink, with both shame and anger.

Then someone laughs. I hear a muffled snigger. "*Look*, she's wearing the *boys'* crown—"

"Maybe she's not Pammy but *Sammy!*" someone whispers savagely.

I bite my lips to keep from yelling back. And I fight my desire to rip the crown from Lynnie's head, make *her* suffer the humiliation of wearing the boys' crown. How I hate her! I hate her more than I can remember hating anyone. I swallow and swallow and swallow: tears, bile, fury. I swallow the terrible injustice of life with a twin who steals your crown, and I swallow the injustice of being Pammy in the red crown instead of Lynnie in the blue.

Carolyn

In the morning I dread the bus ride from our house to the elementary school. Every time we pick up kids, the bus farts black stinky clouds. I hold my breath, but the smell still makes me sick. I stare out the window to keep from throwing up.

Finally we pull up to the school ramp. The bus shudders and dies. I grab my things, slide over the vinyl seat, and squeeze my feet into the aisle.

"Ow! Lynnie, stop pushing!" says Pammy, who is directly in my way. "C'mon, it's not nice!"

I ignore her. Right now being first is more important to me than being nice. Using my red plaid lunch box like a snowplow, I give her a shove, and when she stumbles I quickly wedge myself in front of her. Pammy was born five minutes ahead of me and because of that she gets to go first in everything. I'm always second. Today's our birthday, November 17—today we're six. Pammy's in Mrs. Jardin's class. Because of that I think I have a right to push ahead of her.

I wish we didn't have to go to school at all today. All Pammy can do is talk about the crown, and I don't want to hear it.

Mommy says I should be happy for her, but I'm not. I hate thinking about Pammy getting to wear that beautiful crown. My teacher, Mrs. Connelly, doesn't do anything really special for birthdays.

Mrs. Connelly is very nice and very pretty and she's not strict at all, except she wants things arranged just so. She puts our artwork and papers neatly on the bulletin boards with thumbtacks in all four corners, and she has stuck letters above the blackboard to help us remember the alphabet. Everything is neat. Mrs. Connelly makes us put things away where they belong before we go on to something else.

Mrs. Jardin has stuff everywhere and everybody knows she is the best teacher in first grade and only the smartest kids are in her class.

What I hate the most about not having Mrs. Jardin is the birthday crowns. I saw them once when I passed by in the hall and Mrs. Jardin had them out on her desk. They were carved of real gold—not silly tinsel or painted cardboard—and covered with diamonds and rubies. They sparkled like Christmas lights in December. Pammy says each crown has a center pillow of soft real velvet with nap so thick when you brush it in the right direction it's as smooth and silky as rabbit fur. The queen's crown is a bright royal blue and the king's crown is fire engine red. Today Pammy is going to wear the blue crown and I'm trying to pretend I don't care, but I do. I wish it was me who had Mrs. Jardin, not Pammy.

"*Lynnie? Are* you listening?"

I look around. My teacher hates it when I daydream instead of pay attention. I'm in for a scolding. But when my eyes find her, Mrs. Connelly is smiling.

"Lynnie, would you come up here please."

I get up so fast my pencil goes flying and I knock my chair over with a loud clatter. She grimaces. Tears spring to my eyes as I right the chair and walk carefully to the teacher's desk at the back of the classroom. I'm expecting her to be angry. Instead, her eyes twinkle and she's pursing her lips so tight I think she's swallowed some secret that's trying to come back up. She stoops a bit to my level the way teachers do when they are trying to be friendly and puts a hand on my shoulder.

"I want to show you something, Lynnie," she says with a smile that dimples her cheek. She writes some numbers or letters on a piece of paper and puts it in front of me.

"Do you know what it says?"

I squint and concentrate, but I can't pretend I know. I shake my head and feel tears gathering. *I won't be the crybaby! Not today.*

"I'll give you a hint, Lynnie. It's a date." She points to each number with her finger and says it out loud. "Eleven, seventeen, nineteen fifty-two. Eleven means the month, November. Seventeen is—"

"It's our birthday today! Pammy and me!" I blurt out, my chest suddenly expanding with happiness. Maybe Mrs. Connelly decided to copy Mrs. Jardin and give me a party too. I can barely keep still. I can't stop my feet and knees from doing an excited little jig.

"Mrs. Jardin has invited you to join Pammy for her birthday celebration," says Mrs. Connelly.

Oh, no! And have to watch Pammy show off? Before I can say anything, she takes my hand, walks me two doors down to Pammy's classroom, plunks me in front of the class, and there I stand, alone and grinning like an idiot.

Mrs. Jardin tells Pammy to come up and join me. Perfect as always, Pammy closes her workbook, puts her papers in a neat stack, and places them carefully in her desk. She stands and pats smooth the front of her dress before she pushes her chair under the desk where it belongs and walks to where I stand. Pammy gives me a wan smile and turns toward the teacher. I see her staring at the two crowns Mrs. Jardin has taken out of their hiding place. A shiver of excitement makes me forget I'm not getting to wear one, and I rush over to see them up close. At first I don't believe what I see.

Those are the crowns? *They can't be.* On the teacher's desk, close up, these crowns are shabby and old, not shiny or grand at all. There isn't a single jewel and even the glitter doesn't sparkle. The girls' crown isn't gold, but cardboard covered with ordinary tinfoil. The blue velvet is thin and wearing away completely in places. Somebody's playing a trick—these aren't the real birthday crowns, are they?

Before I can say anything, Mrs. Jardin asks which one I want and I tell her. It all happens so fast it doesn't cross my mind to pick the red one just to be nice to Pammy. Of course I put on the blue one. I'm a girl. The red is for boys.

Spring and Summer 1963

Pamela

I've always been Daddy's favorite. I'm the one who shines at everything and I know it makes him proud. I'm the one he can bring out
and show off to his guests and ask me questions and have me get the
right answers. He likes it when I argue with him about things in the
news, and sometimes, when I know something he doesn't, it makes
him smile and throw his up hands in defeat.

But he doesn't tell me he is proud of me. He never rewards me
when I do especially well, but, boy, do I know it when I don't. Lynnie is neither so favored nor so criticized; she's not as capable as I am,
that's what they always say. Mommy says he loves me, but sometimes
I wish he'd tell me. I love Daddy, despite everything. How can you
not love your own father? Not loving a parent is like the sun not rising, or an apple falling upward from the tree. A kid loves her father,
and that's just how it is. Even when I'm mad and think I hate him, I
make myself think nicer thoughts so the bad ones will go away.

Carolyn

The summer before we start sixth grade we spend two weeks of August at our grandparents' lake house on Cape Cod.

One evening, Martha and Chipper are already in their beds and

Mommy is out walking the dog. Pammy and I sneak out on the porch to play Scrabble at the card table.

It's Pammy's turn. She won't put a letter on the board until she's sure it is the best possible word she can make. As usual she's already way ahead of me, and as usual I am fed up.

"Come on, Pammy, I'm sick of waiting! You can't take an hour for one word!"

"*Your* turn," she announces.

I examine her move. She points, calculates, adds to her total, and circles the number with a flourish.

"Probably cheated," I mutter. Not that she cares what I think; Pammy is so used to winning it's ho-hum for her.

"Girls!" Daddy calls from the house. He sounds mad. "I told you twins to get ready for bed!"

Neither of us answers.

"Put the game away. This instant."

I throw letters into the bag, grab the board, and stuff everything into the cabinet. Pammy just sits there. "We were going to," she says staring straight ahead. At nothing.

"Let's go, Pammy." I pull on her shoulder. "Please don't fight." Pammy can be so stupid sometimes. Giving up on her, I bolt into the house, make a beeline for the bathroom, and start scrubbing my teeth.

From the porch, words are traded back and forth. I turn off the faucet so I can hear. Sometimes I think he's like a train and she's a brick wall and he's coming straight at her and she won't get out of the way. It doesn't make any sense.

Through the door I hear Daddy yell, "What did you say, young lady?"

Uh-oh. Here it comes. Quick as a flash, I dash across the hall into our bedroom. The shouting gets louder. I hold my breath. What's happening? Beat. *Please, Pammy, give in!* Words. Bellowing. Bullets of rage. "Apologize now!" Daddy's voice. Suddenly a loud bang. Silence. I fly into the living room.

Pammy, next to the bookcase, an immense volume at her feet, arms crossed over her chest. Daddy comes at her, his face dark, hateful. "Pick that up. Now!" Instead, she hoists a huge dictionary above her head.

"Pammy, don't!" I scream. *Why does she act so crazy?*

Daddy sees me. "Go back to bed, Lynnie!"

I retreat a few steps. Pammy mutters something under her breath.

"What was that?" Daddy grabs her arm. "Don't you swear at me, young lady!"

She shakes her arm out of his grip but stays silent. Nothing shows on her face. It's like she's in another world. *I don't get it. Anybody normal would give in.*

When I hear a smack and the words, "I'll show you," I tear back to our bedroom, slam the door, and hurl myself into the closet. *I hate her!* I dive into a clean pile of quilts and yank them over me. The hollow closet door doesn't keep out a thing and my imagination goes wild: Pammy shouting. Daddy bellowing. Words crashing. Threatening, swearing, slapping, thudding, kicking, crashing, things toppling, breaking, smashing. Rising, rising, rising to . . . More clattering, banging, shouting. Heart jumping, thumping, panicking, pumping. Everything spinning. *Stop!* Water running. *Stop! I don't want to hear. Water running? No! Hide, you coward.* Pammy screaming. *Don't listen! Where's Mommy?* Mommy! More stamping. Dragging. Again thumping, kicking. I grit my teeth, pull clothes and blankets around me. Gotta keep from screaming. *What's going on? Make it stop!* Water sloshing. Choking sounds. *Is he going to drown her?*

I hurl myself out of the closet. He has her head under the faucet, soap in her mouth. I throw myself at him. "No, Daddy! She can't breathe! You can't do this!" Suddenly I'm screaming too, drowning them both out. I slap him, kick his shins, bite him like an animal until finally Pammy can wrestle free and run for cover.

SEPTEMBER 1963

Pamela

The very first day of sixth grade, 1963, and already it's a catastrophe. I've been out here at the corner for forty-five minutes, but the school bus hasn't come. I know what's in store. More than a half hour late, I'll get my knuckles whacked, I'll be made to stand in the corner facing the wall. And it isn't even my fault. You get punished anyway. Lynnie is horsing around with her friends; she doesn't seem to care. But I do.

When the bus finally arrives, after someone's mom calls to complain, it seems like one of the girls dawdles forever, first pulling up her kneesocks, then dropping her pencil box and taking an hour to pick up the scattered pencils, before sloooowly climbing up the two—just two!—steps onto the bus, which isn't allowed to start up again until she's finally chosen her seat. At last, we're on our way, but my insides are churning and my head feels like a chain is slowly tightening around it as I try to think of what I can say to the teacher to explain my being late. But I know nothing excuses it. Lateness is lateness. It is what it is, and if you're late you deserve the consequences. That's how it was at Wessex Gardens in England last year.

By the time we finish the route and climb up School Street hill and the kids pour out onto the concrete slab at the elementary school, the last bell has long since rung and I feel like I might either cry or throw up, maybe both. The others hustle by me off the bus and push through the outer doors, still chattering happily, making their way into the dark corridors to their classrooms. But I don't know how I can open the door to sixth-grade classroom #16. How can I be so shamefully late on my first day? Tardiness is a mortal sin. I'm a half hour late; in England knuckles got smacked or worse for being just a *minute* late.

Then I spy lanky, red-haired Gary Evans near the driver's seat, ushering the younger kids off the bus. He wears the yellow sash of a monitor and I realize I have a rescuer. Gary can help me. He has to. There is no other way. As he descends the bus steps I snag his shirt-tail and it pulls out of his trousers. I fish him toward me, not letting go even when he pulls away and snaps, "Quit it, Pammy!"

But I'm desperate. I need him. "Listen, Gary, you gotta come with me and tell Mrs. Genet the bus was late. Tell her it's not my fault. I was at the bus stop on time but the bus never came and now it's past the bell time and I don't want her to hit my knuckles or send me to Mr. DeWitt or . . ."

Gary looks irritated at first, but when my chin starts wobbling and tears come to my eyes, he grows wiser, more understanding. He actually puts a hand on my shoulder to comfort me. "It's okay, Pammy. She won't be mad. Buses are always late. Let's go now and I'll tell her. Don't cry. It'll be okay."

I suck back my tears and try not to worry as we trudge past the principal's office then down the dim hallway toward the sixth-grade classrooms, but my heart is in my mouth. Gary flings open the door to room #16 with a flourish, not humbly the way he should, and Mrs. Genet, a tall, slope-shouldered, gray-haired woman with a brown bump on her nose and glasses on a cord around her neck, strides right over to us. Wary, I back away, hiding half my body behind Gary. Just in case.

"The bus was late. She was in England last year and thinks it's her fault. She's just scared," Gary explains, acting like a big brother even though he's only six months older than me. My head down, I trip over my own shoes.

"Ah, you must be Pammy Spiro then," the teacher says, catching me and taking my hands in hers. With a smile, she waves Gary off to his own classroom, mission accomplished. "Come in and we'll find you a desk. You remember everybody, don't you? A year in England, aren't you lucky! I imagine you have lots of adventures to tell us about."

OCTOBER 1963

Pamela

Mrs. Genet chalks our morning assignment on the sixth-grade black-board: "Write a complete sentence using a subordinate clause. Don't forget subject, object, and verb, correct punctuation and spelling. Be creative!"

I grip my pencil so hard my knuckles blanch into little white nuts under the skin, but the words start to form before I even put my pencil to the paper. "The girl tries to scream, but her terror of the dark figure standing in the doorway, dagger in hand, is so great she can't even . . ." *No, I won't write that, I won't!* I fight the impulse, pulling my pencil back from the paper before I write more than the first word.

We have assignments like this every day and I dread them almost as much as I dread lunchtime. Lunches are awful because every third week I have to bring my tray to the secretary's office and take over for Mrs. Baum, who leaves me alone with the switchboard, two phones, and only a door between me and the principal, Mr. DeWitt. For the entire hour I have to sit there, rigid as a washboard, my lips dry, hoping and praying that no one will come in, that the phone won't ring, and that the door, *that* door, never opens.

Though it was an honor to be chosen, that's also why it was im-possible to refuse. How could I explain myself? So when, months later, another honoree, Ann, confides she has so much fun she resents having to share the job three ways, I'm dumbstruck. How can I admit how much I dread every minute? Too late to back out, I'm stuck, and it's my own fault.

For the first time in my life I long to stay home from school. I can't fake being sick; I don't have the nerve. But getting *honestly* ill, with a little help, is okay. So I go to bed with wet hair, pick at my scabs, eat fruit without washing it and cookies that fall on the floor. On the school bus I sit next to little kids with the worst snotty noses and sniffles. I know I must deserve my fate when I stay rosy-cheeked with health despite everything.

The only crack in the façade is those morning sentences.

Mrs. Genet *says* she loves my "wonderful, fertile imagination." She loves my creativity. *But* . . . I wait, knowing there is more. Why do I always write about murder? she asks. I need to "delve" into more cheerful subject matter. What she is really saying is no more murderers. No more burglars, rapists, or child molesters skulking in my bedroom, either.

Now, chewing my lips, I labor to come up with a cheerful sentence, something with rainbows and frilly white lace. My mind draws a big fat blank. *C'mon! You can do it. Write something normal, stupid!*

My brain feels blocked, dead set against it. I know Mrs. G meant well during a parent-teacher conference, when she mentioned the "sentence problem" to my mother, but she doesn't understand how things work in the Spiro family. My mother might have seemed understanding then, but later on she scolded me, saying I "did it" on purpose, as if it made her look bad. But she doesn't understand that the problem isn't *doing* at all, it's *thinking:* I can't *think* of anything but murder. I have no idea why, it just happens.

Despite the trials of sixth grade, one good thing does happen: I'm chosen for the second time since fourth grade for Special Art. This time we have a new art teacher who has recognized my gifts and rewarded me. I'm in bliss using oil paints and canvas and making sculptures out of wire and newspaper mixed with wallpaper paste. But the best thing, the activity I like the most, is copper enameling.

On the last Friday of my childhood, a late November afternoon in 1963, Janet Calder and I are in the kiln shed during art class. I've just inserted some glass-powder coated pieces of copper into the kiln when a whoosh of raw air announces Mrs. Rosen the art teacher, who absentmindedly leaves the door ajar. It's instantly freezing, yet she seems oblivious. The shed, lined with shelves of art supplies, smells like oil paints and turpentine mixed with the earthy scent of clay. It's so cold inside that Mrs. Rosen sniffles. Her squared-off, paint-stained fingers fumble for Kleenex and she dabs at her nose and eyes. What's she doing here? It's much too early for class to end; we've only just started firing our first pieces of copper.

She snaps the kiln off. The orange glow of the On light slowly goes black.

"Girls," she begins, her voice tight, her face pinched and blotchy, "there's bad news. The president—" She stops. Her eyes blink, once, twice, then two more times quickly. Her face twists, her throat contracting so the cords in her neck stand out, as if she's trying to swallow a bite too big to go down. Finally: "President Kennedy has been shot. In Dallas."

The world goes still.

Dallas, I think, not quite taking in her words, trying to picture Texas on a map. But it's so unbelievable I realize she's just teasing. Everything falls back into its proper place. The world starts up again. Though the joke is tasteless, I don't mind; it makes me feel grown up. Mrs. Rosen is usually so serious that her teasing must mean she's treating us like almost-adults. I play along, trying to think of an adult retort. But I can only scoff, "Yeah, *sure.*"

Mrs. Rosen, small and compact, no taller than I, is a painter, but she doesn't look the way I think artists should, costumed in vivid clothing, gold lamé turbans, lots of big flashy jewelry. All of Mrs.

Rosen's clothes are shades of beige or tan or brown, even her hair is a no-color color, cut in a bow-like pageboy she never bothers to curl.

As she stares at me without speaking, almost as if she hasn't heard me, I notice that her eyes are pink-rimmed and puffy, not really like she has a cold. Has she been crying? I feel a dull twinge in the pit of my stomach.

Crying?

Because of something in Dallas, Texas?

I stop giggling. The hush is like a held breath. The clock on the wall snaps onto the hour. I feel as if all my senses have been supernaturally enhanced. A small popping sound comes from inside the kiln, melted glass enamel cracking as the copper pieces cool too quickly. The turpentine and paint tins suddenly tweak my nostrils, their smell acrid, leaving on my tongue the trace of a terrible bitterness, and it is hard to believe all this went unnoticed before. I hear my heart beat, beat, beat, so loud and insistent that I know everyone else hears it too. I hold my breath; if I don't breathe, the moment will pass away like a terrible dream and everything will be all right. I wait and wait and wait. *Please, say something!* I silently beg Mrs. Rosen. *Say everything is okay, say President Kennedy isn't hurt, say he'll be fine. I need to hear you say the magic words, No, Pammy, it didn't happen, it's not the end of the world.*

But she says nothing, and in that instant I understand that my life will never be the same. I will never be just a child anymore, protected, happy, oblivious. Dark bubbles flood my brain. I am drowning, unable to get enough air before I go under. Countless times I struggle to the surface, before being pulled back down.

Mrs. Rosen sends us back to our classroom. As we walk quietly down the empty corridor, I say nothing. I'm shivering when I become aware—"out of the corner of my ear"—of muffled sounds, people whispering behind me, short snatches of music and conversation that echo in my head as Janet and I head toward the sixth-grade wing. I don't dare look around, I don't say anything.

We make our way back toward our hallway and are almost there when the loudspeaker crackles to life. It's the principal, Mr. DeWitt. He clears his throat several times and finally announces in a thick voice the worst possible thing that could happen. "Boys and girls," he says, "the president is dead."

What? My knees buckle. President Kennedy is dead? Impossible. But a general commotion through the closed doors along the corridor confirms it. John Fitzgerald Kennedy, whose infant son Patrick I immortalized in a poem, whose form-letter thank-you note I showed all around the neighborhood, the only kid with a letter from the White House, the president has died in Dallas, Texas, JFK is dead, JFK is dead!

Mr. DeWitt's voice trembles; it sounds as if he's fighting off tears, and he even has to stop for a moment in the middle of his speech. This scares me because Mr. DeWitt is the principal and principals are supposed to be strong, in control. You can tell that something is horribly wrong when a principal cries. Then the whispering comes on again, like the voice on that *Password* game on TV. I hear my name: *Pam, Pam Spiro, Pam . . . Spam . . .* I can hear it right through Mr. DeWitt's voice as he's telling us what happened. My feet plod on, wading numbly through the floor wax, cleaning fluid, and stale cafeteria food smells that drift around me. Now I understand— it is an undertow beneath the ocean of other understandings— everything is connected, even the sharpness of my senses, all is a part of what is happening. These things *mean* something, even though I am not sure what. At the same time something tells me I don't *want* to know, that if I think too hard or try to figure it out, I'll be sorry.

Janet walks alongside me, her nose running. She seems far away, not connected to me, like she only looks like she's there when she isn't. We turn the corner into a glow of light coming from the doors at the far end of the hall. I know suddenly that this is the Light of Truth that will make all things clear because it is made up entirely of shadows. The whispering starts again: *Pam, Pam Spiro, Spam piro . . . piro Spam . . . Spam . . .* Footsteps pad close behind me.

Someone is breathing hard, he's holding a knife, he's going to stab—
I'm ready to scream but I won't look around. If I turn to look, protect myself, the sheer weight of my terror will suffocate me. No one
can help me; no one can protect me, not even Lynnie. If I drown, if
I die, I'll be swallowed up and I'll never get back.

Will you kill you Pam Spiro, Spam pam pam, kill you will you . . .

Ignore it, I tell myself, *pay no attention.* I force myself to think of
other things, clutter up my head with unrelated stuff, make myself
practice the multiplication tables, anything that isn't about what's
happening. I see, in my head, the pictures that hang on the wall over
Mrs. Genet's desk: one, our handsome, glamorous president, who
looks so much like a movie star . . . But President Kennedy is dead,
John F. Kennedy, whose baby son Patrick died and I wrote a poem
about him, the baby is dead and now the father is dead, and again,
despite my intention, I'm thinking about it—somebody shot President Kennedy, they shot him, he died, he's not president anymore,
nobody is, and I'm going to die, we're all going to die—

I feel dizzy, the floor is wobbling under me, my feet and legs
seem far away, disconnected to me, stork legs with my knees going in
the wrong direction. They walk me down the hall. I follow them as
if they belong to someone else because I don't have the will to do
otherwise.

Thrills will kill, Pam Spampamamamam. Will you? Kill you?

In room #16, a woman I don't recognize, her gray hair in a bun
and a thin cardigan draped over her shoulders, wanders between the
desks, placing a hand on someone's bowed head, giving someone
else's hand a squeeze. Her face is paper-pale, the wen on her nose like
a small brown ladybug. Her shoulders are rounded with fatigue, and
though she isn't wearing glasses it looks like she needs them because
her eyes don't seem to focus properly. Then I see her glasses hanging
from a gold chain around her neck . . . Now isn't that strange? That's
just like . . . then I recognize with a start that this strange woman is
Mrs. Genet, my teacher.

The dizziness passes, but I stand in the doorway, not knowing what to do next. I can't seem to figure it out. I wish Mrs. Genet would tell me. Most of the kids are sitting at their desks, stunned and silent. Some bend their heads together, whispering softly, as if they are at the library. A few, pretending they are happy, try to cheer, acting brave and smiling and joking, but I can tell they are shocked too, and when Mrs. Genet sends a frown their way, her scolding face tired and sad, they quickly quiet down and look ashamed.

Without warning, my mouth fills with saliva. I'm going to throw up. I race to my seat in the second row, where I bury my face on my arms, clenching my stomach muscles and breathing through my nose. Then I understand: the whispering people, the bits of music, the sound of footsteps, and President Kennedy, shot dead, dead, dead! It's obvious isn't it? *I* killed him! *I'm* to blame! Isn't that what it's all about? Isn't that what they're saying, the whisperers? That I caused it, that it's my fault, what happened. I could have stopped it, I could have warned him not to go to Dallas in Texas. Why didn't I? I let him go. That's the same thing as pulling the trigger, worse even, because I let him go when I knew he would get killed. I knew it, I knew it, didn't I? And I did nothing. I killed him, *I* killed him.

Killher, killhim, killher, somebody sneers. I turn to find out who is talking, but only Janet is near enough and her face is blank. She looks too numbed, too pale and stunned. But if not Janet, who was it, then?

Killing thrilling willing my oh my it's indeed! someone snipes again. *Public republic enemy numero uno you know who know.*

Uno yoono hoono? Singsong, mocking, both inside my head yet outside it, a voice I don't recognize yet a voice of terrible authority.

When I look up now I can see that Mrs. Genet's mouth is moving. I can hear her speaking, I can hear the sound of her voice, but I can't figure out what she is saying over the din of all the invisible people talking at the same time.

Now everything has turned into music, different strains of awful music jumbled together. The other kids sitting there are pieces of music too, confused and confusing, screaming for attention, and I can't tell one thing from all the others. Sounds and song become things I can see and feel, as if I'm in the midst of a yelling crowd and I see all the people jumping and mixing around, the different colors and shapes and sizes, the conversation and even the quiet make too much noise, a screaming uproar that rattles my body, and it's too much for me, too much . . .

I burst into tears, unable to stop, unable to explain. The president is dead and I'll never forgive God, who will never forgive me, even though I am only a sixth grader and didn't know in the morning that by the afternoon I would have killed my beloved president. I let him die, and I can never take it back, never change it, never make up for it no matter how hard I try. I hate God for letting me live, for letting Kennedy die when he was our president, for watching as this whole thing just happened, for doing nothing. *Please, please, please don't let it be true, God, please let me wake up and find out it isn't true. Kill me! It was my fault. I am to blame. Kill me, God, only don't let President Kennedy be dead. Please?*

The bell rings early and the other kids quietly line up and leave for the buses, but I can't move, and I can't make sense of the hubbub and I can't, can't, can't—just can't stop crying.

Even though Mommy tries to act sympathetic, she thinks I'm pretending to be upset just to get attention. She doesn't believe I could have stopped the assassination; I know that I am responsible. But I can't explain this, not even when I watch Ruby kill Lee Harvey Oswald live on TV because they got the wrong person in the first place, just the triggerman, the last person in a chain that started with me.

When we return to school the following week all seems well again. But I feel ripped apart, and put back wrong. I know that the world is a terrible place, that nothing will ever be the same: I know that I am evil.

Carolyn

It is after lunch and our sixth-grade class has just gotten in from recess. Many of the girls who stayed in are gathered at Sue's or Candi's desk—something to do with the Beatles and their newest record. Candi and Sue collect them all and are constantly arguing about which Beatle is the cutest. On TV news I've seen girls crying and screaming their lungs out until they faint, all because they see the Beatles getting off the plane. There must be something wrong with me—I don't get what there is to scream and swoon about.

Beatles music is okay, I guess, though I don't really like it. For me, "I Wanna Hold Your Hand" brings on dreadful waves of loneliness and a knot of homesickness that aches in my stomach. I know it sounds odd to feel homesick *after* we're back home in the States. But I feel like my real home, the home I remember of kickball games at recess and hours of playing in the neighborhood, is gone forever. I don't recognize the kids I used to know, and I just can't make myself care about a stupid rock-and-roll band.

I stare out the window to the playground field where the grass is clumpy and brown and at the bottom of the hill the stripped trees look like naked skeletons huddling from the cold. Everything here is so boring and ho-hum. I miss England and afternoons on Hampstead Heath with our friends, handstands against the brick wall at school, and hours of playing jacks and hopscotch. The boat swings at the parks. I miss the Golder's Green library where we read every one of the Narnia books and hated coming to the end of *The Last Battle* knowing there were no more books in the series to read. I miss Miss Edwards, who became our babysitter after Mom bumped into her at the local grocery store, and the way she'd say, "Toot sweet, off to bed now," in that really dainty British way. I even miss fish-and-chips drizzled with vinegar and wrapped in newspaper, the rolling ferry rides from Dover to Calais, the six days aboard the ocean liner *Queen Elizabeth.*

Sixth grade in America feels so fake to me; I don't know how to be myself anymore. I wish I were back in England, where I understood my life and I knew how to be me.

I glance back to the classroom where the other kids are fooling around and I realize something must be wrong. Mr. V is never this late. I know I saw him in the corridor as we straggled in from recess and he didn't even yell at us to stop running. With his back to us, he was talking with Mrs. Genet and Mrs. Rosen the art teacher, whispering the way grown-ups do when they don't want kids to butt in. They looked so serious. I thought I saw Mrs. Rosen dabbing at her eyes with a tissue.

I look at the clock again—it's after one o'clock. What day is it? What subject do we have after recess? Then I remember. Math. I hate math.

Suddenly, Mr. V's face appears at the classroom door. Everyone scrambles. Chuck slides into his chair so smooth and easy even his hair doesn't swing. I hate how slick he is—no kid should be allowed to be that cool. Or that cute. If only he'd look my way . . . I have a crush on Chuck. Sue gives a grunt and rolls her eyes as she and Candi sink into their places with such disdain you'd think they were interrupted at their country club. Then there's Tony, with his 1950s flattop and facial expression he stole from Captain Kangaroo. Tony is perfect. As usual he has been sitting where he belongs, his hands folded properly on the desk, waiting patiently, of course. Does he ever do anything wrong? Doesn't he ever whine or complain or even ask for seconds?

Mr. Victor opens the door. His right hand hangs on the door-frame; his left is on the doorknob slightly behind him. He seems worn out, haggard, and holds back for a moment, looking at us as if he wants to turn and flee. He reminds me of an accused criminal on the TV show *Perry Mason*, the background music becoming ominous as the defendant returns to the courtroom to hear the decision that will change his life. It's so weird I almost laugh. But then I see a look flash across his face in a moment I'll never forget. Something terrible has happened, so terrible Mr. Victor wants to make it go away. He turns and closes the door, his back to us too long, working out how to say something. He takes off his glasses the way grown-ups do when they are thinking and holds them with one hand as he turns slowly and plods methodically to his desk. I try to read his face, figure out what he's going to tell us before he breaks the news. He doesn't look mad. He looks wan and drained, old.

Everyone is silent; even Sue and Candi manage to put their records back under their seats without being asked. Mr. V goes to his desk and appears to change his mind and trudges back to the front of the class, his hands in his pockets, and by now we can't stand not knowing what is up. Without any idea what that could be, I feel my heart start to pound in that deliciously excited way when we've just heard that school will be closing early because of a hurricane threat.

"Class," Mr. V says, putting his glasses back on, "in a few minutes Mr. DeWitt will be making an announcement over the loud-speaker, but he wanted me to take a moment to tell you what has happened." He stops to clear his throat and takes off his glasses, buffing them on a handkerchief he pulls from his jacket. My heart starts to sprint. Margie and I throw excited glances at each other. Mr. V continues. "Class, we've just received news that someone has tried to assassinate President Kennedy in Dallas, Texas. We don't know if he is going to live."

Someone in the class gasps and everyone starts chattering. Mr. V holds up both hands and makes a motion for everyone to stop talking. "I'll take one question at a time."

What does "assassinate" mean? It sounds bad, but I've never heard the word before. Ass-ass-in-ate? I look around. No one else looks confused. Assassinate. I guess everyone else knows. Better keep my mouth shut. A lot of kids have their hands up to ask questions, and Mr. V picks one.

"Does that mean we are getting out of school early, Mr. V?" He scowls and answers abruptly, "What kind of question is that? Why don't you think about our president instead of yourself?" I've never heard Mr. V so harsh. Anyway, I'm glad somebody else was stupid enough to say out loud what I was thinking. Still, I wish I knew what "assassinate" means. Mr. V is about to select another question when we hear the cough of the loudspeaker and Mr. DeWitt's voice. Mr. V looks relieved as he withdraws to his desk.

"I'd like your attention please." I've always liked Mr. DeWitt's distinctive deep and commanding voice, even though he's scary because he's the principal, but today he sounds like he has a cold. "I have bad news. At one o'clock, our president, John F. Kennedy, died of—" His voice breaks off abruptly for a moment. In a few minutes he starts again, his voice still shaky and higher pitched, "President Kennedy was shot riding in his motorcade in Dallas, Texas." Pause. "We have just learned"—pause—"that he is dead." Cough. "Let us all bow our heads in a moment of silence." The loudspeaker doesn't click off completely, so we know the principal is still there.

I am totally numb. President Kennedy is dead. Wounded, shot. Dead. Assassinated. Now I know. I wish they'd just say murdered or killed so I'd understand instead of calling it some big vocabulary word that only grown-ups use. President Kennedy is dead, shot to death. Who would want to shoot President Kennedy? I'm pretty sure we voted for him and he seemed okay as far as presidents go. And we still have the vice president, don't we? Kennedy is dead. Don't get me wrong, nobody should've gotten shot, but it seems like in magazines and newspapers people are always getting killed. A murder is a murder; a person is a person, even when they're the president. Someone taps the microphone and Mr. DeWitt's voice returns.

"School will be dismissed early in a few minutes, and in honor of our slain president, I ask for silence as we leave the building. That means no talking in the halls, at the bus ramps, or on the buses. Get your coats quietly, and as your buses are called you will proceed without speaking. Walkers are to observe silence until reaching the crossing guard."

I am so confused. I don't understand what's going on. I understand that the president is dead, but I can't figure out why it is so terrible. The president doesn't mean anything to me. He's a man who's called Mr. President. Presidents are part of history and history is about dead people. He was an old man, even older than Mom and Dad. Old men die. Presidents die. All the other presidents are dead except maybe Eisenhower and he's so old he could die any day. What is the big deal? President Lincoln was shot too—I mean, it's not like I want Kennedy to be dead, but he's just one person. I don't understand.

My ideas don't go over very well at home. Mom and Dad think I ought to care more, but they are so preoccupied with watching the news and listening to the radio that they don't get mad at me. I guess if all three TV channels are talking about it, assassination must be pretty bad.

Pamela

After Kennedy's death, I return to school subdued but more submissive. I finally get the knack of writing those happy sentences, which pleases Mrs. Genet. And one day the following winter, in 1964, I convince my mother to let me go skiing at Mount Snow with my friend Cissy. She worries, because she doesn't trust Mr. Moore, Cissy's father, to watch us properly. But after I plead and wheedle and beg, she gives in.

Now Cissy's father has gone off to the expert trails, leaving us on our own to choose the slopes we'd like to ski, and I'm thrilled that he hasn't made us take a dumb old class like my mother would have. I've never been to Mount Snow, and after it took all my powers of persuasion, reminding her I was eleven years old, and then a sulking fit before I got her to let me go, I'm determined to make the most of it. So far it's been great. I don't know why she made such a fuss to begin with. Now maybe she'll see that I'm old enough to do things on my own, without her supervision.

Kennedy has been dead now for more than three months and Lyndon Johnson is president, with his wife, Ladybug. Despite my efforts, I haven't forgotten what happened, but the whispering people don't come much anymore and I'm beginning to think I'm safe, that the worst is over. In any event, life has gone on, just as my mother said it would.

High above Mount Snow, Cissy and I perch in the chairlift, which swings dangerously as it approaches the top. I'm scared of heights and convinced the cable will break at any moment. Getting off the lift scares me almost as much as riding it, but I'm glad we're almost there. I can't wait to start the long run down the "Experienced Skiers Only" trail spreading out below us.

Lynnie was positively green with envy when Mommy finally told me I could go. When I woke at five-thirty so I could eat breakfast before I left with the Moores at six, I felt bad for her, but not bad enough to stay home. She wouldn't even say good-bye; I can't help wishing she could see me now, riding the chairlift up Mount Snow while she's at home, eating her heart out.

But I don't get as much pleasure from the thought as I expect to. The truth is, I don't enjoy thinking of her hurting or feeling bad in any way, especially if I'm the cause. Even when it isn't my fault, like when Gary Evans got angry a long time ago and bashed her head against the cellar wall and she had to have two stitches above her eye. I was jealous of the stitches, maybe, but the worst part was the blood and her crying, and Mommy taking her to the doctor and me being scared she'd die, leaving me alone without her. I realize, as Cissy and I stare down the mountainside, that secretly what I want most is to have Lynnie here with me, my best friend, the best twin sister in the world.

When we reach the top and the slick ice-covered ground slides beneath our skis, the chair pushes us from behind and a boy in a blue employee parka holds it still a moment so we can slip off and quickly glide to one side. I didn't realize it would be so much colder up here. My eyeballs are freezing; I'm breathing through icicles in my nose. I don't dare open my mouth. But it's worth it. Older skiers, dressed in masks and goggles and using the newest equipment, fly past us, without even pausing to look at the mountain falling away below. Except for the swoosh of their skis, it's ghostly quiet, as if up here ordinary sounds get frozen in winter and no one can hear anything until spring, when all the stored-up frozen sounds pop and fall through the air like rain.

It's like a picture in a storybook—the cut-glass sky, the sparkling white of the slope so pure and wondrous it takes my breath away. Bright-colored faraway figures dot the trails like in a Grandma Moses picture, and the trail edges are decorated with Christmas evergreens drooping under their weight of snow, all that ocean of still white-ness, and the lodge at the bottom not even visible from where we are. If only it weren't so cold, I half wish I could just stay up here and write poems about winter and never come down at all.

But it is cold, and if we're not going to freeze solid, we'd better get going. I look down one last time. The slope doesn't seem any harder than the others we've tried today, and, I remind myself, I skied in *Switzerland* just last winter, and what's stupid Mount Snow to that?

Cissy is off first and I yell for her to wait, but either she doesn't hear or she's trying to race me down to the lodge. No matter. I know I can beat her. Bending my knees, I shove off with my poles, heading down not on gentle sweeps back and forth across the slope, snow-plowing to slow myself and stay in control the way my mother taught me, no, I'm going to catch up with Cissy. I head straight down, the icy surface of the snowpack giving me even more speed than I intend.

I never see the sitzmark. I don't remember tumbling head over heels for yards. I know only that I'm suddenly down, my legs tan-gled, my skis and poles nowhere to be seen. Oh, well, I'll find them as soon as I pick myself up, I think, cursing the delay. I start to pull myself to a sitting position when there's a blast of lightning so in-tense and unexpected I don't at first know where I feel it. Sprawling back on the snow, I realize it's my right leg. I don't dare sit up again. The pain will go away soon. Even though Cissy will get down to the bottom way before me, I'm not too worried. I can hear the breath of skis on the snow as other skiers swoop past me. After a while, I try to push myself to a sitting position again. This time, I'm so stunned by the starburst of pain shooting through my leg, I cry out.

"Hey, honey," calls a female voice, a skier swooshing to a stop just above me. "Are you hurt?"

I feel pain like a stab wound in my leg, and though I want to reassure her nothing is wrong, that I'm just waiting to catch my breath, I nod. I'm surprised to hear my voice trembling and tearful. "I don't know."

There's a scraping sound as she thrusts her poles through the ice crust and carefully sidesteps down to me on her skis. "Hmm," she says, looking me over. She looks at my leg, which I can't see, and shakes her head.

"Sorry, kiddo, but I think you're through skiing for today." She's wearing a red stocking cap, with all her hair up under it like a kid. Her blond bangs are windblown, her fair cheeks sunburned pink. She takes off her goggles. Her eyes are sky blue. Bending over, she unbuckles her skis and thrusts them upright but diagonally into the snow near me, making an X.

I know what this means, and I rush to tell her she's made a terrible mistake. "I'm okay. I fell, that's all. My leg is—just pulled a muscle. Maybe I twisted my ankle." I try to convince her, "Please don't call Rescue."

I can hear her but I can't see her behind me as she waves down a passing skier. Then she kneels in the snow next to me.

"You look like you're freezing."

I realize with surprise that I'm shivering violently, but I don't feel cold at all. She shrugs off her parka and wraps it around me, trying to jostle me as little as possible, even though moving just my shoulders sends fiery explosions of pain through my entire body. "What's your name, sweetheart?"

I tell her.

"Well, Pammy, you're going to be fine. But I'm not going to leave you until Rescue arrives. Don't you worry."

I notice she has a southern accent and vaguely wonder how she knows how to ski when it doesn't snow down south.

When Rescue finally appears in red jackets and ski pants two hours later, she scolds them angrily. I think at first she's mad at me, mad because she missed so much skiing, but she says, "You fellas took long enough! Don't you know this poor kid has been lying in the snow for hours?" I just lie there, listening, unable to do anything to help myself. I notice that the sun isn't above the trees anymore and the back of my clothes is soaked through from snow my body heat has melted.

The Rescue people pack my leg in a cardboard tubelike thing, strapping it so it won't move, but this hurts so much that I scream for them to stop.

The lady with the southern accent brushes my cheek with her fingers. "It's okay, Pammy. I know it hurts, but they have to splint it or it could get hurt worse on the way down. You've been such a brave young lady. Hang on just a bit longer. It's almost over."

They buckle more straps over the blankets so I won't fall out of the sled cocoon. Then we're on our way, the ride so quick we're at the bottom before I know it. Rescue carries me into a wooden building behind the lodge. It's so warm there my glasses fog over. My hands tingle inside my mittens, thawing. There's a crowd of people standing around holding cups of coffee while other people lie on a row of beds against the wall.

Hours pass. Finally a flannel-shirted doctor looks at a piece of black plastic film that he says is a picture of my leg and goes to work, wrapping it in sticky wet gauze. I try to swallow my cries, but it hurts an awful lot and at one point I let a wail through. He frowns, nods to the nurse. She hands me a black mask attached to a tube.

"That's ether," he says to me over his shoulder, instructing. "Breathe deep if this hurts too much." He bends back to his task. The pain is like firecrackers going off in my leg, shooting rockets of pain into my head, but the gas coming out of the mask is so sweet and sickening I can't bear it. I bite back the urge to scream, even when he starts pushing and pulling at my leg as if he's going to snap it off. I feel faint. I'm literally seeing stars, blinding blue light exploding in the black behind my eyelids. And I do scream, I scream and scream, but only in my mind. I beg God to let my mother magically appear. Mommy would never let him hurt me like this. But God says nothing, God does nothing, and my mother doesn't come, and if the pain doesn't stop soon I'm going to die and I know this is my punishment, that if Kennedy hadn't died, if I hadn't let him die, if I hadn't killed him, none of this would be happening. Oh, I'm sorry, I'm so sorry, I'm *sorry*!

With a grunt, the doctor stands, rinsing his hands in a basin of water the nurse holds out for him, and when I look down I see he's cut off my snow pants. My right leg is huge and white in a plaster cast. "Let that set for twenty minutes before moving her," he orders the nurse.

"What is it? What's wrong with my leg!" I cry out. I can't budge the cast. I'm paralyzed. "What's wrong?"

The doctor turns back, giving me a strange look. "Didn't anyone tell you? You broke your leg."

But Rescue said it was probably just a sprain. Besides, Spiros don't break bones. I've never even broken a finger! The idea is so awful, and I'm so afraid that my parents will be mad at me, that I burst into tears.

"It's not so bad, kid," sighs the doctor, a little more gently. He reaches out, almost touches my shoulder but not quite. "Be happy you're not like that poor little boy over there. Seven years old and he'll never walk again."

With that, he turns away.

Sometime later, Cissy finally reappears, with a sad-faced Mr. Moore looming up behind her. He's very careful when he carries me to the car, warmed up and waiting just outside, but every step he takes feel like a hot poker plunging into my leg.

Lying on the narrow backseat, my leg inside the cast bursting with pain every time we hit a bump, I pretend to sleep. Instead, I'm thinking how even though I know my mother will be mad at me and I'll never get to go anywhere on my own again, I don't care, I just want to get safely home again, I want to get home and into my own bed, and I want Lynnie more than I've ever wanted anything in my whole life.

I spend several weeks alone in my room, recuperating, with plenty of models to build, lots of musicals to listen to on my record player, and a cowbell to summon my mother in case of emergency. I don't miss school, my piano lessons, or even my friends.

I do miss Lynnie. Lynnie has stopped speaking to me. She seems angry all the time and she won't tell me why. If I ask her to hand me my crutches she flies into a rage. After a while, I learn to get along without her. I learn to do things on my own. Then I realize I like being alone; I like being *left* alone. This is new for me. It's almost a kind of luxury, and soon I don't want to give it up.

Carolyn

After Kennedy was assassinated, it takes forever for Pammy to get back to being herself. What's the big deal? I don't really believe she cares that much except as a way to get attention from the grown-ups.

Christmas comes and goes, and by January things seem back to normal. Everything changes in March.

I am already wide-awake the morning of Pammy's ski trip. Through the thin wall I hear the door latch click and the creak of the wooden floor as Mommy tiptoes over to wake her up. It's not even six. I clamp a pillow over my head. Last night Pammy tried to be nice to me as she laid out her ski clothes, but it felt like she was sneering, "Nyah, nyah, nyah, nyah!" I sulked, gave her the silent treatment.

I hear her as she finishes dressing, picks up her things, and closes the slider to her closet. Shutting her door quietly, she cracks open mine.

"Lynnie? You awake?"

I don't answer.

"Don't be mad at me. Please."

"Go away," I shout and roll over.

"At least *try* to be a good sport." She sounds like Mommy.

Silence.

"Oh, be that way, then!" She flips on my overhead light, throws my door open wide, and takes off down the stairs.

"You pig!" I leap from my bed and sprint up the two steps that separate my room from Martha's. "I hope you have a *wonderful* time!" I slam my door.

A little while later a car door opens. Boots crackle across the driveway. Voices, more shuffling, the clatter of skis being loaded, more voices, a car door bangs shut. Then they're gone. I jerk the curtain away from my window, hoping to see the car turning onto Ridge Road. Nothing. I am left alone for the first time.

I hate Pammy but already I miss her.

That evening the phone rings. Mom answers downstairs, but before she says anything I know something is wrong.

"Oh, no. What?" Everyone stops talking. I hear her next words clearly. "Is she conscious?"

What's going on? Who is she talking about? I creep closer to the landing.

"Where is she now?" Mommy asks. "Wait, let me put Howard on the line." More whispering.

I'm on the stairs.

"Those girls shouldn't have been on the expert slope! Where were *you*?" After a long pause, he sighs, takes a deep breath. "Put the surgeon on the line."

Surgeon!

Daddy sounds different than I've ever heard him. Is it Pammy they're talking about? Should I go down, find out what's happening? Do I want to know? I hang on the banister, straining to hear.

"Fractured tibia, uh-hmm."

Fractured tibia?

"Did they put her out?"

Put her out? What is he talking about? "Mommy! Mommmmy!" I scramble down the stairs, almost falling over my own feet, careen into the kitchen. Mommy's leaning on the counter.

"What's happened?" I scream.

She turns around. She's wiping her eyes.

"Is Pammy dead? Somebody tell me!"

Mommy shakes her head and holds open her arms. "No, Lynnie, she broke her leg . . ."

Daddy, his expression serious, covers the phone with his hand and motions for quiet.

I begin howling at the top of my lungs. Mommy, crying too, takes me in her arms and walks me out of the kitchen.

Pammy's hurt—what's going to happen to *me*?

It's late and Pammy isn't home yet, but they send me to my room so the adults can talk. What does it matter? Pammy's broken, *my* Pammy's gone. Things will never be normal again. I want my life, *our* life, back the way it always was.

Someone tells me I'll have to take care of my sister now. I'll do anything, *anything*. What does she need? I'll bring her dinners, change the TV channels, do her chores, be her slave. I'll even do her homework!

It is after midnight when they finally bring her home from the hospital. I'm watching from my window and see the car. Quickly I close the shade and sit shivering in the dark. Car doors slam. Voices in the cold. The front door. Heavy. Boots thudding. I steal out to the stairs where I can watch. Four adults. A bundled figure, white as her cast. Somebody trips. A swear word. Pammy screams. I cover my ears. Does it hurt that much? More whispering. More shuffling. Maneuvering her into the living room. Bumping. Creaking of metal bed frame. A whimper. A louder moan. "It's okay to cry, Pammy," Mommy says. Somebody asks for pillows. A question. The whispered answer, ". . . avoid blood clot."

"Clot" sounds really bad. I race back to bed.

She stays in that hospital bed for weeks. I can't sneak by without her seeing me. It seems like hundreds of people come to visit her. Bring her presents. Flowers. Sign her cast. Everyone reminds me to be a good sister. No one visits me. After a while I'm tired of being nice. I have to bite back my fury at all the attention she gets, and I can tell she enjoys every minute of it. How dare she? *I'm* the sickly one. *I* should have broken my leg. She never had to take care of me! Why should I help *her*?

I hate that stupid cast.

AUGUST 1964

Pamela

Just before Lynnie and I start junior high, we have an outside supper with the Bismarck family, neighbors who technically live on the next block but to whom we are connected by adjoining backyards.

Shadows stretch out onto the lawn like pen-and-ink drawings, already long and blue by seven-thirty. Dinner over, the grown-ups are still endlessly talking, now over iced coffee, sitting on webbed chaises and Adirondack chairs on the terrace. My mother smokes cigarettes with Mrs. Bismarck, using long plastic holders to help them cut down on whatever makes cigarettes both dangerous and impossible to give up. The air smells of freshly cut grass and damp asphalt from the sprinkler overshooting the lawn and wetting down the driveway. Lynnie has gone inside to read, and Chip has been told to empty all the wastebaskets for the next morning's trash pickup. Six-year-old Martha plays with Lucy, the Bismarcks' daughter. I sit by myself at the picnic table, sipping a glass of coffee-milk and doodling with a leaky ballpoint pen on a paper napkin someone has left behind.

The grown-ups sound as they always do—everyone interrupting each other and laughing, even the women, though my father's voice is usually the loudest and most insistent. I don't pay them much attention, until someone calls to me.

"Sweetheart," my mother summons me, her freckled bare arm

scooping the air as if to sweep me up and pull me toward her. "Come on over a moment."

I don't like being stared at by a bunch of grown-ups. I drag my toe in patterns on the dusty flagstones. "What?"

"How would you like to babysit Lucy and Jarrod for a few hours? Are you big enough for the responsibility?" Mommy asks, sucking at her cigarette.

I look from her to Mrs. Bismarck, who closes her silvery blue eyelids and smiles. Mommy never uses makeup, only lipstick, so I'm not sure what to make of women who wear blue eye shadow and mascara, especially when it's just to eat supper with neighbors in the backyard. I think her golden-blond hair might have been bleached that color as well. She looks cheap. How can Mommy stand her?

"We'll pay you," she assures me. "Just like an experienced sitter. How does thirty-five cents an hour sound? All you have to do is get the kids to bed and stay with them until we get home."

My first impulse is to cringe. I want so badly to refuse, and not just because of Mrs. Bismarck's makeup. Refusal is my second impulse too, but it's already weakening because I know this is something I'm going to have to do anyway, so I'd better get used to the idea. Posed as a question, it was never one that allowed for any answer but yes.

In the growing darkness of the Bismarck house, I read Lucy and Jarrod a story, Lucy leaning her head against my shoulder the way Martha sometimes does, and after reminding them to brush their teeth, I get them into bed, remembering to let each ask for a drink of water before I give the authoritative signal that ends all the fooling around in *my* house. "Enough is enough, now, toot sweet, go to sleep."

By the time I get back downstairs, it's after nine P.M. I realize in the sudden hush that I'm alone in a strange house that's much too dark and silent and lonely. After fifteen minutes of waiting for the Bismarck parents, I've had enough. I want to go back to my own house. I want to call across the two backyards to Mrs. Bismarck to tell her to come home, tell her, *I don't want to be paid, please just come and take care of your own kids and let me go home. I'm only eleven. I'm not ready to be a babysitter, don't you understand?*

Peering out the back door, I can't see the glow of our patio lights anymore, which means they've all retreated indoors to get away from the mosquitoes. How can they do this to me? They *know* I am afraid to use the phone, and the only one I've even seen in the Bismarck house is in the dark downstairs den where I'm too scared to go because I can't find the light switch. They *knew* that all the time, they *knew* it when they moved from the patio where I could call to them to the living room. Now no one can hear me! And they don't care what happens to me.

I sit in the dim hall on the bottom of the stairs, staring at the wall clock, watching the hands and willing the time to pass. It takes forever for the minute hand to move and just when I think I catch it, the light suddenly changes. And again. *There!* It's inside my eyeballs, too bright, too sharp, so I can't quite see anything. It hurts behind my eyes, the light getting inside and searing my brain. Now it pulses—in and out, in and out—like a fire siren made of light. Outside, the splotches of brightness, thick black lines vibrate. Everything looks cartoonlike and unreal. I push my palms over my eyes, pressing hard. Somehow, the bright light and dark outlines together create suction so that my eyes feel as if they're going to be yanked out of their sockets.

Then the brightness is full of noisy talking, a crowd of people, and I hear my name several times, as if the party's in my honor, as if the large party spilling—yes! out of the house next door!—has been held for me. It's exciting and frightening. I toy with the idea of investigating.

Into the din, the sound of pounding. It's the front door.

"Who's there?" I yell.

"Pammy, it's Mr. and Mrs. Bismarck. We're home."

Like water draining down a sink, the light show and partying noises fade and the normal quietness of reality washes through the house. I run through the living room. Mrs. Bismarck is outside standing at one of the big windows flanking the door. She shields her eyes, peering in, waving. I open the door.

"We thought you'd disappeared!" She laughs tipsily, alcohol loosening her smile. "Any problems?"

I tell her everything went fine.

Two quarters and two dimes in my pocket, I head home back over the fence, but it's truly dark out now, the crickets rasping in intermittent bursts, the heavy moon a deep orange, like that special milkweed the butterflies feed on. In the heaviness of the air I feel like I can smell the end of summer, the last fling of greenness before frost swoops down. It seems ominous and menacing. With an involuntary shudder, I scold myself for being superstitious, a nincompoop.

Most of the backyards in the neighborhood are dark now, but I can see the yellow square of our kitchen window, and so I make my way home by fixing on that square of light and feeling my way like a blind person, trying not to think about anything else.

$\mathcal{F}$ALL 1964–$\mathcal{W}$INTER 1965

Carolyn

Bang, bang. I kick the bathroom door. "Pammy?" No answer. Bang, bang. *WHACK!*

"Stop it, Lynnie."

"Hurry up! It's my turn." She doesn't respond. I put my ear to the door. Nothing. I wait. Glance at my watch. "Pammy, the bus comes in thirty minutes. Pleeease." No answer. "Pammy?"

"Hmmm?"

I can't afford to start a fight. She's weird enough without that. I sigh. "Come on, Pammy." I try not to sound demanding. "At least let me come in with you."

Mom hisses from her bedroom. "Lynnie, shhhh. You'll wake Martha!"

Suddenly, the bathroom door opens. Pammy squinches over to give me space at the sink and shuts the door.

I shouldn't be surprised anymore, but I am. I don't understand what has happened to her. I disapprove and she knows it.

"What don't you like now?" she asks.

I shrug and throw up my hands. I pick up the hairbrush, bend over from the waist, and brush upside down. Then, upright, I flip my hair back and arrange spit curls just so against my cheeks. Satisfied, I lean over the sink, looking for pimples, dabbing Clearasil on the biggest ones and blending. In the mirror, I see Pammy. She's staring at me. "What?" I say. This time she shrugs. I squeeze out some Crest and start scrubbing my teeth. Pammy imitates. We spit at the same instant, rinse, and for a moment our faces are framed in the mirror. Twins. Two sets of crooked front teeth, glasses, brown eyes. Pammy no longer taller. My face a bit rounder. We haven't yet acquired the angles and curves I want. I long to be pretty. But I see something else in the mirror, Pammy.

"What's the matter with you?" I snort in disgust. "Don't you know anything?"

"What's wrong?" She sees me looking at her skirt and picks up the front, scans it, puzzled. "Oh, you mean the *wrinkles*?" She frantically tries to smooth them with her hands. "I was up doing homework last night. I guess I fell asleep in my clothes."

"Liar, you sleep in your clothes all the time. And look, you've worn the same clothes every day this week!" I reach for her blouse, jab at the scabs of old mustard and dingy hem. "When was the last time you washed this?" I sniff the air. "And you didn't take a shower, did you?"

"Shower? I took one last week," she says.

She just doesn't get it. "You're supposed to take one every day." I sound like our kindergarten teacher. God, why do I have to spell everything out for her? "Look, we're in junior high now. People don't know we're twins. If you're filthy, they'll think you're me."

"So?" She slumps on the edge of the tub and looks me up and down. She sighs. "You make it look so easy."

"It *is* easy. Just do it!" I scream, throwing a wet towel at her and narrowly missing. "Why do I have to remind you about everything, for crying out loud?" I snag her greasy hair and yank it in front of her face. "Look at this, feel it!"

She touches gingerly. "What about it?"

"Feel *this*!" I show her my clean hair. I point back at her. "Don't you know all that oil will make your pimples worse?"

"Pimples? What are they?"

"I give up. You're hopeless." How can she be the smartest kid in the class, but taking a shower is too much work? It doesn't make sense. I know it's mean, but I rush out to join my friends at the bus stop. The last thing I want is to be seen with Pammy.

FALL 1964

Pamela

One night, after everyone has gone to bed, I tap on the flimsy drywall between my room and Lynnie's: Morse code SOS. Three shorts, three longs, then three shorts again. *Lynnie, wake up! I'm frightened!* Two short taps of acknowledgment come back almost immediately: *The coast is clear,* she's saying, *come on over, but be careful not to wake anyone.*

It's a school night, and it has been an hour since I heard our mother's measured tread on the stairs, the complaint of hinges as she opened and closed her bedroom door. The glow of light from under my door is dark now where our younger sister Martha sleeps, in a room that connects to ours without benefit of hallway. I'm not worried about waking her; she sleeps like someone run over by a tank. But Mommy has a mother's radar and I don't want her to know I'm still up.

I ease my door open, millimeter by millimeter, holding the knob so it doesn't make the loud click it usually does. Martha snores, mumbles, then turns over. Holding my breath, I slide around the corner, push Lynnie's door ajar, and slip through. A gleam of moonlight comes off the finish of her long dresser, the one we used to share. But I can't see more than that. Fumbling in the darkness, I inch forward until I find her large bed with my fingers. I know she sleeps on the near side, so I follow the edge, finding my way with my fingers to the other side. I lift the blankets and creep under the covers, snuggling up as close as I can without touching.

"Pammy? Tha' you? Wassa matter, you can't shleep either?" Lynnie mumbles. Despite the "either," she's still half in dreamland.

"Yeah," I answer. "Just thinking too much. Can I sleep here?"

"If you set the alarm," she agrees, sounding more awake. "You have to leave before Mommy comes in or she'll be mad again."

I fumble for the clock, set it for five-thirty, then put it on the floor by my side of the bed.

"Thinking? What about?"

For a moment, I can't remember what she is referring to. My eyes are getting used to the dark and I can see her now. Turning to me while lifting herself on one elbow, she asks again, "Thinking about what?"

"Oh, well, about something really—you know, it's kind of hard to explain, it's just this weird feeling and—" I'm deliberately vague, not sure how much I can tell her. "First this afternoon. Then it happened again tonight, my hands got blue and—"

The silence was suddenly eloquent.

"Lynnie?"

I can see her silhouette in the dim glow from a streetlight coming in the window. She is lying on her back now. Her eyes are open and she stares at the ceiling; her fingers tap impatiently against each other while her arms rest on her stomach.

"What's wrong? Are you mad? I'm really sorry for waking you, I mean it."

"No," she says, her voice thin and sounding angry nonetheless. "But if you're talking about what I think you are, I already know."

More silence as I take this in.

"You do?" I finally answer and wait for her to explain.

She takes a deep breath, then pushes herself up against the headboard till she's almost sitting. "It's like this feeling"—she hesitates, as if it's hard to describe, and spreads her arms to encompass the feeling in the air—"like my hands are blue and huge, like those parade bal-loons from Macy's—"

"Yes! I was *all* hands! And then—?" I push her, wanting her to complete the thought.

"I don't know how to explain it, but then this idea that took up all the room. Pammy, it was so weird, I don't know *what* it was."

My face has gone icy; I can hardly breathe. The *last* thing I want is for her to say three critical words, because then she really has un-derstood and that means it was *not* just my imagination. It was some-thing real. This possibility is too horrifying to contemplate.

"You know what I'm talking about, don't you?" she whispers. "Three words?" Even in the darkness I can tell that her eyes are wide open, staring at me. I nod.

"Gray. Crinkled. Paper," we whisper at precisely the same time.

I gasp and sit bolt upright.

She looks at me with astonishment and, to my surprise, relief is written all over her face. She's almost smiling. "You too?"

I nod. I don't trust myself to speak.

"Wow, that's so—" She sighs. The worried rigidity of her body washes away, vanishing. "Gray Crinkled Paper. I thought I was the only one. I was so afraid. But you felt it too, honest? What a relief."

I'm not so easily reassured. What allays her fears only makes mine worse. Even after I go back to my own bed at dawn, I can't sleep. I lie awake, still troubled, thinking and trying to puzzle out what happened and what it means.

Lynnie doesn't mention Gray Crinkled Paper the next morning, or the next. It's like she has completely forgotten it. She acts as if the conversation never took place. Or doesn't matter. I want to forget it myself, so I say nothing to her or to anyone else, but it never leaves my thoughts.

Mr. Kimball, the seventh-grade guidance counselor, is pulling his hair, shaking his head, his mouth and nose pinched into a disapproving snout. *How*, he wants to know, can someone who tests in the 99.99 percentile be getting Cs? Why am I not working up to my potential? Don't I know that even in seventh grade bad marks will condemn me to a second-rate college? Why, Radcliffe won't even look at me with grades like these, he lectures, sounding coached by my father.

Luckily for me, the ten minutes allotted for my annual conference with Mr. K are leached away while he shuffles official-looking papers with my name at the top, so I don't have to answer his questions. Questions I couldn't answer even if there *were* enough time.

How could he understand how fear makes me shrivel? I'm afraid of everything in junior high: the ninth-grade greasers slouching down the hall in their leather jackets and slicked-back hair; their "fast" girlfriends with bleached manes and too much mascara; the rough, menacing crowds spilling out into the corridor when the bell rings; and especially gym class where my modesty is offended by obligatory gang showers, supervised by the teacher who watches to make sure everyone washes properly. Worst of all, the disembodied voices and Gray Crinkled Paper, and the Strangeness—I could never tell him about such things.

He finishes stacking his papers and clears his throat to get my attention. "I'm afraid we're out of time this afternoon, but I hope you manage to bring your grades up next year."

I stare at my shoes. "I won't be here next year."

He stops in the middle of rising and sits back down. "What do you mean? You won't? Why not?"

"I'm going to Dayhill Girls' School."

This gets his attention, much to my dismay, and when I repeat that I'm transferring to DGS, a private school in New Haven, he looks both wounded—what, public school isn't good enough for me?—and relieved at the prospect of one less underachiever in his charge. He seems to think, however, that this can't possibly be my choice, that my parents, or at least my father, have to be behind the decision. I don't care. Let him think what he wants; I'll be just as glad to see the last of him as he of me.

Finally, ending the interview, he stands. He looks like he's going to add something more, but I am quickly out the door before he can open his mouth. I don't want to hear anything he has to say. I'm going to Dayhill, end of discussion.

SUMMER 1965

Pamela

Even though Daddy is a salaried professor at Yale Medical School, not in private practice, I always feel guilty for what I have, as well as a burning need to share it. This is strange, given that I have grown up sharing everything with Lynnie and have precious little to call my own. My behavior drives Lynnie crazy; she thinks I'm trying to be little Miss Perfect, Saint Pamela or something. And maybe I am. But it's not for the sake of praise. The more people praise me, the more people see or know about what I do, the less good it is and the worse it feels. I don't know if I believe in God or not. I mean, I do believe in God, but I know as a Unitarian I'm not supposed to, and part of me agrees it *is* silly, there's no two ways about *that*. But another part of me wants the kind loving father part of God so desperately she'll do anything.

It is for God that I do things like giving away my Christmas presents or instigating my sixth-grade Sunday school class to make wooden toys for "poor children." That happens one Sunday morning in early September. While the other kids are haggling over how much of their allowances to contribute every week to the church, I stand up in the back of the room, my voice rising like I'm some white-bloused, plaid-skirted Elijah, and I suggest that investing time and effort is a better way to donate to church and society than just coughing up a few quarters. Chastened, they turn to what we can do and how we can do it.

Maybe it's because of this, which leads to an article and pictures in a New Haven newspaper that I refuse to allow myself to read, or maybe because I'm so terribly shy and quiet that she has mistaken it for maturity—whatever it is, one evening in April, not long after I graduate to my last walking cast, my mother asks me to come with her to church to see a slide show about a special Unitarian summer camp.

Lynnie's ears perk up when she hears that Camp Channing is coed. "Can I come too?"

"I don't think you're ready for this kind of camp, Lynnie, but there's no reason you can't see the slide show," Mommy concedes.

I don't feel ready either, I want to say. I've attended Girl Scout camp for years, and each summer I've been miserable. Why she wants me to try yet again I don't know, and it makes me feel like screaming, *Can't you see anything? Don't you know I hate camp?*

At church, the slide show is narrated by a young man with a scruffy beard and owlish eyeglasses. He talks of "group this" and "group that" until I can feel panic rising in me like swirling green water and all I can hear is my heartbeat in my ears and I lose track of everything and don't see the slides or hear anything the man is saying, all I want is *out, out, out*. I want nothing to do with the "unique Camp Channing experience." I can barely breathe. I'm getting dizzy just sitting in my chair. It's all I can do not to get up and run.

Finally the lights come up and the man asks for questions.

"I've got to go to the bathroom," I mutter, racing out the door, frantic to get away before I have to offer a reaction. By the time I return, the group is having coffee and cookies and Lynnie and my mother are deep in conversation.

"Are you sure, Lynnie?" my mother asks, shaking her head. "I can't drop everything and drive up and rescue you if you don't like it. It's a commitment. You have to be sure you can make it through all three weeks."

"I'm sure, I'm sure," Lynnie begs, hopping from one foot to the other. "I really want to go. I *promise* I won't call."

Mommy looks up and smiles when I approach. "We were waiting for you. So what do you think? It's exciting, isn't it? Even Lynnie wants to go."

"Good. Let her." I am off the hook and no way is this chance going to get away.

"What do you mean?"

"Let her. I don't want to go."

"But Pammy, it's just your cup of tea—"

"No it isn't. It *isn't*. I hate camp. Don't you *know* that by now?" My voice is getting loud. The other parents and teens start looking at us, so I turn stiffly and walk off. I figure I'll go sit in the car and wait until they are ready to leave.

The car, of course, is locked. It's dark out and a cold rain is beginning to fall.

That summer, while Lynnie attends Camp Channing for three weeks, I spend my time with the family at our summerhouse on Cape Cod. I do a lot of reading and swimming, and most of the time, I don't miss Lynnie.

One morning my mother starts cleaning the house like it suddenly matters. She snaps at me for swimming in the lake then tracking sand in on my bare feet instead of showering it off downstairs.

"But Ma, there are too many spiders in there!"

"I don't care. You shower before you come inside next time, do you hear? I'm not your personal maid!"

I'm stung. She knows I'm a neatness freak and never expect her to clean up after me, but it is hard to scrape off all the sand on the mat by the door before crossing the living room. Besides, the basement shower, open to the world, is dark and smelly and infested with creepy crawlies. She's never made us use it before. So what's up now?

It soon becomes clear. Daddy's old friend, Rob Panzer, whom

he's known since high school, is bringing his family from California to visit, and Mommy wants the place to shine. I try to pitch in, but she's in such a bad mood I can't do anything right. Finally I decide the best thing to do is just to stay out of her way.

The Panzers arrive with so little fanfare you'd have thought they lived just down the street. Dr. Panzer is wearing a striped polo shirt and worn khaki shorts and looks like a kind of tall elf, potbellied, weak-chinned with likable eyes, and if his wife is forgettable, she isn't objectionable either. I'm looking around for the kids, figuring I'll be drafted as babysitter. *No* kids? Boy, am I lucky! Then I notice the boy sitting on the car fender, carving up a thick twig.

"I see you've found our son, Paul," says Dr. Panzer. "He's just about your age, thirteen, if I'm not offending the young lady by guessing how old she is. Paul, put that infernal whittling away and come say hello to—ah . . ."

"—Pam," I answer. "I'm twelve." I say this to Dr. Panzer. Then to his son, "Don't put it down 'cause of me. No, you're almost through. Just cut the hole out and you'll be able to use it."

Paul looks up, eying me with curiosity. I'm ashamed of myself for showing off the way I just did. Still, I can tell he's impressed. It's not every day he meets a twelve-year-old girl who knows how to carve a whistle.

The Panzers are staying a few days. I didn't sign up for entertaining this Paul guy, and I want to get more reading done, but the grown-ups are always throwing him and me together. One afternoon, they have cocktails on the lawn and someone suggests that Paul take me out on the lake for "a row." I groan. As if I need anyone to row me anywhere. I'm perfectly capable of taking myself out on the lake anytime I please, thank you kindly.

But Paul surprises me. "Why not, Pammy? It'd be nice to go out together, just you and me." He smiles at me in such a way that I know this means something different from what his words actually say, but whatever he really means, I'm not getting it all.

We go down to the dock and untie the rowboat, and Paul ceremoniously lets me get in first, before he lowers himself in and casts off. But soon I see he barely knows how to row at all, and I know I shouldn't but I'm dying to tell him how to feather the oars to scoop water more efficiently. When we're out in the middle of the lake, Paul ships one oar then the other and looks me over with a puzzling half smile.

"So now what?" I ask.

He's quiet, just sits there, dangling his fingers in the water. I copy him.

"Isn't this romantic?" he finally says. The sun casts long after-noon rays on the sparkling water.

Romantic? The notion makes me very nervous. I don't think I'm ready for whatever "romantic" means. I know I don't *feel* romantic. So I sit up high, pretending to stretch, and casually crane my neck.

I feign surprise. "Uh-oh, I think they're waving at us! They want us to come in. Look at those clouds! We'd better hurry."

Paul looks disappointed. Without a word, he grabs the oars, but he rows so poorly it takes us a half hour to get back to the dock. I'm relieved when we finally tie up the boat and I'm free to go off by myself.

The next day the Panzers go off sightseeing, and Daddy and Mommy drive up to the Berkshires to retrieve Lynnie. Later I hear the car pull down into the gravel drive. I dash up the steep steps, ea-ger to see if three weeks away have changed her.

To my surprise, she emerges from the front passenger seat, next to Mom, which by rights belongs to Daddy. He gets out of the back like it's no big deal.

"Hey," I say softly. "How was it?"

She groans lightly, like someone who has feasted too long and hard, her knees giving a bit. "*God,*" she exclaims, before rebounding, "it was fantastic!"

I notice the "God" before the "fantastic." "Lynnie, you swore!"

"What? Oh, you mean, 'God'? Psht, that's nothing. You shoulda heard us!"

"But swearing, Lynnie?"

A great deal of the three-week experience has indeed been fantastic, literally, I gather, as Lynnie tells me the details. She loved camp, especially the drama classes and twice-daily chapel, but more than anything, she liked being near boys and spent a great deal of time fantasizing about them. Her biggest disappointment was that she never had a chance actually to talk to one face-to-face.

The Panzers return later in the afternoon. I've forgotten to warn Lynnie about Paul, who greets me like an old friend, then asks me who *she* is.

Openmouthed, stricken, Lynnie looks at me with anguish and an accusation of treachery in her eyes. From that moment on she declares war, and Paul is the battlefield. What Lynnie doesn't understand is that I don't care to fight. As far as I'm concerned, Paul is hers.

Carolyn

I feel like a hero the summer I go to Camp Channing for the first time, alone, without Pammy. At last *I'm* the one our parents talk about with admiration. I'm sure they see *me* for the first time, no longer just Pammy's shadow. I like this. It makes me feel grown up. Although initially they expected Pammy to attend, when she refused, they were surprised that I wanted to brave this venture without her. When I return from camp I've had an epiphany of the wholly intellectual sort; for the first time I understand what it's like to feel smart. It's odd. I never realized that I could have my own ideas, that my brain operates independent of Pammy's.

At Channing, Unitarian-Universalist camp though it is, we start and end each day with a church service. At thirteen, more than anyone knows, I look forward to those services in the tiny stone chapel with real pews and colorful stained-glass windows. At home our church, if you can call it that, is made of concrete cinder blocks in the shadow of a significantly grander synagogue. We aren't Jewish enough to go there. Unitarians aren't anything enough. To me, the chapel at Channing is a real church. Though I don't say so out loud, I feel like God is actually there.

The second year, Pammy decides to accompany me. We are assigned to separate cabins and groups, and spend very little time together. Other campers know we're twins, of course, and as usual I feel inferior when they compare us. Although I wanted her to come with me, I didn't expect her to take over; Channing was *my* place— I never would have encouraged her to come if I'd realized how much I'd lose. What's happened to me? Last summer I felt so easy, relaxed, confident. This summer I'm back to feeling second.

It's eight o'clock on one of the last nights at camp. All the campers hike two by two as usual down the dusty camp road, past the Bonnie Blink where we eat, the barn, and outer cottages. We tramp across the wooden bridge, our footfalls clattering like rifle shots, until finally we trot down the paved main street to the chapel. In the fading twilight the chapel is lit from within and glows ethereally, warm and inviting. The end of camp is already on our minds and heavy in the air with the smell of dry leaves and moist earth and in the sorrowful echo of feet.

Counselors motion for silence as we approach. One by one we mount the stairs, enter the darkened church, and file into the long worn wooden benches. Soft, indefinable music seems to emanate from above and mixes with the fragrance of burning incense, infusing the space with a deep mystery and awe. As the last camper takes her seat, the music fades, the electric lights dim, and a hush of anticipation and excitement fills the room.

Then suddenly, from the rafters comes an amplified female voice intoning slowly, dramatically, "Some say the world will end in fire." The lights fade up just enough to see, coming down the aisle, dancing figures, each clad in leotards and tights and holding a stick with a cardboard mask in front of her face. On each mask is a simple marker drawing of a facial expression. The first dancers carry masks of happy, smiling faces. The dancers whirl and stamp down the aisle until, reaching the proscenium, they stop, frozen, facing away from us while the next line of the poem is read.

"Some say in ice . . ." And the next series of masked dancers enters, their faces grim, sad. They dance to the front and end up also facing away, their backs to the audience.

"From what I've tasted of desire, I hold with those who favor fire." Dancers with laughing masks. The background music accompanying the reading grows even louder with each line.

"But if it had to perish twice . . ." Music becomes noise. Masked dancers raging. Faces contorted, angry, hateful.

"I think I know enough of hate, to say that for destruction . . ." Dissonance, crashing cymbals, breaking glass. All the dancers have turned their backs to us, cutting a thin line across the stage.

". . . Ice is also great . . ." Blam! Cut lights!

". . . and would suffice." Cut sound! Momentary black. Then lights flash.

In the startling glare, we see the line of dancers facing us, their masks completely blank. We gasp in unison.

The whole camp talks about the service for days, debating its meaning and admiring its powerful impact.

The author, director, and producer of this event turns out to be guess who: Pammy.

Pamela

In 1966, the summer after Lynnie went to Camp Channing alone, we both attend, and I earn the nickname "Silent Sam" because I won't talk.

One rainy afternoon, two counselors gather our cabin and the boys from our brother cabin for a camp specialty known as a "snowflake." In the empty arts building, we lie on our backs in a circle, heads toward the center, legs extended outward like the spokes on a wheel or the snowflake for which the exercise is named. The rain pecks at the tin roof and wind seethes through the cracked windows. We close our eyes and are told to lie still, letting our minds wander.

Paula, the counselor, gets us started. "I am on the beach on a warm summer's day, the sun on my face, the air is sweet and salty. Someone is lying on the sand next to me—" She stops and lets the silence carry her words.

"She offers me a stone, perfect, round and smooth. She is smiling," murmurs Ted, the camper lying next to me in the circle.

Lloyd's voice takes up the train of thought. "She says she misses me and wishes I could stay with her."

"Suddenly, a cloud passes in front of the sun and I feel a chill—" Waiflike, pretty in a "Jesus freak" kind of way, and sought after by the boys, Augusta wears a leather bracelet to hide the scars on the inside of one wrist.

"A tornado rages up the beach and sweeps me into the darkness," I whisper and am shocked to hear the sound of my voice. "I'm drowning in Gray Crinkled Paper, but the voices just laugh and mock me—"

Silence. All that can be heard is the rain's fitful tapping. In an agony of regret—how can I have been so weak, so stupid? as if anyone here cares!—I wait for someone else to take up the story, praying that my inadvertent disclosures will be ignored.

"Sam, what's wrong with you?" someone says. "We want to be your friends. Why don't you trust us?"

My face burns with shame. "I'm fine!" I yell, my eyes flying open. "There's nothing wrong with me. Leave me alone!" I jump to my feet and dash from the room. Barefoot, I run through the rain all the way back to the cabin, the voices jeering, *Sicko! Sicko!*

The empty cabin smells like woodsmoke and bug spray and the faint mildew of damp bathing suits hanging on a string across the cabin. I fling myself onto my bunk, pushing myself deep into my sleeping bag, breathless and shaking. To drown out the voices, I have to cover my ears and drone loudly. Finally, exhausted, I fall asleep, and when the others return, I am calm again, lying on my stomach, pretending to be absorbed in writing in my journal. No one mentions the snowflake disaster.

After our three-week camp session at Channing, I begin to crumble. We join the family again, spending the summer at our house on Cape Cod, and my friend Katie comes up for a visit. At first, things go well—we spend time bicycling to the ice-cream parlor or rowing the boat out on the lake. Once we bicycle to Woods Hole and take the ferry to Martha's Vineyard, where we sleep overnight in the backyard of our English teacher's summerhouse. Though unathletic, Katie seems to enjoy herself. On rainy afternoons, we pore through my father's big dictionary, trying to guess the meaning of various strange words and learning them in the process. Although I complain that he isn't "singable," which Katie flatly contests, we play

Otis Redding's "Dock of the Bay" over and over. Frictions develop, however. My mother interprets Katie's extreme shyness as aloofness and arrogance, and my apparent complicity as betrayal. Naturally, I side with Katie. It seems to me my mother is deliberately picking fights. Finally, there is a blowup and Katie is taken to the bus station to go home early.

I lie on my bed, furious and hurt, thinking about how I should just run away from home, where it's clear no one cares about me. *Do it,* murmurs someone, the same flat, robotic sort of voice I first heard after JFK's assassination. *Do it, run away, teach them a lesson!*

An unearthly Strangeness fills the room. I feel like Alice in Wonderland, except that I've eaten the eat-me cake and drunk the drink-me drink at the same time so that everything is wildly and frighteningly distorted. Noises seem both too loud and yet muffled; light seems only to emphasize the utter foreignness of everything in the room, including my own body. I am suffocating, but I can't do anything but clutch myself and wait for it to pass.

Finally, I manage to get myself to my feet and am relieved that the floor levels out. I'll take the dog for a walk in the fields on the other side of the lake, I decide, too unnerved to leave the house without company of some sort in case the strange feelings return.

At the field, I unsnap the dog's leash, letting her gambol off into the weeds, making sure she stays within view and doesn't wander off to the road. I stomp down a seat in the golden grass, then sit, back to the lake, fiddling with the pebbles, bottle caps, bits of broken glass my fingers find in the weeds.

Why don't you die? asks a soft, persuasive voice. When I don't respond, it gets louder. *You're useless! Why don't you just go ahead and kill yourself? Nobody cares about you anyway!*

I think about this and decide it is true: Nobody does care about me. Tears fill my eyes. I pick up a shard of glass and, extending my wrist, drag the sharp edge across the skin. Again, this time deeper but still not much more than a bad scratch, though blood begins to seep out along the inner side of my wrist, jump-starting me back to myself. *What the hell are you doing?* I think. I hurl the glass into the lake. *You can't do that! You want people to think you're crazy?* The wind rustles the weeds and little glassy wavelets slap the shore. Everything now seems perfectly normal—no voices, no Strangeness. I stick my index fingers in my mouth and whistle for the dog, then walk home, beelining it to the bathroom to wash off my wrist and put on long sleeves before my parents notice the scratches.

Pamela

I'm in ninth grade now. Snow falls early and lies in patches of glittering crystals beneath the evergreens. One day, for many hours, a malaise infects me. Faint spatial irregularities distort my perceptions, deepening stairs and telescoping school corridors. Although no voices intrude, a vague jumble of noise interferes in the background. In English class, ordinarily my favorite of the day, Mrs. Hamilton has to call on me three times before I understand my own name and can respond. By the time school is over and I'm on my way home, the disorientation of the day has begun to resolve itself into the separate reality governed by Gray Crinkled Paper. I feel as if I'm straddling several universes without fully belonging to any one of them.

Grunting a hello to my mother, who is in the kitchen preparing supper, I flee up the stairs, through Martha's bedroom, and into my own. Lynnie and I were given separate rooms in seventh grade. I've kept our old bunk beds, though I use only the upper one. I've dressed both beds with red, yellow, and green print quilts, arranged a bookcase, cricket rocker, and small round table so that the good-sized room, sunken two steps below the level of the adjoining second floor, serves as a kind of bed-sitting room. Melancholy prints by Goya and El Greco are pasted on the ceiling that slopes overhead and a homemade bulletin board of acoustic tiles, the seams concealed with fluorescent-hued "flower power" wrapping paper, hangs on the wall. Unlike my brother and sisters, I keep the room meticulously neat, with a place for everything and everything in its place. It is my haven, my refuge. Now, locking the door, I creep into the double closet and slide the door shut behind me, surrendering to the Strangeness and Gray Crinkled Paper.

"You bitter pig—change the upper climate," my mother says when I finally emerge and come downstairs, joining her in the kitchen. I stare at her, frightened, until, an instant later, I translate it into what she's actually asked, which is for me to walk the dog. "Daddy's due any minute now, so hurry. Supper's almost ready and you know he likes to eat as soon as he gets home."

I do know. Usually on a diet, he eats little during his long day at the hospital, so by the time he gets home from work he's starving and irritable, liable to explode if the meal isn't just then being put on the table. He never likes to wait, for anything.

In the mudroom off the kitchen, I leash Tina and bundle into my jacket again. We head out into the cold of early evening, the dog tugging eagerly at me. Inside, I need the hall light left on when I go to bed because I'm afraid of the dark, but outside I don't mind it so much: I find the darkness comforting, less intrusive than sunlight, and nighttime—like overcast drizzly days—seems to match my state of mind, which is increasingly one of sadness and despair.

Despite the darkness, the snow reflects moonlight so I can make out houses, their windows brightly lit. I look up at Gary's window as I pass the Evanses' house and see someone silhouetted in the window. I wave, but the figure turns away without response. I wait to see if whoever it was will come back until the light goes out.

Farther down the road, the streetlamps are spaced farther apart. When we start down the hill on Tokeneke Drive, it is almost pitch-black in between them. I don't know any of the families on this end of the street, and watching unknown people moving about inside the lit-up houses gives me a pang in my chest and makes me want to cry. I don't even know why. At the bottom of the hill, Tina halts, sniffing and pawing. Finally she relieves herself in the leaves next to a fire hydrant set in front of a clump of leafless birches. Fire hydrant? I see a nun, tiny, wizened, swathed in a black habit. Tina whines, impatient for the return trek, but I stand in a trance, less scared than amazed. It seems to me that as a reward for not running away, a cosmic revelation is to follow. Finally the black-robed figure speaks, her voice pitched low, almost like a man's. "Remember St. Sebastian and the arrows, remember," she whispers. I do remember, how can I forget the arrow-pierced man in a loose robe, his anguished face thrown heavenward in the picture I had to analyze for art history?

Amazement and curiosity turn to terror and Tina and I flee, racing neck and neck up the hill, my lungs on fire, the muscles in my legs growing rubbery with fatigue. My only thought is to get home and lock the door before the apparition overtakes me.

In my increasing misery and confusion, I make another person equally miserable, my ninth-grade science teacher. Mrs. Kato is new to Dayhill and inexperienced as a teacher. She has large, wide-set, rabbity eyes rimmed in pink and always seems to be on the verge of tears. Even her voice trembles. With her compact but petite frame and her light brown hair, cut like a bowl, she could pass for a teenager, except that up close you can see fine lines in her face. Sensing her weakness, wanting her to be stronger than I am, so I can trust her, I go out of my way to be obnoxious and rude, gloating over my consistently high grades because I know she can't flunk me in order to get revenge.

It must seem to her that I enjoy being nasty, that I get a kick out of it, but she doesn't know me, so how can she understand that her emotional fragility only heightens my own feelings of insecurity? I don't enjoy being the "ogre that ate Manhattan," but I am too scared to let her see what lies behind my unrepentant front.

Mrs. Kato puts an equation on the blackboard, writing a plus sign where it is obvious she should use a minus sign. I speak up. "I be-leeeve you've made a mistake again. Don't you know it's supposed to be a minus sign?"

She stares at me, but I stare back, forcing her to look away. She turns to review her calculations, changes the plus sign, then turns back, flushing. "Pam, I'd like to see you after class."

When the bell rings at the end of the period, I casually stack up my books and papers and remain seated until the other students leave the room. Mrs. Kato, her back to me, is writing on the board again. When she turns to face me, her features are contorted, her hands shaking.

"You wanted something?" I bait her, still wanting something from her I can't explain.

Her hands twist themselves over and over. "Why are you so mean to me?"

If she'd asked only why I'm so mean, I might have been able to let down my defenses and talk to her. But she makes the mistake of personalizing the question—"mean to me"—when my behavior is generalized: I'm not deliberately mean to *her* so much as to the weakness and lack of confidence she represents. In truth, I resent being put in a position where I *can* make her cry, where I *can* be the ogre. If she'd assert herself in any way, if she'd stand up to me, I'd be relieved. But she asks, "Why are you so mean to me?" so I have no other option but to respond chattily.

"I don't believe that pointing out mistakes is mean. You would have had everybody learning the wrong thing."

She shakes her head. Then she lifts her face and stares at me, her eyes tearing. This time I'm the one to look away.

"Are you through? Can I go?" I ask, getting to my feet.

"Yes, you may go," Mrs. Kato whispers.

I stomp out and go in search of one of my classmates who loves to talk about Mrs. Kato behind her back.

Because I broke my leg in sixth grade and my weight did not increase commensurate with my height that year, I entered seventh grade weighing eighty-two pounds. By the time I was in eighth grade I still barely topped the scales at ninety-five, but in tenth grade I reach a weight of a hundred and ten pounds and this, compared to my former Twiggy-like build, makes me feel cumbersome, though at nearly five foot three I am not overweight. I begin to feel my body is a burden to the world, and one afternoon when I feel my thighs chafing against one another, I resolve to go on a diet.

Lynnie, who has already reduced her weight to under a hundred pounds, concurs. "You've got to stop eating so much. You can't eat five Toll House cookies in a row. If you want to lose weight you've got to keep your calories below a thousand. Five cookies at five hundred calories—that's half a day's worth! And you have to exercise a lot. I run in place for half an hour every night. If you want, we can exercise together." Although at ninety-eight pounds she doesn't look fat to me or in need of any more exercise, I agree that would make it more fun.

The next morning we tell our father that we'll make our own breakfast and each sit down to a single hard-cooked egg in a custard dish and a dry round of what we've always called "half and half bread," a yin/yang combination of rye and pumpernickel that comes in very small slices. We eat slowly, savoring each bite because we've made a pact not to eat anything else until suppertime. This pact is something Lynnie will find easier to fulfill than I, since at DGS attendance at lunch is mandatory and carefully monitored, while she can simply skip the cafeteria and go to the library instead.

That night, after we've done our homework, we dress in our leotards and head to the basement, where we light a candle, turn off all the lights, and run in circles, leaping over the candle in the center of the room as music plays. The dimly lit cellar, combined with the music and manic exercise, makes us giddy, and we keep at it until somebody's feet start down the cellar stairs. Then we collapse, giggling, on the torn leather settee, vowing to keep the reasons for our giddiness a secret.

Under this regimen, I rapidly lose weight until, when I reach ninety pounds, the other students at school begin to notice. Rather than pleasing me, the comments embarrass me, not because I don't want to be thin. I do, but we've long been taught that dieting, with its unwholesome fixation on the body, is something to be ashamed of, revealing a vanity unworthy of a Spiro. Our cognitive dissonance, a concept I've recently learned from a Yale senior who is teaching us social psychology, arises from the fact that both our parents are overweight and obsessed with it. They continually start new regimens, only to break them in a matter of days. We always know when one or both have started a new diet, because my mother starts cooking up cauldrons of low-calorie cabbage soup and diet Jell-O for dessert.

Every spring, Dayhill allows students to wear their own clothes instead of the hot winter uniform of wool kilts and blazers. In tenth grade, Lynnie and I sew me a spring wardrobe. One day I wear a sleeveless green shift with a halterlike neckline. As usual, at lunch I plead vegetarianism so as to avoid eating anything but lettuce. Hungrily, I watch the others, unconcerned, eating their cheeseburgers.

Sarah Wimble looks up from her plate. "Why don't you eat anymore, Pam?"

"I do," I assure her. "But I'm a strict vegetarian and prefer to eat health foods."

Mrs. Zellman, the dance teacher who sits at the head of our table that week, looks at me. "I hope you don't lose much more weight, Pam," she says. "You don't want to get sick."

I laugh. "Oh, don't worry. I won't. I'm healthy as an ox."

"You don't look like any ox to me," Sarah adds. "Look how bony your shoulders are."

I wish they'd just leave me alone. I laugh and make a face, as if

Sarah's comment is ridiculous. Then I excuse myself to go to the bathroom, just so they'll change the subject.

Scuttlebutt has it that the year before, a tiny seventh grader was hospitalized for losing too much weight because she "didn't want to grow up." At the time, I felt bad for her, wanted to comfort her and help her feel better. It horrified me that anyone would try to starve herself to death. She didn't want to grow up; at fifteen, in tenth grade, I *am* grown up. There's no comparison. No, my problem is that I take up too much space, intrude on people with my massive body. I refuse to eat because I am desperate to reduce that unwanted burden, because I know everyone finds it as loathsome as I. After all, isn't that what the whispering behind my back has been about for years now?

From that very first morning that Lynnie and I abstain from breakfast, I am determined to reduce my bodily presence in the world, to take up less space, to be "one with the wind," as discarnate and spiritual as a spring breeze. Already I have symbolically reduced myself to a disembodied "pair of ears": Others are always seeking me out to listen to their problems while I divulge none of my own. Now I strive to divest myself even of that.

By eleventh grade my behavior is attracting attention, less because I engage in worrisome activities than because I stop doing things I formerly enjoyed. Little by little, I lose ground. Though I manage to keep my grades up, except in my old bugaboo, algebra, I no longer participate in class or pursue extracurricular activities—glee club, school drama productions, current events club—unless they are solitary ones. Perhaps nowhere is this change more obvious than in dance class.

My body was never flexible enough for gymnastics. True, I could place my palms flat on the floor, bending from the waist and keeping my legs straight, but I was never able to master even a basic backbend or walkover. Nevertheless, in dance I was graceful and creative and as a child was often singled out for starring roles in recitals. Then, for no apparent reason, starting in tenth grade and within the space of a year's time, I begin to lose it all. My body feels foreign, no longer connected to me. At the same time, I feel it's my responsibility to keep away from others, to reduce the potential for harming them. Soon, physically expressive movements in dance class feel so dangerous that I abbreviate them into the smallest acceptable gestures, suggesting arm movements by fluttering my hands in the correct direction or merely inclining my head instead of bowing. Mrs. Zellman is perplexed: How could I have been so transformed, turning from her graceful swan into a gangling ugly duckling? That semester Mrs. Zellman gives me my first C.

I may be stuck living in a body, I think, but I don't have to be involved with it. I vow to separate my essence from this *thing* that takes up so much space in the world.

Lynnie and I are vigilant in monitoring each other, so when she starts attending a nighttime adult education yoga class at a local school, I am compelled to go along. As it turns out, the yoga exercises and accompanying aerobic workout are not the worst of it. It's a popular class, taught by Glory, a vivacious, well-liked woman who still has a dancer's body in middle age. Because her classes are sought after, the entire gymnasium is needed to accommodate all the participants, who are female, middle-aged, and, most of them, carrying unwanted dimpled flesh around their thighs and stomachs. All things being equal, I might have escaped notice, dutifully exercising while not calling any attention to myself. But all things are far from equal. For one thing, not only are Lynnie and I the only teenagers, and noticeably underweight to boot, but Glory is a friend of our parents.

That the class is a source of dreaded torture for me doesn't change the fact that I force myself to attend whenever Lynnie does. At first I blend into the background, unnoticed amid a sea of fat, sweaty, inflexible bodies moving more or less to the music. When Lynnie is remarked upon for her considerable talent—she loves dancing of any kind—I feel no jealousy, only relief that Glory's focus is not on me.

My feeling of relative safety in numbers does not last, however, if only because the contrast between Lynnie's perfect execution of yoga and dance steps and my own terrified awkwardness is so striking. Barre exercises threaten me the least, because I am near the wall and have something to hang on to. But it also takes the least time. Because so many of the women want to lose weight and get into shape, Glory incorporates running to music into our routine, all forty or fifty of us panting as we run in a large circle, Glory in the middle banging a drum and issuing commands: "Tess, run faster, you're holding everyone up!" or "Work those gluteals, ladies!" I wouldn't mind running alone; it's decent exercise and fairly straightforward. But my inhibitions have grown to the point that I cannot allow my arms to swing freely but keep them locked at my sides, no matter how fast she has us go.

"Move your arms!" Glory orders the class, then proceeds to diagnose "those people whose arms don't swing" as "sick." I don't want to be sick; I want to be normal, I want to blend in with the crowd instead of sticking out like Pinocchio's nose, all my faults, all my *symptoms* on public display. I'm terrified that Glory will talk to my mother, enlisting her against me so that even at home they'll notice and comment, and I'll have no escape anywhere.

Even after my transfer to Dayhill, I'm convinced that my father thinks I'm a failure and evil incarnate. I'm sure he has people spying on me. We no longer speak to one another except when it is absolutely unavoidable. I won't sit near him at dinner, making Martha, the youngest, sit between us. He doesn't understand how afraid I am of him and so he makes fun of me. I don't understand why I still want his love.

I withdraw, spending hours in the basement, alone with my art projects. But on party nights, once or twice a year, I'm expected to participate, passing around hors d'oeuvres and taking coats. I don't mind replenishing the trays in the kitchen or stacking dishes in the dishwasher, but when my mother pushes me through the swinging door to "mingle," I beg for any other chore, even though I've known since kindergarten that I am expected to do as I am told.

On one such night, Chipper and Martha are banished upstairs while Lynnie and I help out in the kitchen. Lynnie and I love to be around food, preparing it, serving it, even if we won't eat. Now, nibbling, we artfully arrange hors d'oeuvres on the serving platters. My mother hands me a full tray of blue-cheese-filled celery stalks, asking me to offer them to the guests.

"I'm kind of busy, Mom." My voice is low and I hope she'll finger Lynnie for the task or give in and do it herself.

"Mmm. That looks beautiful the way you've arranged it, Pammy." She samples, then checks the canapés baking in the oven. "Pass them around, there's nothing to be afraid of—they're all people you've met."

"But I don't want to," I say louder.

She says nothing. I see her jaw tighten, so I pick up the tray and back carefully through the swinging door. I stop the moment it closes: There are too many people. *Stupid jerk!* someone mutters. I look around; no one's there.

"Well? What are you waiting for?" My father has appeared out of nowhere. "You're supposed to pass them around in the living room."

"Can't Lynnie do it?" My voice is so small I can barely hear myself.

"You do it. By yourself!" he bellows, his eyes dark. "You don't need Lynnie to hold your hand!"

My mother would say that he hates shyness in me and Lynnie because he's ashamed of his own shyness. But knowing this doesn't help me hold back the tears. I bend my head over the serving dish, hoping to hide my tears and praying he'll leave me alone, hoping against hope I'll be allowed to relinquish the tray and return to the kitchen.

"*What* is wrong with you?" he roars.

"I can't, Daddy, I can't! There are too many people out there."

"I don't care. You'll do it because I say you will."

His voice is catching the guests' attention. He demands again, "What's wrong with you?"

I don't have an answer.

"You're pathologically shy. Sick! I won't have it."

Lynnie's eyes are round, her mouth agape. As I run toward the privacy of the bathroom, she follows, takes the tray. *Sick, sick, sick!* the invisible people scream. *She's a sicko!* When I finally emerge, I find her talking with my father's administrative assistant, a longtime friend of the family. I've never understood what makes her so fond of us. Maybe, I think, it's because she has no daughters of her own.

". . . then he said, in front of everyone, that she was psychopathically shy!" whispers Lynnie in horror.

The poor woman looks confused at first, not understanding. Then her eyes clear and she reaches out to me. I pull away.

Carolyn

"How long do we have to wait? I feel like I'm going to throw up," I say to Mom. She gives a noncommittal hum, inclines her head a bit as if to say, *I see,* but doesn't even look at me. She's brought a bunch of boring-looking papers stapled together like the handouts we get in high school. I take the top one off the pile. "On the Causes and Consequences of the—" "Ughh!" I slap it back on the pile. She squeezes me a tolerant smile and turns back to her book. At forty she's trying to get her degree at Southern Connecticut State University, and for some stupid reason they are making her major in history. Chemistry, math, biology I could understand; she's a born scientist. But history?

We've been sitting here at the Department of Motor Vehicles for hours. I don't know why I thought getting a driver's license was going to be fun. Pammy and I took the written test, then were told to sit here and wait. Pammy gets called to her on-road driving test, and when she comes back she acts like it's nothing. Now she's got her nose buried in a book and I'm still waiting to be called.

I wish this test were over with. I'm so nervous it's like I'm on death row. I can't believe how many grown-ups are here taking the same test; I thought all adults already knew how to drive. I wonder how many of them fail. I wonder how many sixteen-year-olds fail. I wonder how many fail multiple times. It'd be just my luck. I'm sure

Pammy will pass and I won't. I'll have to watch her get her license knowing I have to go back and get tested again. I'd better practice sounding sullen and impatient instead, in case I flunk. I can stroll out of here acting cool—maybe it would make me popular. I know one kid who didn't pass the first time and he acted like it was just hilarious. In the cafeteria I heard him telling a bunch of sophomores, "Like, so what's the big deal, there was nobody at the stop sign. I just didn't expect Mr. Driving Tester to be timing me with a stopwatch. He had it in for me the moment I got into the car . . ."

Usually I stay away from the cafeteria at lunchtime—it is scary walking into that huge room when you don't know anyone to sit with. Even if I could find friends, I'd still feel uncomfortable. Everyone else seems to know how to be normal and not feel so fake. But I get tired of pretending. Besides, if I did go to the cafeteria I couldn't eat anyway. I don't want to let Pammy get skinnier than me.

Ever since a couple of summers ago, I've been afraid of getting fat. I can't say exactly why—maybe it happened at Channing. One counselor was so worried about her weight, it became contagious. Then I got on the scale at Margie's summerhouse in the country and was shocked to weigh over a hundred pounds, one hundred and three, to be exact. Everyone wants to look like Twiggy, and magazine articles tell girls how to do that. Everywhere you go there are books about weight loss, calorie counters, and diet instructions. It seems so unfair that girls have to worry about their weight and their hair and their looks. No one puts that kind of pressure on boys. Boys can eat anything they want, look any way they want, and still make fun of fat girls. I'll never give any boy the chance to laugh at me. The girls at school are envious. They always ask, "How'd you get so skinny? I wish I could do that." It's nice to have people admire me for something. Ever since I started eating less, Pammy's been trying to beat me at being thin. Mom and Dad complain about their weight all the time, Mom especially. She thinks she's fat and ugly, which is crazy because to me she looks like Miss America.

At the Ridgetop swimming pool you see all the mothers in

lounge chairs at the side of the pool, wearing these ugly old-lady
bathing suits that cut in so tight under their bottoms it makes their
thighs pop out like the legs on those balloon-twist animals. Most of
the women don't actually swim, and the ones who do stuff their hair
into ridiculous bathing caps with flowers and ugly doodads all over
them. Swimmers or not, they all complain about being too fat.
When a thin woman walks by you can hear envy in the silence that
ripples across the water.

I look at my friends and admire our smooth muscles and firm
bottoms and resolve never to let adulthood happen to me. I'm never
going to get a huge puckered rear end and disgusting fat-dimpled
thighs that rub together and jiggle when you walk. Mom is always
trying some new diet, the grapefruit diet, the high-protein diet, the
no-fat diet, Weight Watchers, etc. Given her complaints about dieting you'd think she'd be happy I was trying to keep from having the
same problem.

Even Margie's mom tells Margie in front of me, "See how nice
and thin Lynnie is?" She'll run her hands down her own ample hips
and sigh. Then she'll say something about her daughters, like, "All
you girls got my hips. If you're not careful you're going to end up
looking like a cow . . ." I always want to slink out of there when she
starts in on that subject. Margie should hate me for being skinny.
Mom and Dad do.

Dad thinks his bellowing will force us to eat more, while Mom
just gets sarcastic. Neither approach works—why would I want to
get fat and suffer like them? Supper with them is hell, and more
nights than I can count somebody ends up leaving the table in
tears—usually Mommy or me.

Some girl just came out crying after her driving test and has a few
words with her mother. The daughter, taller by a few inches, rests her
head on her mother, who looks close to tears herself and keeps
smoothing her daughter's hair, tucking strays behind her ears.

Shortly after, the instructor comes out carrying a clipboard and a booklet. He calls a name and the girl's mother stands up. As he starts over to meet her, his eyes meet mine and he gives me a smile like he knows me. "No license yet?" he asks. I don't know why he's being so nice—he probably thinks I'm Pammy—but I return the smile, shrug, and say, "Still waiting." He talks to the other kid's mother and I hear, "Next week sometime," and he hands her the booklet.

About fifteen minutes later a woman comes out and announces who is to line up for license photographs. She reads my name and then Pammy's. I haven't taken the road test yet, but maybe they just want to get pictures taken and I'll be called soon. Pammy says no, only the people who have passed the road test are in this line and she thinks I should tell someone. I don't. I smile for the camera. Shortly after, I am handed a brand-new State of Connecticut driver's license. Mine looks as authentic as Pammy's, but we both know it isn't.

Pamela

It's senior year at Dayhill, a month after we've finally gotten our driver's licenses, and the voices, though intermittent, have become familiar. Still, when they appear they do so without warning. Because of an orthodontist's appointment, Lynnie drives our parents' behemoth of a Chrysler station wagon to pick me up at school. Our mother is student-teaching only a few blocks away but is too busy to deliver us there herself. Since Lynnie got to drive the distance from home to my school, I insist it's my turn. We head toward where she's parked and argue about this until she concedes my point, though she has dibs on driving home.

The car smells of leaking oil and gasoline, and driving it is like piloting an unseaworthy boat. Getting it out of Park and into Drive takes concentration, but finally we're about to turn onto a street that will take us to the main drag, when someone yells in my ear, *She's off on a joyride!* The voice sounds so astonishingly like the headmistress's voice that I swivel to look behind me. As I do so, the car swings wide around the corner and heads directly into the path of a man on a motorcycle speeding up the hill toward us. Slamming on the brake, attempting to avert the accident, I hear Mrs. Boyd yell again, *Not that pedal, you fool! The other one!* Without thinking, I press my foot to the accelerator, and with a sickening crush of metal, we hit the cyclist. My bladder empties in shock as I watch his body brush the windshield, fly over the hood, and land crumpled yards behind. *I killed him!* I think. In the background the voices giggle with glee.

I bolt from the car, running toward the injured man, who groans and thrashes about in pain. I remember the cardinal rule: Don't move the victim. "Stay where you are, don't move!" I scream, motioning for him to lie still until help arrives.

In a matter of minutes, the police are at the scene. I know the other cardinal rule: Never move your car after an accident until the police direct you to, so I've left the car catty-corner in the middle of the road. An ambulance follows and soon a substantial crowd of on-lookers collects. On the verge of shock, I cannot control my shaking, and I can tell from one glance at Lynnie's face that I must be at least as pale and stunned-looking as she. My legs go wobbly, my head spins. The blood seems to drain away from my brain, pooling in my feet. I am about to pass out when a policeman takes my elbow and guides me to the patrol car. He settles both Lynnie and me in the front seat.

"Am I under arrest?" I whisper, my lips twisting in an effort not to cry.

"No, sweetheart. But we need to get everyone who is not necessary away from the scene so the medics can do their job."

Lynnie says nothing. We exchange not even a glance but remain fixed on the scene in front of us. I can tell that she too lost bladder control on impact. Someone slides into the backseat, leaving the door open. I turn around to find Mrs. Boyd, my headmistress, sitting there, her look of concern so abhorrent to me that when she lays a comforting hand on my shoulder, I shrug it off, telling her to leave me alone.

The injured cyclist is loaded into the ambulance, which roars off, siren screaming. All I can think is that we're going to miss our appointment and someone should call to let the dentist know.

Later that evening, my mother summons me. *This is the day I killed a man,* I think, creeping toward the landing. *Nothing will ever be the same.*

"He's going to be fine, Pammy," she assures me from the bottom stair.

"Thank God!" I crumple into a crouch and hug my knees.

"Your father has been to see him and talked with his doctors, but apparently his injuries are minor—a broken leg and a punctured scrotum."

The broken leg is a relief. Since I broke my leg in sixth grade, I know he'll be fine in just a couple of months. But while I'm aware the scrotum has something to do with a male's private parts, I'm not sure what it is or what puncturing it does to a man. At seventeen, I have only a rudimentary understanding of sexual matters. All I know is how important sex is to men, all men. I have visions of a lifetime supply of sperm leaking out, resulting in devastating impotence, whatever that is. I can't ask my mother to explain, so I skirt the real question—will he be able to have intercourse?—and ask, "Will he be able to have children?"

"I think so. It should heal, though it's extraordinarily painful for a man to be hurt, well, in that area." She averts her gaze. She doesn't convince me she knows what she's talking about, but it's clear that we're not going to be able to discuss it further. All she says later is that he was given a ticket for not wearing a helmet, and that when he found out Daddy was a doctor he dramatized his wounds. Fabricating internal injuries and complications is a shameless way to establish a basis for a lawsuit, my mother explains, but he was soon thwarted.

That summer, Carla, a girl I know from Dayhill, invites me to stay with her and her father and stepmother in Newton. Jobs are plentiful there, she says. I've been fired from a fabric store in New Haven for letting Lynnie, who works nearby as a waitress, help me at the cash register, and I've had no luck finding other work, so I agree and take the bus to Massachusetts.

I feel awkward and out of place, sitting at a table in the country club lunchroom where Carla is a waitress. I wish she'd appear. Finally, she bustles through the red padded swinging doors from the kitchen. Her face is pink and shiny with sweat. "Hi, Pam. You're looking"—she gives me the once-over—"thin."

I ignore this and say hello, wondering if I've been foolish to come. Then I remember: a whole summer miles away from my father, a summer to give myself a complete makeover. I'm going to shed, like a puppy's milk teeth, all the fears and concerns I know are so childish: I'm soon to be a college freshman, an adult, no room for anorexia or the Strangeness, the voices.

No time for second thoughts, either. Carla removes her apron and steers me toward her car, ready to go home.

At the house, Carla shows me around, telling me I can choose between an empty bedroom upstairs, where the rest of the family sleeps, or one down in the basement. I love basements; at home I begged my mother to no avail to let me use ours as a bedroom. So I have no trouble choosing. No one else is home yet so she can't make the customary introductions, but she tells me to make myself comfortable while she showers and takes a nap.

I head for the basement and unpack my suitcase, prowl around a bit. I have a private bathroom, and in the bedroom there's a record player, books, and a long table built in against the wall. Then I sit on my bed, waiting for Carla to come and get me. Time passes, the sky outside the windows high up in the walls darkens. I hear noise upstairs, people speaking, real voices that I assume belong to Carla's father and stepmother. Carla will be down anytime now, I think, far too shy to go up and introduce myself without a direct invitation. More time passes. The invisible voices are oddly quiet. Thirsty, my stomach nags me to fill it. I drink water, wondering why Carla hasn't come to get me yet. Finally, it's night and I fall asleep, fully dressed, on the bed.

The next day I wake to silence. It's ten o'clock, far later than I usually rise. Carla has probably gone to work, but I don't dare go upstairs to take a look, fearful of coming across people I don't know. Or who don't know me. So, again, I sit on the edge of the bed and wait for Carla, and wait and wait.

Hours pass. I hear footsteps above me. People talking in muffled voices. Finally, hunger like searing heartburn makes me desperate. I venture up the stairs and stand hesitantly at the top, wavering behind the closed door, trying to work up the nerve to open it. I can hear voices clearly now and the clink of silverware on plates. The smell of cooking wafts under the door and I actually salivate. It is this that finally gives me the nerve to force myself to turn the knob and push open the door. Cautiously, blinking, I step out into the kitchen. Everyone turns to look at me.

"Well, what do you know! Look who's here! Our visitor has come up for air!" jokes a man who must be Carla's father. "Are you starving? We thought you'd never decide to join us. How about a cheese omelet?"

Too hungry to care about calories, I sit at the table next to Carla and down two servings before I stop myself. Bewildered, she asks me why I didn't come upstairs earlier. I murmur an excuse, ashamed to admit that I was too scared of meeting strangers, even if they were her parents.

BOOK TWO

FALL 1970–FRESHMAN YEAR

Carolyn

In high school, when looking like Twiggy is the teenage girl's dream, I lose twenty pounds just to prove I can beat Pammy at something. In other areas to reduce competition we divide our world into hers and mine: Pammy writes, I dance; I sing, she paints; and so on. As long as competition is eliminated, we can enjoy a degree of mutual dependence; we can finish the other's sentences, sense each other's thoughts, and tune out the rest of the world. Pammy understands me completely; she is my best friend. Through high school I am addicted to this ease, but inside I sense it isn't good for me and I'm lonely.

I dream of dancing, acting, Broadway, ballet. My sister is supposed to become a doctor. Except for international folk dancing, she stops all dance after eighth grade, leaving modern dance and ballet to me.

Pammy is an original in everything she does: She won a science prize in sixth grade, wins swimming races, plays piano better than I play flute, and, as far as I know, never gets a grade less than an A. People always compare us, and I am tired of always coming out the loser. It seems pointless for me to try very hard at anything; Pammy's accomplishments make my efforts seem childish and laughable.

We all know, in the Spiro household, that real talent reveals itself in childhood. After all, precocity and giftedness are synonymous. Received wisdom holds that if you are capable of something, you are good at it from the get-go. Having talent means you need no instruction, and of course talent always trumps effort. The most esteemed prize is won *on the first try*. Pammy has that down pat. To any Spiro worthy of the name, "The Little Engine That Could" is only a dull-witted plodder. Better to recognize failure before others do and quit before inevitable humiliation scalds you. That sinks me.

When Brown University accepts both of us, I assume it is because I am Pammy's twin; my own SATs and grades are immaterial.

Carolyn

DEAR DIARY,

I want to start my diary at Brown with three resolutions:

1. I start college today as Carolyn Standish Spiro, not Lynnie anymore; I am becoming a grown-up. I'm exhilarated but also a little afraid. This is my first solo. I've always thought of myself as part of Pammy, limited by her but safe. Now I'm finally on the verge of freedom,

I've told everyone to start calling me by my birth name. Carolyn Standish sounds so aristocratic and it's cool to be related to Myles Standish. Cár-o-lyn-Stán-dish-Spí-ro has a nice musical rhythm to it. It'll be a bit weird to remember to answer to *Carolyn* when I've been *Lynnie* for seventeen years, but I'm looking forward to it.

2. I need to stop thinking I can't put words on paper simply because Pammy has always been "the writer." This journal is for me alone, just for practice, to find out what I like and what I can learn. I did write some things in high school, but I didn't want her to read them so I tore them to shreds and threw them out. Now I wish I had kept them.

3. This is related to the first two: I have to start thinking of myself as *I*, not as *we*.

We got to Brown a few hours ago and I didn't even want Mom to help me unpack I was so excited to get started. In spite of a letter we sent asking Brown to please put us in different dorms, they put us in the same one! Thank God we're at opposite ends. Pammy is in West

Andrews, I'm in East Andrews. I hope it won't keep me from learning to be on my own. Even though she will probably always be my best friend, we've agreed not to spend much time together.

I hope she doesn't hate me. She doesn't realize how hard it is for me to be independent when she's around. I can't help it—everything she does seems so fantastic to me that I don't bother to try anything on my own. I worry that I'll never be able to feel close to anyone except Pammy. More than anything I want a boyfriend. But I want girlfriends as well. To others it might seem stupid to worry about this. I don't want to go through life always feeling like an outsider and only really, truly comfortable when I'm alone with Pammy. Right now it is hard to be with other people, people who don't know me, and it takes such an effort to be sociable. Most people don't understand how hard it is to make the effort with other people when you've always had so easy a connection with your twin. I am so used to the ESP I have with Pammy that I don't know how to be satisfied with less.

Maybe it'll help to be in mostly completely different classes. I'm signed up for anthropology, Christian ethics, Russian, and a literature class. Also, I auditioned for the advanced dance program, though I guess most freshmen don't get in. Keep your fingers crossed.

Oh, and one more thing—there are so many cute guys here! The ratio of males to females is something like four to one. I want a boyfriend so bad it hurts.

DEAR DIARY,

Tonight at supper a couple of girls were homesick, crying because they miss high school. I don't get it at all. Go back? No way! I just hope Pammy and I can make this work and still be friends.

The dance audition went pretty well, I guess. I got called back for the next level tomorrow! But I don't want to get my hopes up. This junior guy named Andy came over and said he thought I was very good. He's in the advanced program himself and he thinks I'll get in. I hope, I hope! He's so cute, with curly dark hair and sad dark eyes, but one of the older girls told me he has a girlfriend back home and he's very loyal. Too bad.

The people I've met so far: My roommate's name is Annmarie. She's okay but she's an art student and the first thing she said to me was, "I'm very serious about my work." I think she is hinting not to plan parties or stuff in our room. I don't think Annmarie and I are going to be great friends.

I met a girl in line at the bookstore. Her name is Nan and she lives in the dorm just across from mine. She's from Manhattan and she seems cool, not at all snobby. We go to the Morris-Champlin dining room for dinner every night, and you wouldn't believe how many boys sit with us.

Then there's Emma who lives down the hall from me, and she's the funniest person I've ever met! She is so unselfconscious and she knows everything there is to know about boys. She says she lost her virginity at thirteen or fourteen; she makes talking about sex so easy it's like breathing or brushing your teeth. And there is so much I don't know.

DEAR DIARY,

It's been a week since I wrote, but I've been really busy. I got into the advanced dance program! It is so cool, but two hours of dance class every day—my muscles are killing me! The dance teacher is beautiful, and she's also a twin! Her sister dances with Paul Taylor, which makes me wonder if my teacher feels like the loser. Anyway, she is married and pregnant, but she still dresses in a leotard and tights like the rest of us. I've never seen a pregnancy up so close. It's weird to think there's a real live baby in there. I can't imagine ever wanting to have a baby. I hate babysitting, so that ought to tell you something.

DEAR DIARY,

It's October and it's already getting cold outside. I ran into Pam yesterday and she didn't seem really happy. I saw her eating by herself in a corner of the dining room and I joined her. I guess she has a boy who likes her a lot, but she won't give him a chance. After a while she said she had to go study, but I think the real reason was she saw Nan and my other friends coming in for lunch. When we are alone, it's like nothing changed and we can talk like old times, but in public she's so uncomfortable, it's like she's made of wood. I wish she could just relax, have a good time. I think she will soon; it just may take her longer than me.

A few days ago I was jogging to a dance class on the opposite end of the campus when I ran into an old high school friend. We ended up spending the day together, and when he took me to dinner he remarked, "How come in high school I never noticed your beautiful white teeth?"

In high school I never smiled.

DEAR DIARY,

This weekend one of the junior guys with a car took a bunch of us to Cape Cod and I showed them the Cape Cod Mall and the restaurant where I worked last summer.

Being a waitress was fun—I didn't feel shy and I could even joke and talk with people! It's amazing the different things people do for a living. Sometimes customers asked me questions about myself and I felt *interesting* for the first time in my life.

One day Mom and Dad, Chipper, and Martha totally surprised me when they came in for lunch and ice cream. I could tell Dad liked seeing me acting normal, especially flirting a bit with some of the waiters. I don't know why, but it makes him happy to see me with a boy. Most fathers I know try to keep their daughters away from the opposite sex. My dad practically throws me at them. I can't say that I mind.

DEAR DIARY,

It's November 18 and we're eighteen! Happy birthday—for yesterday, that is. Of course I didn't forget, but it was so late by the time I got back I just wanted to go to sleep. Pammy and I made an exception to our separation rule and opened our presents together. So I brought my stuff down to her suite and we sat on the floor. Mom sent us both identical "care packages" with cheese and crackers and all kinds of stuff to share with other kids on the hall. For a while it felt like old times. Pammy seemed relaxed, maybe even happy.

The biggest surprise was after dinner when Nan dragged me over to a friend's dorm. I wasn't really all that interested in going, but she insisted. When we got there it turned out to be a birthday party *just for me!* They'd all managed to keep the secret so I had no idea anyone was planning this. The bad thing was that it never occurred to some of them that it was Pammy's birthday also—so they had invited her there as a guest! When they realized what they'd done, they tried to make her feel like it was her party too, but obviously it was too late. Pammy stayed for a while, but I could tell she was uncomfortable. So I couldn't really enjoy the party even though she said she was okay.

DEAR DIARY,

Providence seems a lot colder in December than it was at home. Only ten days and we break for Christmas. I wish I felt more excited. I really don't want to leave all my friends and go home. Winter break is almost a month long! At least Mom and Dad are letting me go to New York City for a two-week Martha Graham workshop. I'll be staying with Nan, who lives on Central Park West.

I sort of dread going home with Pammy because she's acting weird and I don't want to get pulled into it myself. Today I found her in the dorm common room. She had pulled a chair over to the window and was reading almost completely hidden behind the heavy drapes. When I called her name she spread the curtains and I pulled in another chair and she released the brocade fabric around both of us. It was odd, but I was getting used to odd with her. Her drapery den reminded me of other comforting enclosed spaces we created for ourselves when we were kids. We swathed paper umbrellas with bedsheets to make cozy tents, the wooden toy box billowing with our dress-up clothes became an imaginary ship. Pammy's refuge did feel sheltered, safe.

She looked terrible. Her eyes were puffy, and she was as thin and nervous as in high school, with worry lines indenting her forehead. I couldn't figure out what was bothering her and she didn't tell me.

"See, I'm protected in here," she said, with a half smile. "They can't find me." Who? Sharon, Gemma?

January 1971

DEAR DIARY,

Pammy is getting worse and worse, and I wish she'd get some real help. I'm torn about this. Part of me wishes I could run away, not have to deal with her. When I started at Brown, I wanted freedom, independence, my own life. I don't want to take care of Pammy, but I need to know she'll be okay, and right now she has no one else but me. When she calls home, she never tells Mom the truth, and Dad refuses to talk to her.

"They'd only see me as a failure," she said when I suggested she let our parents know. "And maybe I am."

I've been calling and visiting her every day, trying to cheer her up, keep her going. I know that Pammy isn't "acting," I know she's genuinely miserable, but I don't know what I can do about it.

Pamela

It seems as if every day in early January, the year I'm a freshman at Brown University, is bleak, steely-cold, and miserable. I walk aimlessly for miles, trying to clear my head, trying to still my brain. Instead, everything provides fuel for rumination and involuntary wordplay going on full tilt in my head for most of my waking hours.

One afternoon when I'm striding parallel to the river I notice a sign saying "Seekonk," and with a flash of intense interest I realize I've solved a riddle: Seekonk is not merely an Indian word no one understands anymore but is cleverly composed of two or three words: "seek" and "see" and "konk." This understanding seems to me sheer brilliance, a once-in-a-lifetime insight, perhaps a contest winner, with levels of significance and connections many times above and below the obvious.

I am a seeker, I have sought, and now I see. That is, I *see;* I am seeking truth and seeing it, which is Holy See-ing, a sacred pun, meaning I'd been given a nod of approval from the Vatican, the Vat-I-Can. I can see that I am at sea, that I will get Cs in all my classes, the gentle*woman's* Cs, for good attendance and sitting for every test, though I am no Lady Bird Johnson, I don't wear white gloves or send invitations for tea. I don't garden or beautify America's highways. But there is the matter of the piano's high C and canned orange juice

drink, and high seas and . . . seven seas and . . . seize the day and . . .
Eat drink be merry for tomorrow we die, and . . . konk out.

Thoughts like a storm of tossed confetti whirl through my
brain, ricocheting back and forth between the walls of my skull,
evolving through a frantic train of association into revelations about
the secrets of life and death, space and time. Without sensible connections, they segue on and on dizzyingly until all my thoughts stop,
coming hard up against the inescapable conclusion that Yes! *I* killed
President Kennedy . . .

I am frightened by my careening train of thoughts, thoughts
that, when I can stop them long enough, I know—vaguely,
distantly—don't make sense. This can't go on. I can't keep up the
pace, the peace, my end of the bargain, my head above water. It's exhausting me, mentally more than physically, but physically as well:
My bones, my muscles, even my skin and hair ache with the desire to
sleep.

Looking up from the sidewalk in front of my feet, I find myself
at the edge of the river. It's getting late and through the needles of
freezing rain I can barely see the water. Picking up a flat stone, I hurl
it against the not-yet-frozen surface, but instead of skimming in
shallow arcs, it makes one blip, then a doubled plopping noise. "See-
konk," it blats, then sinks. *There!* I think, *Isn't that proof of everything?*

People start whispering behind my back, talking about what
they're going to do to me, but no one will tell me anything to my
face. Gemma, the red-haired Unitarian who is my roommate and
with whom I was once best of friends, now hates me with a passion.
She and her friends—once *my* friends—start playing a cat-and-
mouse game with me, but my safety depends on pretending not to
notice. I learn to recognize that the red sweater she sometimes wears
signals bad days, days when they are going to torment me, though I
never let on I know that anything at all is afoot.

Confused, exhausted, buffeted by voices that now seem to be in
cahoots with Gemma and the others, I begin to stay in bed day and

night. I no longer make an effort to join people for supper or to walk to the library. Now when there are midnight bull sessions in the room Gemma and I share, I stay in bed under a heap of blankets, my face covered and my presence unacknowledged. I know they are talking about me, but I rarely speak.

My stomach hurts and I'm terribly constipated. I haven't been able to move my bowels for more than two weeks, not even after taking half a bottle of milk of magnesia, mixed with cocoa to make it palatable. I suspect that Gemma has put something in my food, some poison. My stomach is tight and it's harder and harder to eat anything. In a way this is a relief, as it gives me an excuse not to go to the dining room with Gemma and the others anymore, which is obviously no longer safe.

Carolyn

DEAR DIARY,

It's intersession before the new semester, and I finally have a boyfriend. His name is Jim and he says he's in love with me. I like him a lot, but I'm not "head-over-heels" for him or anything. Partly it's because he drinks and he's way more into pot than I am. I hate it when I smell alcohol on his breath. His roommate Bok is really nice, and I like how mature he seems compared to Jim. Sometimes even when Jim is out at class or something, Bok and I will hang out just studying or talking. He's a philosophy major, but he's thinking of going to medical school.

I'm torn. I wish I could run away, not see Pammy, not have to worry about her. But I need her to be okay. I have my own life and I cherish my independence. I don't want to have to take care of her. But I'm the only one she talks to. One morning last week I checked in on her.

"Go away and leave me alone!" she shouted from behind her locked door. I knocked again. "Go! For your own good!"

Oh, the drama queen! Annoyed, I banged repeatedly. She can be so frustrating sometimes! I was about to quit when finally Pammy unlocked the door. She was in old clothes and her hair was a mess. Her eyes were swollen and dark with exhaustion; she hadn't slept for days. A thick film clung to her teeth and lips; cracks festered raw and irritated at the corners of her mouth. At first she wouldn't let me in, but when I didn't budge she backed away from the door. I pushed through and demanded to know what was up.

She skittered behind her desk, a barricade arranged to keep her back to the wall and everything else in her view. Was she afraid of me? She watched the door. Looked around the room. Back to the door. "I am no good." She couldn't meet my eyes. "Even Daddy says so."

"Who cares what Daddy says? You two haven't even talked to each other for years."

"It doesn't matter. It's the truth. Everyone knows it—" She broke off. Seconds later another flood of words. I listened. I offered advice. What else could I do? After a while she stopped. She thanked me for listening. "I'll be okay."

JANUARY 1971

Pamela

The last days of winter vacation soon pass. Classes are about to start up again, but I go deeper and deeper into a fog. My eyes seem to have trouble focusing: I can no longer make out anything except what lies directly in my path, as if the world were far away, at the end of a long gray tube. But it is more than just a visual distortion; my impression is that the tube is somehow constructed of sound-webbing, as if the voices have finally taken on physical form and are themselves the tangled fibers making up the tube's walls. It is dizzying, even nightmarish, but I am so discombobulated it is more numbing than scary. Because the tube reduces what gets in, the amount of the external world I have to pay attention to, I welcome it.

I am tired, tired beyond bearing, yet sleep brings no relief. Mesmerized by the sound-webbing of the tube and barely aware of anything else, I don't care what other people think. For the first time in my life, it doesn't matter whether I keep up the front and try to attend to the world, a world that feels increasingly to be *their* world, period.

The end will come in two weeks, when all will be resolved. I decide I should take a couple of sleeping pills every few hours, just enough to get me through the worst of it. Still bone-drained, still numb, still in the fog, I drag myself to a drugstore off campus where

I snatch up a bottle, Sominex because it is closest at hand and people are staring at me, sending out their rays. The pharmacist doesn't want to sell to me, I can tell from the way he is acting. I worry he will call the police, think maybe they are already monitoring me. When he hands me the bag, I grab it and, without waiting for my change, run out of the store and race back to my dorm.

Both rooms in the suite are empty. Gemma is gone for the weekend and Sharon is not yet back from the library. I hide the Sominex inside my desk. Music is playing softly, and I think maybe I've left the stereo on, or maybe the voices are creating the music. "Eleanor Rigby," "Sad Lisa," "Lucy in the Sky with Diamonds"—these pieces have been written for me; they are also about me. But something is wrong. The songs are all recognizable, yet they've been distorted, a word changed here and there, the tune subtly dropped into a different key or switched from major to minor, changes so slight as to be almost imperceptible. Except that now there is a sinister quality to the music that focuses my attention. I seat myself on the windowsill, curling up against the window despite the sharp chill of the glass against my cheek.

Earlier in the year, some of my dormmates and I made one iron-clad rule: Fearing that a bad trip might make one of us do something crazy, like jumping out a window while trying to fly, we agreed never to take drugs alone, not even marijuana.

I tried grass in high school but didn't enjoy it; the overintensification of my senses and the fact that I could not control the high or make it go away when I had enough terrified me. Even in college, unlike other people, I never get the munchies when I smoke; I just slow down to the point of immobility: Sometimes I freeze in one position, unable to move or speak yet aware of everything. Paralyzed, suffocating, I panic, thinking I'll never come down. I try desperately to tell the others I am scared, but they are always too stoned to notice.

That night, in an act of defiance, I pull out the Baggie we keep hidden in a coffee can. Clumsily, I roll a small joint. It is dark outside and I keep the room lights off; only a thin line of yellow seeps under the door from the hall. Back on my perch on the sill, legs drawn up to my chin, I try to drag in as much of the sick-sweet smoke as possible, but I keep coughing. I can't hold it in long enough to feel any effect. I've already stubbed out the roach when I hear a key turn in the outer door.

"Pam? You home?" Sharon calls.

"Yeah," I answer. There is a pause. She pushes the door open and cautiously sticks her head inside. Her nose wrinkles, she sniffs the air and frowns. "Have you been smoking, Pam?" I can hear the disapproval in her voice.

I narrow my eyes, stare hard at the wall, and don't reply.

"Pam, what's going on with you?"

"Sharon? Sharon?" I look straight at her. "Why don't you fuck off?"

She blinks. Her head jerks back as if I've slapped her. The silence is thicker than the smoke.

"Fine," she says finally. "Have it your way. I know when I'm not wanted." She pulls her head back and stalks off to her own room. I hear sounds of puttering around, her muffled voice on the phone. Shortly afterward, the outer door opens and closes again, and the key clicks in the lock. Then all is quiet. I notice that the music has stopped. From somewhere nearby, somewhere inside the walls, I hear a laugh, someone taunting me. *That'll teach you a thing or two, you asshole Oswald, whore of Satan. . . .*

Something gives. All my last shreds of hope fall away. *Stop the world, I want to get off,* I think. And then I understand the real reason I bought the Sominex. Instead of taking them spaced out over several days, I upend the bottle into my palm and gobble them all at once, washing them down with hot cocoa. I lie back on my bed, waiting to see what will happen. Will I get sleepy, or just pass out? Probably neither—over-the-counter pills have to be mostly harmless or you'd need a prescription for them. But don't people die from taking too many aspirin? Isn't that possible? I don't want to die; I just want . . . I don't know exactly . . . I want it to stop, but what is "it?" . . . And what do I mean by "stop"? . . . *Stop the world,* *I want to get off*, someone calls, distantly, or maybe it is just me, thinking, remembering . . . a line from a play, something I've heard . . . if it's Brussels this must be Tuesday, the rabbi's day off, or something . . . the pills . . . not really dangerous, of course not, but the woozy feeling . . . scary . . . probably not, no, I'm just making a big deal over the mountain, I'm coming around the mountain . . . or is it the mole of a, no, Muhammad coming to the . . . mole . . . hole . . . whole mount, um . . . mole . . . hill . . . mill . . . hill . . .

I shake myself, trying to wake up. The room spins, my stomach lurches. *Maybe I'd better go find someone*, I think. I scrawl out a note, though I know no one will be back for hours. I've taken, I write, a few too many pills, I'll sleep them off by morning probably . . . but just in case . . . I'll be in the downstairs lounge. . . .

I reach the second floor, taking care with my feet because the floor is rippling underneath me. As I turn the corner on the landing, I hear footsteps coming up toward me. To my complete amazement, it's Lynnie.

"Hi!" she says, smiling as if she is genuinely glad to see me. "I was just looking for y—" She peers at me, on alert. "What's wrong?"

"I left a note near . . . the sink . . . maybe you should . . ." I hand her my keys, then start drunkenly down the stairs again. "I'll be in the lounge," I mumble back at her, "in case you think . . . I don't know . . . if it's important . . . serious . . . you know . . ."

I am curled up inside my armchair, cocooned inside the curtains that I've draped around the large wings. Lynnie finds me. She's brought my coat. I put it on and we cross the campus in the frosty darkness, heading for the infirmary.

"Why, Pammy?"

I drag my huge feet across the frozen grass, stumbling over a pink and yellow lizard that has popped out of nowhere. It takes some doing, just walking over the undulating ground. Concentrating furiously, I try to answer. "Because . . . I needed everything to stop . . . the world, you know, get off . . . because I can't . . . talk . . . expl . . . talk to anyone, people . . . you know . . . not even you . . . you know?"

She doesn't respond. The sound of her breathing is raspy, like an animal panting. Or is it me? It's hard to tell.

"I know—" she finally says. As she nods her head, it gives off dizzying waves of colors like the refraction patterns of oil on water. It seems very important to note and remember this.

The nurse on duty is waiting at the door. Making nervous, unintelligible noises in her throat, she hurries me into a white room with a hospital bed in it. She takes my coat and hands me a cup of reddish liquid. It isn't as bad tasting as I expected. "Here, drink this, all of it." She hands me a glass of water, her fingers trembling. When I've finished, she fills it again and makes me drink that too. And another. "I can't," I say when she hands me a fourth glass. I belch noisily, clutching my stomach. "I'm going to throw up."

"You'd better," she answers, pushing the glass toward my mouth again. Under her breath, she keeps muttering in a nervous voice, "Jesus, Mary, and Joseph, Jesus, Mary, and Joseph—" Her eyes are bright, squirrelly. Her hands won't stay still and she peers at me with what I realize is panic.

It occurs to me that maybe I'm in more danger than I thought, but I don't have time to get scared: A sudden wave of nausea distracts me. Seconds later, I feel a groan rumble involuntarily up my throat and I heave huge quantities of liquid into a large basin. Mostly water—brown-colored from the cocoa—no pills. Again and again, I throw up.

During a lull, when I can stand, I run to the bathroom and kneel in front of the toilet bowl. Almost immediately I begin retching again, until I am so light-headed I can no longer keep myself upright. The room grows gray and the lights dim. I hear what sounds like the ocean booming in my ears, deafening me. Just before I go under, I understand that Lynnie, standing in the doorway, is watching everything, that her last memory of me will be how I died right before her eyes on the tiles of a sterile infirmary bathroom. I feel immense sadness at this. I want so much to apologize, to beg her forgiveness. But I can't get the words out, my tongue is too huge and clumsy. Before I can finish the thought, I feel my body give way and I slump into a thick cushiony blackness where the hard floor should be. As everything fades, a mild curiosity like a small stirring of the air—*What's all the fuss about?*—passes through me. I hear scuffling nearby, someone's panicky wail. Then nothing.

Oof! What hit me? An ammonia smell like the banshee screech of chalk against blackboard. My head clears and I struggle to sit up. The nurse is waving a broken vial under my nose. *Stop that!* My body barely obeying my commands, I manage to shove her hand away. Moments later I faint again. Another sucker-punching whiff of ammonia. Between bouts, I can hear the nurse, still more scared than I am, wailing, "Jesus, Mary, and Jo—No, no, no, no!"

Finally, I'm able to stumble back to the bedroom. Shimmering green snakes parade across the walls, each wearing a pink dotted necktie. I point them out to Lynnie.

"There's nothing there, the walls are plain white."

It is after midnight. The nurse and Lynnie peel off my clothes and stuff me into pajamas and Lynnie is told to go back to the dorm. The shift changes. A new nurse bustles in. "Go to sleep," she says brusquely, extracting my arm and wrapping a blood pressure cuff around it.

I know what she is really saying: I'm going to die, there is nothing they can do about it, but it will be easier on me, and easier on the nurses working that night, if I go quietly, in my sleep, so they aren't telling me. They don't want me to make a fuss about it. I am exhausted, still seeing the shimmering snakes even on the insides of my eyelids. I try to hold my eyes open, afraid if I sleep I'll die. But I feel myself drifting off anyway. Maybe it would be easier if I give in, then I could rest . . . if I . . . then . . . if . . .

What am I thinking?! I bolt upright, trembling, breathless. I am still hyperventilating when the nurse comes in again.

"Still awake?" she asks. "Thought you'd be dead to the world by now. Scopalamine will do that."

Dead to the world. Aha! So I'm right! I *am* going to die.

The cuff squeezes off the blood in my arm. I watch the mercury rise. "Your BP's still pretty low," she says, a frown on her face. "Go back to sleep."

I knew it. There is nothing I can do: I am going to die. She is merely acting kind so I won't make a fuss and will get it over with quickly.

"I'm dying, aren't I?" I manage to croak.

She looks at me appraisingly. "No, you're going to be okay," she tells me, her voice somber. "But I'll need to monitor your pressure for the next few hours. Just in case."

Just in case. What does that mean? But I can't fight off the pull of darkness any longer. Knowing I might never wake up again, I surrender to whatever fate has in store, toppling into a drugged, exhausted sleep, as deep and silent and cold as outer space, an eternity of light-years away.

January 1971

Carolyn

DEAR DIARY,

Since the new semester began, I haven't felt like writing. So much has happened and I don't know how I feel about anything right now.

Since Christmas, Pammy's been really down. Last weekend I was at Jim's, but I had a stomachache that hurt so much I decided to go back to my own room to sleep. On my way back, I figured I'd stop by and say hi to Pammy—I haven't seen much of her since the new semester started and I felt a little guilty, even though she completely understands my spending time with Jim. I know she's depressed. She's been studying all the time and has definitely lost weight, which is scary to me. But I can tell it's different for her this time—it isn't about her weight and mine anymore. She says she wants to disappear, somehow take up less space in the world. I can't really believe she'd kill herself, but she's miserable and crying, and though I know she appreciates it when I visit, I can't make her feel any better.

So it was a surprise when I ran into Pammy going downstairs just as I was coming up to see her. She said she'd done something and I should go read the note. I ran up to her room and saw that she had taken a whole bottle of sleeping pills. Her roommates were away and I knocked on some doors in the hall, but no one answered. I don't know why I didn't panic, but I just got her coat and went down to find her in the lounge. Her note said she didn't want to die, and I convinced myself that she simply needed a rest. By then she was really drowsy and confused. I was glad the lounge was on the first floor because her walking was unsteady and if she passed out I couldn't have gotten her down the stairs by myself. Even walking across the quad she had to hang on to me or she would have fallen.

At the infirmary, when we told what happened, the nurse insisted I stay. She didn't make any sarcastic comments about what Pammy had done, and I was glad for that, though it surprised me. Giving little concerned sighs, the nurse did her exam, made phone calls, and had Pammy drink something to make her throw up. The nurse let me leave only when she was sure Pammy was going to be okay. On my way out the door, Pammy begged me not to call Mommy and Daddy.

Numb, I walked across the silent quadrangle to my dorm. Slept. Went to class. Went to meals and activities as usual. Didn't call the infirmary. Didn't visit Pammy. Didn't telephone home.

A couple of nights later, Mom called. I don't think she was angry or even disappointed, but I knew a question was coming. "Lynnie," she asked. No rancor, no accusation. "Why didn't you call us?"

Patient silence.

"I don't know," I said. "I thought she'd get better and call you herself."

I couldn't tell Mom that I knew they wouldn't have believed Pammy anyway. Did I think she was depressed? Yes. Suicidal? No way.

Pamela

A nurse I don't recognize leans into the white room of the infirmary and tells me I have a visitor. This formality is strange. Usually visitors—Gemma, Sharon, Lynnie—have walked right in, their smiles tentative yet presuming a welcome I try to live up to, though I weep afterward from the effort. It never occurs to me to talk with them about what happened, what I did, what I have been going through. It's not so much that I think they won't understand as that I am profoundly ashamed of myself. I believe that I have proved, to them as to myself, that I am spoiled beyond saving, that, in the words of my mother's favorite cliché, it's my own bed and now I have to lie in the mess I've made of it.

But instead of Gemma or Lynnie, a heavy, dark-suited man, another doctor probably, lumbers through the door and stops just inside. The atmosphere is immediately charged, thick with ill will even before I glance up and realize it's my father. He grunts something that might or might not be a greeting, then sits down heavily in the single chair next to the bed. I turn away, facing the blankness of the white wall. I stare into space, pretending to ignore him, as if his presence is meaningless to me. But inside I'm already preparing myself for being attacked, steeling myself, making my body and mind go blank, wooden, and impenetrable.

Silence, thick like the inside of a wad of cotton, but without its softness. I can't hear any of the usual busy noises going on outside the room, I don't even hear the voices. Then, like an egg cracking, there's a gurgling, strangled noise, like smothered laughter. It's not so unexpected, to have him mocking me, making fun of my "Sarah Bernhardt dramatics," which is what he calls it whenever I feel something he doesn't. Still I'm shocked, and despite myself, I turn my head to look at him. For a moment, in the muffled quiet, an odd feeling of distance, even superiority, fills me and I appraise him coolly, almost surgically, the way a stranger might. His heavy body is bent slightly forward, his big hands spread over his face, as if he's trying to stop himself, as if he's ashamed of himself. I am about to turn away again when, for reasons I don't understand, I glance again. Maybe I'm wrong, I think, maybe he's not laughing, maybe he's—? It seems impossible, but that disgusting retching sound is my father crying.

At the same instant that I understand this, I believe his tears are not for me; they're for him. They are tears not of sadness but of outrage, humiliation, and selfish rage. I turn away, confused. When I show no reaction, he stops crying almost as quickly as he started. Maybe he says something, maybe he doesn't. I won't acknowledge him, certain he feels nothing for me but fury. I want to make him hurt as much as he hurts me. But it doesn't register. He leaves abruptly, without saying good-bye.

I stay in the infirmary for a week, and though I won't—can't—explain to the college psychiatrist, or any of the nurses, what drove me to the overdose, I assure him I am not suicidal. After a pep talk about the difficulties facing young adults away from home for the first time, he gives me the name of a local psychologist and sends me back to the dorm.

Classes have already started, but nothing else has changed. The game continues, with the twist that now everything, no matter how trivial or irrelevant, is an alias for something much more sinister and important. I'm not going to make it. I am relieved but also scared when I realize making it doesn't matter anymore. My mother drives up from North Haven to see me. Picking at my food at a nearby Pancake House, too distressed to eat, I try to tell her, without mentioning the voices or the game or the cascade of strange thoughts and wordplay knotting up my brain, that I can't go on, that I'm desperate and on the verge of another overdose, one I'm not sure I want to survive.

That evening she calls from home. She spoke to a psychiatrist at the Medical Center of New Haven. He wants to see me. Immediately. As it happens, my father has a lecture engagement in Providence. He'll drive me to the hospital in New Haven, where she and Dr. Schein will wait for me. She wishes she could pick me up herself, she says, but she is so drained and exhausted she can't safely make the trip again that day.

I say I understand. But I know better. This is a test. If I fail it I'll die. *Just play along. Do what they say. Why won't somebody help me!* I agree to do as she asks.

It is nearing ten o'clock by the time I reach the hotel. Daddy acknowledges me with what I assume is a look of disgust and for the two-hour drive neither of us says a word. I am convinced he feels only contempt for me. I am already being dressed down by voices he can't hear but with which I am sure he would fully agree: *What a loser, little Miss High-and-Mighty! Now you'll get your comeuppance, now you'll come down a square peg. Shake a leg! You're not crazy, you're lazy!*

What amazes me is that this is synchronized perfectly, almost choreographed, with the flashing red and blue lights of five police cruisers escorting us the entire way across two states. I soon realize that FBI and CIA agents in the escorting cars are communicating with one another by means of crude headlight/taillight flashes of Morse code that I have no trouble interpreting. This ease of understanding—the very fact that I've so quickly picked up on what is going on—gives me genuine pleasure, however short-lived.

My mother is standing against the wall in the deserted hospital corridor. She reaches out to give me a hug. I submit but quickly pull away. A short, compact man in a dark suit emerges from an office nearby. She introduces him as Dr. Schein.

I can sense his gaze and feel exposed. I look away.

"Gut eefening, Pam," he intones, his voice thickly German-accented, sounding just like the Freud of bad jokes.

Bowing slightly, he escorts us into his office. The corridor is dim, but the inner rooms stun me with such brutal blues, blue so shocking and assaultive I understand at once that he redecorated that same afternoon and has chosen carpet, upholstery, wall covering, even the coruscating blue flashes coming from the overhead bulbs to test me, to attack me. Ordinarily, blue is my favorite color, but Dr. Schein has deliberately chosen to use it against me. The hue is so powerful and so agonizing to my eyes that I can barely think past my terror.

He has placed three chairs in front of his desk. My parents sit down on the ones on either end. Feeling threatened, I drag the remaining chair into a corner, trying to get as far away from all of them as I can.

"Well now, Pamela, tell me why you are causing your parents so much *tsuris*," Dr. Schein demands without preamble, his hands folded on his desk, his eyes glinting and cold. He has never met me. *Why is he angry?* Something doesn't make sense. Psychiatrists are supposed to help people. He only seems to care about my parents. I glance around, looking for a way out.

"Pamela, you will answer me!"

I hug my ribs and keep my face still, afraid to let my confusion show. *Little shit,* someone needles.

Again and again he demands answers to questions I can't understand. Finally, I mumble something hostile.

"You are how old, now? Eighteen? Hmmm. An adult, are you not? You attend an expensive university for which your parents are paying? Yet you treat them like this!" He glares at me. I look away. Now I understand. He is on the other side. He has been all along.

I've had enough. I bolt up from my chair and dash for the door, wrenching at the knob, pulling desperately. It won't turn. It won't budge. It's *locked*. The bastard has locked us in! Schein springs up from his desk and is behind me at almost the same instant I reach the door, as if he has expected me to run. He grabs my fists, pinning them in his. Contact is like electrocution. I can feel the blast as my brain blows apart.

"Don't TOUCH me!" My head explodes; bolts of electricity surge through me.

"Aha, so you don't like to be touched!" He is still gripping me so I can't pull away. "I thought as much."

I wrestle free. Or perhaps he lets me go. I shrink as far away from him as I can, trembling. I am trapped. Nowhere to go, no place, not even a corner where I can hide. Smiling without kindness, he strides across the room, picks up my chair, and slams it down between my parents.

"Sit down and behave yourself!"

I do as I am told, drawing my feet up under me and clamping my arms around my knees. I make my face go blank. *Go ahead. Kill me. What can I do?*

Suddenly he is calm. I don't know why, but now his questions make sense. I answer in as few words as possible. The fight is gone out of me. The acid blues of the room sap all ability to resist. Also gone is any hope that he can—or would, if he could—help me. After a while, he sits back, steepling his hands. "Young lady," he finally says, "I'm going to give you this choice. You may go home—Marian, you are not to let her out of your sight one single moment, not even to use the toilet. Or you can be admitted upstairs. It is up to you."

What kind of a choice is that? I stare at him.

"Well? Which is?" he demands. "You have made me to come all way into town to see you and it is now after vun in the morning. I have not got all night."

"I can't go home with them." Tears start. "I just want to go back to school."

"That is not an option."

"Can't you see? That would be horrible. I—" I rise to my feet.

"Then you agree to be admitted." He picks up the phone and jabs his finger in the dial.

"Wait! That's not fair."

"Not fair? Why? You said you couldn't go home, did you not? I told you what was the choice. Now, zit down." After a few phone calls, he finally unlocks the door and escorts us upstairs. My father, who knows the way, goes first, then my mother and me. Dr. Schein brings up the rear in case I decide to bolt.

As we head down the long hallway, I create mental static, silently reciting nonsense words to defend myself against Dr. Schein's telepathy, cringing as we pass the gauntlet of night nurses and aides. All I can see are sneering faces full of mockery and contempt. *See? I told you. There she goes* . . . I want to crawl into the dark space inside me, tuck my head into my chest, retract my arms and legs like a hedgehog, just a ball of quills.

It's after midnight, but before I can be admitted the resident on call has to do a physical. I follow the rumpled, groggy-looking young doctor into an examining room lined with stainless-steel counters and glassed-in cabinets.

Every time the doctor touches me, I have to steel myself. He doesn't seem to feel the shock he gives me. Maybe the electricity flows in only one direction, like a cattle prod. Suddenly he leans toward my face. I recoil.

"Whoa. It's okay. I'm not going to hurt you." He shows me the ophthalmoscope. "I just need to look in your eyes." Stiffening, I hold my breath, trying not to wince, or pull away. *Don't give him a reason to touch you.* He says little, except to ask me to sit or lie down or breathe or say "ah."

"Good girl," he mumbles, jotting notes in a small spiral notebook. He looks at the ceiling as if mentally reviewing a list. I don't look at him. I sense him nod to himself. "Okay, yes," he mutters. He puts out his hand. "Squeeze my fingers, please."

I look. His index and middle finger are held out together. I balk.

"Pam, can you squeeze my fingers for me?"

I've never seen a man's sex organ, except by accident. This is another test. How to pass? If I squeeze as he asks, will I be right or will I be wrong? If you are supposed to squeeze, maybe the test hinges on how hard. And what does that reveal about you? I don't know. Nothing, not wild horses, not wild mastodons, *nothing* is going to get me near that . . . thing he has turned his two fingers into.

"Pam? We're almost finished here, if you'll do me a big favor and just squeeze my fingers for me?" He sounds impatient, but the "for me" is a big giveaway. This is a psychological technique to see how perverted I am. But I'll never do it. Of course I can't explain why, not if I want to survive.

Finally, he gives up, tells me I can get dressed again, and leaves. I take off the flimsy gown. The room is lit only by fluorescent bulbs, and the clanking steam radiator gives off no heat. My skin prickles into goose bumps. I put my jeans and sweater back on, dressing slowly. *Loser.*

Pamela

That night, a bed on the unit is not available, so my mother is asked to watch me through the night while I sleep on an office sofa. I'm too wound up, too stunned to sleep. I don't know why a nurse keeps poking her head in the door, but after her third round she comes back with two small paper cups.

"Here, this should help."

I look at the cups, one with a tiny white tablet in it, one half filled with water. I've heard about the stuff they give people in mental hospitals. I shake my head. "I don't need a pill. I'm okay."

"It's just Trilafon, a sedative. You need to get some rest. Tomorrow's a busy day."

"I don't need a sedative." There is an edge in my voice. "I'm fine."

The nurse glances at my mother for support. I look at her too. "Go ahead and take it, Pam, it's just for tonight. It won't hurt you."

So she's on their side too, my own mother. I feel a terrible sadness at this, but I swallow the pill.

A short time later I fall into the restless chop of semioblivion, but it is so cold in the office that I wake up every few minutes and I'm too shy to ask for a blanket. Very early in the morning, when it's still dark, Mommy crawls into bed with me and holds me in her arms. We whisper a bit—I say I'm sorry and she says she's sorry too. But mostly we just share tears that it has come to this.

When morning finally grays the sky around the edges of the window shade, a dark-haired woman in a dress with white cuffs bustles in and flips on the overhead lights. I sit up, shivering, shawled in the rumpled sheet and blinking because I don't know where I've put my glasses. She is Lindsay, Psy-1's head nurse, she explains, and she's brought me a glass of orange juice. She tells my mother it's okay to leave now, that I'm in good hands and can see her that evening during visiting hours.

I follow Lindsay into the hall but immediately shrink back. It's not yet seven in the morning but the unit is already crowded with people, all dressed in street clothes instead of hospital pajamas or nursing whites. I can't tell who is a patient and who a doctor or nurse.

Phyllis is assigned to "special" me, Lindsay says, introducing me to a matronly nurse, one of the few in a white uniform. She explains that "specialing" means Phyllis will be staying close by me for the rest of the day. Phyllis inspects me, looking me up and down, then comments, "She's pretty skinny. Don't tell me we got another anorectic!" The head nurse grunts noncommittally, as if embarrassed by the inappropriate candor, and without answering strides down the hall.

Phyllis leads me to a row of chairs lined up along the wall. She takes my temperature, pulse, and blood pressure, all the while talking about Daddy, who is "a brilliant physician, one of the most famous" she's had the opportunity to work with. My throat goes tight, but I choke out a reply that I hope will pass if not for agreement then for proof I'm paying attention.

Brilliant, schmilliant, tootsie. She's one of theirs. The usual commentary first thing in the morning.

In baggy yellow corduroys and carrying a clipboard, a gamine young woman, not much older than I yet with oddly wizened features, marches down the hall shouting, "Breakfast! Time for breakfast!" Phyllis urges me to follow into a large, dingy common room, the solarium, which, despite its name, sunshine barely dusts. Patients have crowded around a steam cart, helping themselves to hot cereal and eggs and toast and melon slices. "Go ahead." Phyllis gestures. "It's self-serve."

I hang back, pressing my shadow into the wall. "Could you come with me?" I'm as afraid to ask as to go alone.

"All right. Just this once. But after that you're on your own."

To extend my arm far enough to snatch a triangle of cold toast feels like I am plunging my hand into fire. Cradling my arm as if it has actually been burned, I follow the nurse to a round table where other people are eating. A few heads turn and look at me, but I scuttle back into my mask and ignore them: Like the child's drawing toy, I lift the magical plastic film and erase them. Despite butter, the cold toast is dry. It sticks in my throat, refusing to go down. After a few bites I give up trying.

Although it seems to me the voices drifting around my face like wisps of smoke are garbled, words spoken through thick webbing, eating noises have metastasized. The crunch of someone biting a piece of toast seems to contain the slime of his saliva as well as the gummy, disgusting mess inside his mouth. The slight slurpings of coffee or juice revolt me. Even the ding and clatter of silverware against cheap china are unbearable acoustic assaults, which my mask of indifference cannot muffle.

After breakfast, Phyllis shows me to the large room where I am to sleep with other patients who are being specialed: On the right are "staff specials"—patients considered dangerous or suicidal and supervised by a trained staff member; on the left are those who have moved up the "privilege ladder" to being specialed by another patient. "Specialing" and "privilege ladder" are such strange terms I have a vision of patients scrambling up a rope net, clambering toward the top, only to reach it and be pushed back to the bottom again.

Phyllis takes my knapsack and empties it onto the bed. She goes through everything, examining each article I've brought and summarily confiscating items that aren't allowed—nail file, a pair of scissors, my quilting supplies, needles, pins, and all. She pats my jeans pockets while I am still wearing them and even opens my wallet and counts my change.

Feeling violated, I am allowed to put the rest of my things in one of the lockers against the wall. Yellow Corduroys comes stomping down the hall with her clipboard again, yelling, "Patient-staff meeting in the solarium!" Phyllis looks at her watch. "She's right. It's almost nine. We'd better get you a seat."

She ushers me to the solarium door, where I balk, afraid to enter and sit within the large oval of people forming. Desperate to remain inconspicuous, safely in back, I slide into the nearest chair I can find. Lindsay approaches, scrutinizes me.

"She's stubborn. She won't sit with the others," Phyllis announces, as if I can't hear her discussing me in the third person. "And she ate only three bites of toast this morning."

"You'll have to sit in the oval next time," Lindsay tells me, as if she hasn't heard. She smiles warmly at me. "Are you scared, Pam?"

Wondering what she really means, afraid to let her see my face move, I concentrate on staring through her and don't respond. She nods as if she understands something. "It'll get easier once you're used to us. Give it some time."

Yellow Corduroys, who turns out to be a patient, takes attendance with amazing officiousness considering her size, then sits. A youngish doctor, seated among patients at the far end of the oval, calls the meeting to order. He looks around. "I hear we have someone new this morning."

I freeze.

He stops to glance at a sheet of paper. "Her name is, uh, Pam Spiro. Pam? Where are you? We like new patients to introduce themselves and say a little about . . ." Searching the oval, he calls, "Hold up your hand, Pam."

I don't move or breathe.

"Does anyone know where Miss Spiro is?"

Several necks crane. I hear the rustle of clothing as people move in their chairs. The seconds tick by. Gripping my ribs, I cling to the hope that by remaining mute and utterly motionless, I will not be seen. If I am not seen, I cannot be murdered. I fix my eyes on the floor, trying not to breathe, trying to squeeze myself into a speck, trying to will my presence into absence. I close my eyes. My ears ring with the expectant hush that overtakes the room. And for a moment I feel reprieved, as if I have actually been granted a cloak of invisibility.

Then, to my horror, Phyllis stands. Her voice dripping with sarcasm, she says, "She's in hiding over here," and she points me out. The whole sea of faces turns at once.

I jerk one leg up to my chin and hug it, then the other. But I remain silent, scared that if I say anything I'll be in danger. Again the doctor asks me to introduce myself. I struggle but can't force the words past my teeth. He asks again. Growing impatient, he interprets my silence as opposition. If I can't say my own name, how can I tell him he's all wrong? There is no escape; I see that clearly: The only way I can get him—all of them!—to stop torturing me is to steel myself and do as he asks, terrified or not. I hold myself as tightly as I can, swallow once, and whisper, "I'm Pam Spiro."

"I can't hear you," the doctor calls at once, seconded by a chorus of patients.

"I'm Pam." Louder.

"I'm afraid people still can't hear you," the doctor sneers. I am on the verge of tears when it occurs to me all this is deliberate; it is an initiation ritual, another test.

One more time I croak as loud as I can, "My name is Pam. I'm Pam Spiro, okay? And I *don't* belong here!"

There. Now go on to whatever the meeting is about and leave me alone!

Unable to stop rocking and jiggling, I sit with my head down. I pray everyone will take their hands and minds off me.

Sicko, sicko, sicko! This time it's the voices jeering.

But they won, I protest silently. They've proved they have the power to make me do what they want. *Please, please, please, now make them leave me alone.*

"Well, it seems the young lady can talk after all. When she wants to," the doctor says, as if he has uncovered an incontrovertible truth. He makes a kind of faucet-turning motion with his hand to conclude the matter, as if literally changing gears. Then he looks around the oval.

"All right, let's start, people. Issues for the morning?"

A tall, acne-scarred young man I noticed on the way in raises his hand and starts complaining about not getting on the "buddy system" the week before. A debate folllows about whether or not he is now ready for an increase in status. "Status," I slowly gather, means which privileges a patient is granted, in his case the privilege to go outside with a "buddy," another patient. A woman in ragged bell-bottoms and a tight poor-boy sweater breaks into the middle of the discussion. "They're always telling me dirty things," she mutters, sucking at a cigarette. "Those fuckers tell me to kill myself, whispering all the time, 'Listen, Franny girl, you are no-oooooo good.'"

A male nurse, in jeans and a polo shirt, interrupts. "Don't tell us what the voices say, Francis. That's crazy talk and unacceptable. You should know that by now. Either tell us what you want or—"

"But they want me to off myself!"

"We understand you refuse to take responsibility for yourself; you'd rather blame someone or something else. But it won't wash, not here. Now either talk about yourself appropriately or you go back on checks."

Franny leans forward, frowns, about to object. Then realizes she is outnumbered and decides it isn't worth it. She slumps in her chair, her scrawny body collapsing like a balloon that has lost its air.

Although I am left alone for the remainder of the meeting, it feels interminable, with endless discussions of status and pass requests, the assigning of patient specialers, and finally the election of a monitor to take over for Yellow Corduroys. When it's over at last, there is only half an hour before lunch.

During the meeting, I would have fallen asleep from boredom if rocking and jiggling hadn't kept me conscious. Afterward, sitting by myself in the solarium, my head nods. My whole body is so exhausted I'm ready to topple from my chair. *Why am I so sleepy?* If I don't stay alert I could miss signs of danger I need to respond to quickly. But I can't keep my eyes open. In agony, feeling my lids closing of their own accord, I stumble to the large dorm, lined with beds crammed side by side.

"You can't sleep during the day," someone crisply informs me as I fling myself down. Phyllis again. I've forgotten all about her. Clearly she hasn't forgotten me.

I drag myself to a sitting position. "Why not? Can't I rest for just a few minutes? I'm so sleepy."

"Isolating isn't healthy. People need other people," she recites, appearing not to realize that her words of wisdom sound an awful lot like a Barbra Streisand song. It makes me want to shred paperbacks, to smash things. I'm also aware I could never admit to such wrong-think.

"It's better for you to interact, to socialize." Phyllis continues her spiel, looking over her glasses at me. "You should learn to sleep at night like everyone else. Now, no more isolating."

"Isolating"—that word again, a transitive verb used intransitively, like screeching blackboard chalk. I shake my head, trying to clear my brain.

"You can't give in to the meds. If you sleep now you'll only want more."

Meds? What are they? Then I understand: Oh, she means *medications.* I remember the pill I was given early in the morning. But knowing why I'm so drowsy doesn't comfort me. My brain feels shrouded in heavy layers of canvas, like straitjackets I've seen in the movies. I can't take any more "meds." I can't. I have to stay alert, stay prepared. There will be signs to discern, more tests to pass. I need to be ready—for anything.

Phyllis takes pity on me. "Stay active. Beat the sleepiness."

Active? She has to be kidding. I look around. Except for sitting in the solarium, there is nothing to do.

"How about some fresh air?" she asks. *Air? Outside?* I jump to my feet. She goes to one of the ceiling-to-floor windows and raises the bottom half until I can duck under the sash. "There. You can stretch your legs on the porch."

"Porch" means a narrow, caged-in walkway running the length of the unit. Filthy and nearly empty except for two rusty metal chairs and a pile of debris at the far end, it is technically outside, which is better than nothing. I walk back and forth in the cold, until Phyllis knocks at the glass, waving me in.

Lunch is self-serve again, she tells me, and this time I'm on my own. If I want to eat, I'd better start fending for myself.

Waiting for the steam cart, I sit in a corner, trying to shut out the din, feigning rapt interest in the linoleum. A young man with flecks of dried spittle in the corners of his mouth and sagging beltless trousers trespasses into my visual field. His T-shirt has "Mulvin" emblazoned across the chest.

"You're isolating," Mulvin declares, as if it's any of his business. I recoil. His voice is so insistent, so pompous and grating it makes me feel exposed, in danger, pinned by people's eyes like a pithed frog.

"Don't you know? No one isolates here. It's against the rules." He's too loud, too gleeful telling me this.

I pretend to ignore him, trying to wait him out in the hope he'll leave on his own.

"Didn't you hear me?" he shouts. "Man, you are really sick, you know?"

I clamp my lips together, silently begging, *Go away, go away, go away!* I try to influence him telepathically so he'll think it is his own impulse to leave.

"I told you, you're not supposed to isolate!" Then, again so

loudly everyone who wants to can hear him, he diagnoses the situation: "You need a *lot* of help."

Gripping the arms of my chair, my fingers have gone numb. I
am on the verge of yelling back that "isolate" is a transitive verb, you
stupid fuck, when the steam cart rattles into the room. With a grunt,
Mulvin, who likes eating even more than embarrassing new patients,
shambles away.

When everyone is seated with his or her plate, I make myself
small and cross the room. Grabbing one of the remaining dinner
rolls and a container of what turns out to be flamingo-pink yogurt, I
slide into a chair at an empty table. Immediately, a girl about my age
brings her plate over and sits next to me. Her dull brown hair falls
the length of her back, like mine, with the part in the middle. Her
eyes are ringed in black that isn't entirely the effect of makeup. She
looks like she hasn't slept in weeks.

"Hi-iiiii." She draws out the word as if in pain. "You're new
here. Is this your first hospital?"

My *first* hospital? Should there have been others? "Yes," I answer,
which seems easier than figuring out what she is really getting at.

"You're lucky. This is my third." Sorrowful face. "My doctor
says I'm a hopeless case. I'll probably spend the rest of my life in
hospitals."

I don't know what to say. She doesn't seem crazy to me, but
what do I know?

"Why are you here?" she drawls.

As it turns out, I don't have to answer; she's not interested in
me. Before I can open my mouth, she segues into how she attempted
suicide three times and once almost died, except her boyfriend
found the empty pill bottles. Even after "gastric lavage"—having
your stomach pumped, she explains—she was in a coma for fifteen
hours. "The ICU was so awful," she confides, "all those machines
beeping. I had tubes everywhere, my mouth, my nose. I couldn't eat
or talk." She picks up her fork and pokes at her food. "I have a death

wish. That's what my doctor says." Finally, a pause. Then, "Did you OD too?"

I must look blank because she elaborates, "Overdose, you know, taking a shitload of pills. That's what most people are in here for."

I am tempted to deny it, because even though I took the Sominex, I never wanted to die. But to explain, I'd have to reveal the game, its attendant signs and their significance. I'm not ready for that. Besides, who is she? Maybe an agent or examiner. Luckily, just then two dietary aides bustle in, announcing that all plates must be returned at once.

I toss my half-eaten yogurt into the trash receptacle. The sad raccoon-eyed girl with a death wish murmurs, "Hey, if it's cool with you, we'll rap more later on, okay?"

I walk away without answering, trying to figure out what subtle meaning lies hidden in what she said.

While Phyllis stands in the doorway, gabbing with the other nurses, I collapse facedown on my bed to take advantage of a permitted nap. As usual, I pull a pillow over my head. Seconds later I feel it roughly tugged away.

"What?" I lift my head. Without my glasses I'm barely able to see.

"Are you trying to suffocate yourself?" Phyllis demands.

"Huh?"

"It's not allowed. Understand?" She sounds genuinely angry. I explain that for as long as I can remember I've slept with my head under a pillow. "My twin sister does the same thing, and there is always plenty of air getting in."

She isn't buying. "Sorry, you'll have to sleep some other way. I can't have you endangering yourself in my care."

There is little point in arguing, especially as the precious minutes are skidding away. I replace the pillow at the head of the bed and turn on my side, but I know I'll never fall asleep. A tiny, elderly Chinese woman, who wears white socks but no shoes, comes into the room. She walks with her back elegantly straight. Standing between our two beds, she closes her eyes, makes a graceful arch with her arms, and does a series of deep pliés and relevés without holding on. I finally fall into a drowse.

"Is Pam Spiro in here?" A male voice with a New York accent. I hope the nurses will tell whoever he is that whatever he wants, he should come back later. No such luck. "Pam? Pam? Please get up. I want to talk with you."

I open my eyes, feel for my glasses, and glance at my watch. It is only a little after one, still twenty minutes left. "Wha—?"

"Wake up, Pam. You can sleep tonight," Phyllis admonishes. She grabs my shoulder and pulls. Instinctively, I jerk free and roll to the opposite side of the bed, keeping all parts of me out of reach. I drag myself to a sitting position.

"This is Dr. Daud."

"Hello, Pam," says a short, shaggy-haired man in a white shirt, somber tie, and dark trousers. He offers his hand but I barely graze it with my fingers. I feel his eyes scrutinize me, trying to read my mind. I start the multiplication tables to confuse him.

"You're our new patient, Pamela Spiro. Did I pronounce that right?"

He didn't. He said "Speero," not Spyro," but I don't correct him. Rather than meet his gaze, I study the air to one side, getting a sense of mustache and glasses.

"Please, come with me."

I follow reluctantly, with Phyllis close on my heels. Past the nursing station, just before the exit, we turn, passing through tiny interconnected rooms into a windowless office, bare but for a desk and three chairs. Dr. Daud stops at the door. Sweeping his arm in a mock-courtly gesture, he motions me in.

"I'm specialing today, Doctor." Phyllis, ever present, ever accommodating. "I'll wait for her outside." She glances at me. "Unless you want me to stay?"

Special you! Special youhoo! What a load of crap! a voice carps.

I shake my head. Another test: if I ask Phyllis to stay, Dr. Daud will interpret it as my being afraid of him, which is true, or of fearing all men, which is at least possible, or of hating men in general, which is absolutely not the case. All of these, founded or unfounded, lead to tangles I don't need at the moment. Being in the hospital, dealing with the life-or-death obstacle course of all these tests, is confusing enough. I don't have the energy to figure out what every sentence I speak might indicate. I have to survive, that's all.

So I shrug and say nothing. I feel them exchange looks. Phyllis leaves, closing the door behind her.

Watch it, watch it, watch it. Watch for trouble on the double.

Dr. Daud takes a seat. I stand where I am, staring straight ahead, too petrified even to move my eyes.

Silence. Papers shuffling. A cough. A pen clicks. "Wouldn't you prefer to sit, Pam?"

I don't answer. I can't move or sit because there are two other chairs. Too many choices.

"Here," Dr. Daud says finally, taking one chair and setting it opposite him. "Sit right here." He pats the seat with one hand, directing me over to it with the other.

I sit but immediately push back with my feet until I am as far away as the walls permit. I feel him looking at me but can only stare at the floor, mentally scrambling my thoughts so he can't hear them or interfere.

More silence.

"Pam, this is your time." His voice soft, seductive. "Aren't there things bothering you? What would you like to talk about?"

I think to myself, *All I want is to get out of here safely, before checkmate, before you kill me!*

More silence. The minutes stutter by. I feel like I am "being thought" by the zillions, as if thoughts themselves—and not even *my* thoughts—are in control. One of those, on one of the many levels of reality involved, concerns Dr. Daud. He has no compunctions about intruding into people's minds. My only defense, my only protection, is to prevent his gaining access. I avert my eyes, the easiest portal.

Little by little, and I dare move only in almost imperceptible increments, I swivel in my chair until I am facing the other wall, leaving just my profile exposed. But I have to talk—about something, about *anything*. If I don't, he'll think I'm crazy and keep me locked up.

It is almost too late.

"You seem to be lost in your own little world, Pam," Dr. Daud observes, his voice dripping with false kindness. I know what he is getting at. He is calling me nuts.

"I'm fine. *I'm fine!*" I burst out. "Don't get any ideas! There's nothing wrong with me. I just want to get out of here." I glance in his direction. Under his mustache, I sense a smile, as if he has scored a point. I've said enough.

"So, you want to get out of here," Dr. Daud repeats.

I nod. Too tired to think. *Stupid shithead! He's got your number!*

"Fine. How are we going to make that happen?"

"We?" I hear my voice echo.

"Well, I am your doctor, you know. We'll be working together as long as you need to stay here."

"I don't need to be here now. I want to go back to school." This is my prepared response.

"Things were going well for you there. You enjoyed school."

"Of course I did. Why wouldn't I?"

Silence from his corner.

"No matter what you think, I'm *not* crazy."

"No one said you were. But there is the matter, which you seem to believe is incidental, of your very serious overdose. That doesn't sound to me like something a person does when everything is going well."

Oh, no you don't, I think. *You're not going to trick me, it's not going to work. I'm not telling you anything. I know all about your techniques, the questions that make people spew their guts, only to get locked up forever.*

I take a deep breath. "It was a mistake," I finally answer. "I meant to take a couple of pills and by accident took too many. By *accident*. Now I just want to go back. I've missed too much already."

"Let's talk about that."

"You mean I can leave?" *Where would I go? What would I do? How can I go back to school? Doesn't he get it? They want to kill me!*

"I didn't say that. But in large part it's up to you just how long you stay. Let me explain how things work around here."

Four weeks, he tells me, is the average stay. If I cooperate and work hard, I might be out before then.

Four *weeks*? How can I tolerate four *weeks*?

He assures me that with several meetings each day, group therapy and other activities, I'll be lucky to have an hour to myself. Which is the point: You keep patients from isolating, because isolating is what has made them sick and, if allowed to continue, isolating will make problems more difficult.

Now, will I turn my chair to face him?

Huh?

"You've gone around so far, all I can see is your back."

I grunt to let him know I've heard and shrug. I'm too scared to turn even partly toward him.

"Pam? Can you face me the way a polite person would or do you need help?"

Help? I don't want any help . . .

"Pam?" He ups the ante. "Are you going to answer me?"

This isn't fair. It's not a matter of being polite, and he knows it. It's a matter of survival. I make a noise of protest, but I can't explain any of it.

"Do you want to say something, Pamela? Then turn around and say it to my face the way a *normal* person would." Then his tactics go from firm to brutal. "Come on, let's see you do it." He grabs the arms of my chair and starts pulling me around.

I push away with my feet, forgetting that the wall is behind me. My head slams back against it. I yank my knees up against my chest, putting a barrier between us. When his face comes right into mine, I swing out with my elbow and get him in the cheek.

"Nurse!" Dr. Daud calls. "Nurse!"

The office door opens and Phyllis rushes in. The two confer quickly, suggesting they've done this before. Then they are upon me. Phyllis grabs the back of my chair while Dr. Daud yanks on the arms and together they roll the chair with me, whimpering, into the center of the small room. Dr. Daud sits down and draws up close to me while Phyllis takes her position behind me.

"Now, then, let's see if you can behave when forced to," he says.

The room beats in my ears, a gigantic thundering drowns out everything else. I can barely hear or see or breathe. Despite his proximity—he crowds me on purpose, while Phyllis plays rear guard—I manage to twist myself to one side, draw my knees up, and tuck my head into them with my arms folded over the top for protection. This becomes ammunition.

"Do you think, Nurse," queries Dr. Daud, more to the air than to Phyllis. "Do you think Pamela knows she looks like a crazy person, all twisted up like that, refusing to speak to us? Or is she too far gone?"

Phyllis sighs. "Oh, Doctor, I don't know. She seems pretty far gone to me."

I wrench myself out of the chair and dash for safety to the other side of the room. I stand in the corner, my arms crossed, clutching my own shoulders. "I'm *not* crazy! Why don't you leave me alone?" I start crying. "Please, just leave me *alone*."

At that moment, I feel an arm go around my shoulders. "It's tough, kiddo, I know." Dr. Daud hands me some Kleenex and leads me back to my chair. "But I *can't* leave you alone, it's my job *not* to. You've been alone too long and that's what needs to change."

This sort of therapy is what Psy-1 is known for, but it is good only in small doses. As standard fare, it comes more and more to feel like abuse. In any event, after four months, I am still mostly mute and unable to interact, and I remain on one of the lowest status levels. My parents ask for a consultation with an outside psychiatrist, Dr.

Saul. He's a tall, white-bearded man who holds the door for me and smiles in a gentle way that makes me like him. We go on walks; he seems to understand that it is too hard for me to talk or to look at him. His voice is soft and kind. He's not sarcastic like the other doctors. After six visits I come to trust him.

Then he recommends long-term hospitalization and my parents explode. Not caring who hears, my father shouts, "Behave like a normal human being! Do you want to be *institutionalized*?"

Dr. Saul also recommends a switch from an antidepressant to an antipsychotic medication. This is finally effective. I begin talking and rise in status. I am even elected head of the patient government.

Discharged a month later to a halfway house, I get a job at a local hospital pushing wheelchairs and stretchers. Despite the lip service given to "follow-up," within a week I have no doctor, no medication, no future.

Carolyn

New semester, new year, moving day a couple of weeks ago. Started classes, and in biology the realization hit: She isn't coming back. There's no "Spiro, Pamela" following my name in the Brown class handbook. Out of curiosity, I walk by her old room. The door is wide open and smells of fresh paint. A spattered drop sheet covers the floor, but the paint cans are tightly closed and the painters nowhere to be seen. I peek in. Of course, the bed is bare, the shelves empty, waiting for the new occupant. What did I expect? Already somebody's cardboard boxes are piled in the corner.

At home no one mentions it, but I know they're holding their breath. Will I fall apart like Pammy?

Except for a brief visit, I didn't go home this summer. Even now, I barely think about Pammy and I never call. But Daddy phones me every Sunday morning.

"I feel fine." I tell him. *It's seven o'clock, for God's sake.*

"You don't sound very happy."

Who sounds happy at this hour? "Dad, I said I'm fine."

"You ought to socialize more." His answer to everything. "It's not healthy to spend so much time alone."

I'm trying to keep my voice low. The phone is on the main stairwell of the old mansion they've turned into a dorm and there's no privacy. Besides, everyone else's parents know better: They wait for their kids to call *them*.

"Dad," I say, "I live in a house with sixteen other kids. I'm *never* alone."

"You know what I mean."

"But I'm *too young* to get married." I sigh with heavy drama. "We've been through all this before—"

"Oh, stop it, Lynnie. It's not that I want you to get married."

"I know. You just think I should settle down, make some decisions about life."

Pause. "Pick. A. Major."

I just started sophomore year, but Dad is already nudging. It's okay. Actually, I like his nervous attention. I never got much before.

I haven't called Pammy in months, and he doesn't mention her. When I ask about her, he passes the phone to Mom. I can tell he leaves the room.

"How are you, sweetie?" She sounds tired.

We chat for a while. Then I ask about Pammy again. But I don't really want to know. Mommy seems to understand.

"She's up and down, out of the hospital, at the halfway house. They want me to visit less. I guess I'm part of the problem."

"Part of what problem?"

"I'm overprotective or something. Pammy's too dependent on me."

Pammy never depends on anyone as far as I know. She was a loner in school, never needed help with her homework, was never given help anyway. Mommy used to feel snubbed by Pammy's *inde*-pendence. Pammy was too smart to *need* anything.

"You overprotective? No way."

"Don't worry about it, Lynnie. Your sister's going to be fine. You need to focus on your own life for now. I'll take care of Pammy."

On my visits home I see the toll it's taking on her. She's lost weight. She's smoking again. There's high-voltage tension between her and Dad. It's a strain on everyone, including Chipper and

Martha. Daddy says Pammy is willful and obstinate, that she needs to grow up, snap out of it, stop being so self-absorbed. He says he wants nothing to do with her. Mommy's worried. She thinks Pammy is sick.

The next September I take a year off to dance in New York City. Mom and Dad hope I'll get it out of my system and consider a more reasonable career. I figure this is a way to ease them into the idea of me dropping out of college. I have a new boyfriend who's a med student at Yale. I take the train to New Haven every Friday night to be with him. What different approaches to the human body: Doctors look at what doesn't work, dancers look at what does. I don't know which is better.

One day, I pick up a used copy of Watson's *The Molecular Biology of the Gene*. They assigned us excerpts at Brown. Now, a few pages at a time between dance classes, I read it like a novel. The other dancers think I'm weird, but I don't care.

I meet up with my old friend Bok from Brown. He's in medical school now and goes by his real name, Stephen. We eat, talk, and go for a walk after dinner. Crossing town on Thirty-third Street, we hike over to Fifth Avenue and head north with no goal. I am dressed in only a T-shirt and jeans, and the night is cooler than I expected.

Waiting for the walk light, I cradle my arms for warmth. Bok notices and takes off his blazer, drapes it over me, and encircles my shoulders with his arm. It's only a platonic hug, but for a moment I envy his girlfriend. He asks me about Pam.

"I haven't seen her much since she was in the hospital." I squeeze his arm. "But thanks for asking." He pulls me close. Our strides synchronize as we cross the street and continue up the avenue. "How did you remember?"

"Actually it was my girlfriend who knew Pam. She's always wondered what happened. I hope she's okay."

"So do I."

I feel his eyes on me. "Carolyn, how are *you* doing?"

"I feel guilty . . ." I say. *Guilty?* Is that what I feel? "I know I should feel guilty. I shouldn't go on with my life as if nothing has happened."

"What else can you do?"

"A person should have the decency to feel, well, at least upset."

"Says who?"

I stop abruptly at the curb and nearly trip Bok.

"Says who?" he asks again.

"Her life has fallen apart and if I cared—"

"Says *who*?"

"*I* say, that's who!" We stop at a street-side café. "I have no business enjoying anything—"

"You'd stop living your own life?" He pauses as a waiter pours us coffee, then adds, "How would that help?"

My fingers drum the table. If I don't look at him, I won't cry. Bok covers my hand gently with his own.

"It wouldn't . . ." I cover my face. "It's totally crazy!" He taps my shoulder and I look up. A smile slides over his face and he puts his finger to an invisible blackboard, giving himself the winning point. I grin and slap his hand away.

"So, it's Stephen Bokar now?" I tease. "When's it going to be Dr. Stephen Bokar?"

He tells me about his first year, and it's obvious he loves what he's doing. I tell him about reading Watson between dance classes and my fantasy about med school.

"Of course, it's only a dream. I'm no scientist, just ask my mother—"

"You don't have to be a scientist," he says, slouching comfortably. "You have to work hard, of course, but so what? Carolyn, you'd be a great doctor!"

I argue with him and am happy for once to lose. He ends the discussion with a clincher. "Take a chance, Carolyn. You want to go to medical school, go. If a philosophy major can get in, so can you." I want to believe him. Me, a doctor? Maybe it is worth a try.

In September 1973 I transfer to Sarah Lawrence College with a plan—one science class at a time and then I'll see. But just in case, I'll continue dance classes. Inside: *Too good for the rest of us, are you? Who do you think you are? Pammy?*

April 1975

Carolyn

In December 1974 I get my first medical acceptance letter. At Christmas, my parents look at me differently. I withdraw my other applications except for Harvard and Yale, where I applied to please my father. Yale turns me down.

Late one night in April 1975, I open a fat envelope with the Harvard insignia. With trembling hands I pull out the letter and read "Congratulations." Yes? No! I reread the letter several times before I let myself breathe. That fall I am to enter the Harvard Medical School class of 1979. Lynnie Spiro, going to Harvard! I wake my parents at midnight.

I call Pammy the next day. She's still at Brown. After a few minutes of chitchat, I tell her.

"Harvard? Oh, wow. Really?" Deep breath. "Congratulations!"

"You don't hate me?"

"Why should I?" She sounds genuine. "Lynnie, I couldn't do what you're doing. Your going takes the burden off of me."

Burden? What does she mean?

We talk and it feel like old times. Things are getting better, she assures me. She'll graduate soon too. Not so sure what she'll do after that. Maybe for once she'll follow in *my* footsteps. We laugh. That would be reversing roles but good.

April 1975

Pamela

One evening, still at Brown, reading for finals, I am in my dorm room. The phone rings. It's Lynnie. Something's up. She never calls me.

Should she call back, she asks, is this a bad time? She has news, she says, good news, but her voice is strangely tentative.

Yeah? So? Good news for you or for me? "What?"

She takes a breath, then admits she's been applying to medical school.

I put down my cup and sit back, thinking quickly. *Wow. Wow . . . and I didn't even know.* I try to picture Lynnie in a white coat, stethoscope around her neck, Lynnie, a doctor.

Then she says she's gotten in.

"Congratulations," I manage, feeling a band tighten around my chest. "That's really cool. So, where?"

For the briefest of moments, she pauses. "Please don't be upset, Pammy—"

"Where?" The band cinches two notches tighter. I know her answer. *Of course. Where else?*

"Harvard."

I swallow. *Harvard.* For the first time in years, I feel the weight of what has happened to me. I am not supposed to cry. I am not supposed to care. But I am supposed to say something, brave and preferably gracious.

"*Harv*—Harvard?" I croak at last. "Well, I couldn't do it." And I couldn't. That hurts like hell. We talk about a lot of little things. I tell her everything is fine, that I'm happy for her. I *am* happy for her. But when we hang up, I burst into tears.

BOOK THREE

Pamela

I graduate Brown magna cum laude that May. Both my parents are thrilled by my acceptance into Phi Beta Kappa and join me on the day of the ceremony. I pose for pictures with each of them. In one, my father, thawing for once, looks at me with real pride.

One afternoon not long afterward, my mother suggests a walk to the tower on top of Sleeping Giant, the local hiking spot. I'm at loose ends, wondering what to do.

"Come on, Pammy," she urges, knowing my soft spot. "You love walking. It'll do you good. Besides, we need to talk."

We take the dog, as usual, and on the way up say little of importance. I identify the wildflowers for her and she points out which rock face is made of granite, which of sandstone. Once, she starts to mention the fact that I can't live at home forever, but I change the subject and don't respond.

We climb the old tower, look out upon the greening landscape, and let the retriever off the leash for a while. Then we head back down the path, the dog trotting obediently alongside. It's then, in a rush, that I confess my fears. What am I going to do, what am I going to be? I worry out loud. I haven't planned for this. I start rapidly listing my options: I could take courses; I could join a writers' group; I could apply for a job at the newspaper. It's then it occurs to me: If Lynnie can attend medical school, why can't I?

"Oh, Pammy," my mother says with certainty. "You could always do anything you put your mind to. Of course you can go to medical school."

It's the first time since freshman year that I've considered it. It's the first time since that year I've made any plans at all. But with Lynnie in, it no longer seems an unattainable goal. Sure, with two hospital stays on my record, some schools might not take me, but with a Brown degree, surely I could get into the state school. I could do all the premed courses I've missed over the next two years. The more we talk about it, the more excited I become. Maybe, just maybe, I have a future after all. By the time we reach the car, I'm joyful with relief. Maybe I can attend medical school. Maybe I can do what Lynnie is doing. Maybe we can both be doctors!

The next year, I work part-time and take chemistry and calculus. One evening I find a notice about Scottish dancing held every Tuesday night at the Graduate Center. Despite a horror of human touch, I am as wild for folk dancing as Lynnie is. I used to attend every chance I got. And I miss it.

However, dancing doesn't come easily. I always arrive early and sit for a while behind a barricade of folding chairs, preparing myself with a mental lecture: *No, Pam, holding someone's hand will not kill you.* Or more likely, *No, you don't have to date the first guy who asks you to dance!*

One evening, I find myself paired off with a thin, sandy-haired man about my age. He makes me nervous, especially when he smiles, and even more nervous when he tells me to *look* at him while we're dancing. When the set is over I leave the floor and scurry back to my seat; I don't want him to think I'm counting on being his partner more than once. I'm pleasantly surprised, if scared, when he follows me. His name is Bryce, he says, he's a Yale graduate student in economics. "You're a good dancer—you catch on quickly. You must have danced before."

I stare at my hands, glad he doesn't embarrass me by mentioning my lack of eye contact. Shyly, without once meeting his gaze, I murmur a few sentences about doing international dancing since my junior year in high school.

"Ah, well, that's why you're so good. You've had a lot of experience. That'll be helpful here. Some of these people can't tell their right foot from their left!"

When the next dance starts, he takes my hand and pulls me up from my chair. After that, we are all told to take different partners and I lose track of him. At the end of the evening, he finds me taking off my dance shoes and switching to my scruffy old moccasins.

"Would you care to join me for a TJ downstairs?" he asks.

I don't know what "TJ" is. There's a bar on the lower level, so I assume it's something alcoholic. I'm afraid I'll look out of place wanting ginger ale or Tab, but I don't know how to refuse. I don't *want* to refuse, either, not exactly. It's just that I'm sure I'll make some stupid gaffe and look completely out of place.

Bryce finds us a table away from the others, and when he brings back two glasses, I am relieved to discover TJ is nothing stronger than tomato juice.

Next week is Thanksgiving, and Bryce asks where I'll be spending the holiday. I tell him I'm staying home alone. I admit that I hate the holiday gorging and will be just as happy not to have to endure it. I am sure he'll find this strange. My face flushes, regretting the confidence. He only grins. "How perverse!" he says. "I'm not going home—Michigan's too far away. Maybe we . . . Well, how about we spend the holiday together? We could fast all day. A kind of anti-Thanksgiving. We could study in my room, then at midnight have a ritual breakfast. What do you think?"

Stunned but eager for company on the holiday I least enjoy, I mumble, "Sure." All the way home I tell myself this is what normal people do—they talk, socialize, spend time together. I'm going to prove to Bryce I'm an ordinary young woman who takes being asked to spend time with a guy for granted. If the voices have any reaction to this, I am determined to ignore them. I refuse to let anything, not even Gray Crinkled Paper or the Strangeness, spoil my mood of giddy pleasure.

After Thanksgiving, Bryce and I spend a lot of time together, much of it studying silently for our respective courses. Although I am fearful of his touching me, I also wonder why he hasn't tried, why our relationship is so platonic. Is there something wrong with me? Do I secretly repel him? Is my body intrusive? Do I, despite all efforts, still take up too much space? The last idea seems possible— at ninety-seven pounds, my weight is higher than it has been in years. He's had other girlfriends, he tells me, although he isn't currently dating anyone special. From this, I conclude there must be something loathsome about me that makes him keep his distance.

In the spring of 1977, my parents travel to one of my father's speaking engagements in a foreign country. I'm staying in the house alone, looking after the dog. Earlier that afternoon, I pick up Bryce in my used Opel Kadet, which has a bashed-in front headlight and no radio. We bake bread and share hot mulled cider. After nightfall, the house is cold. Even in my heavy sweater I shiver uncontrollably. Noticing my bluish fingers, Bryce builds a fire in the fireplace and arranges sofa cushions on the floor to lean against. I don't know what to make of this. Does he really want to sit close to me, or are the cushions only for him?

"Go ahead," Bryce says, indicating the cushions. "Make yourself comfortable. I'm going to bring us both a cup of hot tea." I huddle upright with my arms hugging my knees. When Bryce returns with two steaming mugs, he sprawls lengthwise on his stomach, propping himself up on his elbows. I notice with alarm that there's now scarcely half a foot between us.

"Talk to me, Pam," he says, shifting his weight and making the space between us even smaller. "I don't bite."

"People who don't know, think they're safe, but they don't realize the poison is infecting them."

"What poison?"

"The poison that one exudes."

He laughs. "But you're not poisoning me. What are you talking about?"

"Just the poison coming off a person."

"Well, I don't know about any poison," he says with a puzzled look on his face. "All I want is to find out more about you. You never talk about yourself, you know."

I stare into the bright fire and try to open up for the first time. Although I talk in riddles as usual, whenever I clam up, not wanting to bore him, he urges me on. "Don't make me pull teeth, Pam," he says. "I don't understand everything you're saying, but I'm interested in you, I really am."

The fire burns down. At one point he says he sees a therapist and asks if I've seen one myself. "I occasionally talk to a doctor who specializes in mental processes," I answer. I glance at my watch. I need to cut this off; he's getting too close to home, though part of me is sorry to find it's past midnight. "Uh-oh, I'd better get you back to school." I rise, searching my pocket for the car keys. "I didn't mean to keep you so long."

"You weren't keeping me. I wanted to stay. And maybe I don't have to."

"Don't have to what?"

"Well, these cushions are pretty comfortable, and it's late for you to drive me back. Why don't I just sleep here? We can make beds out of the cushions, both of us, and sleep in front of the fire."

I look away but know he's seen the beginning of a smile on my face. That night we sleep, fully dressed, each on a separate pallet of cushions, only a foot apart. Sometime during the early hours, I stir to find Bryce's hand touching mine while he sleeps. Carefully, I pull away, not because I recoil at the contact but because I'm certain he'd never touch me voluntarily or without disgust if awake.

When I get up in the morning, I am surprised to see Bryce still asleep next to me. I'm late for work, so I wake him and we put the sofa back together, then head out, Bryce for the bus stop, me for my job. Walking side by side, neither of us speaking of the night before, I torment myself with uncertainty, desperately wanting to know if he regrets staying over, fearing he does.

We reach the bus stop. I'm babbling apologies to defuse the awkwardness of the situation, when Bryce puts an arm around my waist and pulls my body to his. I go rigid. "Relax, Pam. Getting a hug can't be that bad." A long moment passes before he lets me pull away.

I know I'm blushing and look down, but he lifts my chin with his finger and turns my face to his. "You know what, Spiro?"

"What?"

"I really like you. I like you a whole lot."

I step back a bit. "That's nice," I stammer.

"Only nice? Boy, you really know how to build up a guy's ego, don't you?"

"I meant, well—thanks. I'm glad. I like you too, I think." In my nervousness, I'm zipping and unzipping my car coat. He puts a hand on mine to still it.

"That's better," he says as the bus draws to a halt and the door sighs open. After another quick squeeze, he jumps on board, and I'm left to wonder what his liking me means. I know he hugged me on impulse and I also understand he will come quickly to regret it. Nevertheless, even the sneers of the voices can't deprive me completely of the bubbly, euphoric feeling in my chest.

Pamela

One day, a month before I start studying medicine at a state university, the only school that accepted me, I have another long and tearful phone conversation with Lynnie, who is just finishing her second year at Harvard med school. We both know I'm smart, but she knows I'm afraid to touch people and I think she's worried about my emotional stability, though she tries to assure me I'll do fine.

The next evening she calls again, this time with a proposition. "Pammy, listen. It turns out my psychiatry prof is doing twin research, so I talked to him about you. I realize I don't know a lot of the details, but I told him what I knew. Anyhow, he offered to see you on Friday for a one-time consultation before you go off to University Hospital med school. Maybe he can help."

I can't say anything. I don't know what to think.

"Pammy? Are you mad at me?"

"No, no. It's just that I . . . I didn't think you would tell anyone about me."

"But he's interested, Pammy; he *really* is. It's his field. And he knows *me*. Why don't you come and meet him? What harm could it do?"

I haven't seen Lynnie on her home turf ever, and haven't been seen *with* her for years, not since our first semester at Brown. We've carefully orchestrated that. The problem is we look so much alike that people are always comparing us to see who is prettier, smarter, thinner, better. I hate competing with her. She thinks I always win and I'm tired of feeling guilty, so for years we've made sure that our visits home never coincided. Even so, we would never say we were anything but close; we talk by phone for hours several times a week. Whenever I want advice or help, it's Lynnie I seek out first; likewise, I assume I'm the one she turns to.

In the end it takes little encouragement for me to drive up to Boston, but once I am left off in Dr. Llosa's waiting room, I begin to imagine disaster. Luckily, he is on time, so I don't have to imagine it for long.

He asks me what's the matter. What am I supposed to tell him, I wonder, that I'm hearing voices and cutting myself with razor blades? I'm not that crazy. If he knew, he'd call University Hospital and they'd never let me in.

"Your sister is worried about you. She thinks you won't ask for the help you need."

"Help is relative," I say. "Sometimes one is in need of lifesaving, but preserving one's life may involve the help that is relative."

He raises his eyebrows.

"But the one who is in need may need to be protected from the need one feels maybe within, without the words to say it."

He's not getting it. After several more questions, he suggests that I take a break and get a drink of water. When I get back, we try again. The problem is, I want him to read my mind, but I'm afraid. If I let him in I may not be able to get him out. Still, I know how little he understands because each time he writes a note, he reads it out loud.

"She mutilates her vagina."

"What!" I leap up.

"Isn't that what you said?" he asks in mild surprise.

"All I said was that I have scars that wouldn't show in a bathing suit!" Who does he think I am? *What* does he think I am?

"I'm sorry. I misunderstood." And he crosses it out.

I take my seat again, but the interview is over as far as I'm concerned. Several questions later, he asks if I would mind seeing a psychiatrist when I'm in medical school. This seems like a trick question. What does he really mean?

"No, I don't think so," I answer slowly.

"Good." He fingers his pencil. "That's good. Even with a chronic mental illness there's no reason you shouldn't study medicine. As long as you're in treatment. I know a couple of docs down there. I'll write to them and refer you if you like."

He offers his hand before I leave, and gets my limpest, dead-fish fingers. I can't forgive his "mutilates her vagina" comment, pulled right out of the thin air of his dirty mind. I say nothing about it to Lynnie but I stew all the way from Boston back to Connecticut. I'm so embarrassed, I never tell anyone.

Bryce and I continue to see each other until I'm ready to leave for University Hospital medical school. He teaches me everything I'll ever know about sex and as far as I can tell he is a good lover—kind, attentive, interested in my pleasure. But the truth is, I hate it. After the first flush of euphoria, discovering my body is not too loathsome for him to touch, my fear and distress return. Also, we begin to fight over small things that I can't understand. One evening when I've consented to stay over again, he admits he's taken another lover. He is afraid of my reaction, and it is true I am angered. But not for the reason he feared. I'm angry because he didn't tell me earlier, so I wouldn't have felt obliged to go ahead with sex just to please him. For some reason, I know I come first in his heart, and his having sex with another woman only relieves me of a burden.

Nevertheless, my distaste is coming between us. I've begun to sense that he depends on me too much; his caresses and hugs feel intrusive and even pawing, clingy. After some hard thought, two weeks before the semester starts, I tell Bryce we have to break up. I claim to want to meet other students and not have to worry about being attached, but in truth our physical relationship is so repellent I can't stand it any longer. He is devastated. Up till now he's thought we had a long-term thing going, he says, trying to keep me. He hates economics and can't get through graduate school without me. But his naked desperation only repels me further.

In the end, he decides to switch to law school, a move I agree would be good for him. Despite my discomfort with physical contact, I still care deeply about his happiness and I know he'll enjoy law a lot more than studying economics. He has a lot of the meticulousness that the law demands, and since he wants to save the world, or some small part of it, surely law school would be a good place to start. I want to make this a clean break, but he insists we plan to see each other at Christmas. Assenting reluctantly, I warn him not to count on it. When I move up to Farmington a week later, I feel bad admitting to myself I'm relieved not to have him around anymore.

The final thing I do before departing for University Hospital med school is to change my name. My father and I still do not speak, and while I warn him of the impending legal move the night before, he only laughs as if it's unthinkable; that I should want to lose the advantage of being known as Dr. Spiro's daughter and take on my mother's maiden name seems to him the height of foolishness. Still, the day I officially become a Wagner, I feel as if my real life has finally begun.

"... *Two forms* of respiration, anaerobic, or fermentation, and aerobic," the first lecturer of the morning drones. I struggle to keep up, scribbling notes as fast as I can. My eyelids desperately want to close. I feel like I've been up for days and struggle to remain alert. A sudden blankness. The next thing I hear is, "That's it for today. Thank you, ladies and gentlemen."

There's a bustle as students rise to their feet, crowding the exits of the amphitheater.

"Wake up, sleepyhead," someone says, jostling me. "Man, you must have had some wild night!" Karl, a classmate who sneaks in behind me late every morning and is constantly telling dirty jokes, laughs at the sexual implications of his comment. I sit in the back too, but only because I'm afraid of the other students, overwhelmed by the noise. I need to have space free behind me and to be able to leave at a moment's notice. He never seems to care that I move over a seat to be closer to the aisle and farther from him whenever he sits next to me.

"We're still in the middle of biochemistry. Why is everyone leaving?" I ask, bewildered.

"Lecture's over. You slept through it," Karl explains dryly. "You already know biochem, it's that boring to you or something?"

"Are you kidding? I'm totally lost. But how could I sleep through the whole class?" I'm stunned. "The heat must have made me drowsy," I decide.

Karl studies me, a quizzical look on his face. "You're the one who's kidding, right? The—ahem—AC is going full blast."

I realize with sudden embarrassment that he's right: My bare arms have goose-pimpled from the chill.

Karl and his friend Randy are going for coffee at the caf. They invite me along but, as usual, I turn them down. I have a heating coil and instant coffee at my lab station and I want to read up on what I've missed. I don't tell them I'm terrified of the always-packed cafeteria where I can't control the assault of incoming stimuli. And of course I can't say anything about the voices. But I need some time by myself. Wrapped in my shawl, my arms full of books, I keep my face blank, skinning the wall, making myself as small and inconspicuous as possible. In my flight upstairs to the lab, I try not to touch anyone in the crowded hallway. I avoid even accidental eye contact.

The voices hold off until I'm alone, but as soon as I close the door behind me, they burst out in a torrent. *Dumb floozy! We'll take her down a peg. What a tub of lard.*

I have ten minutes before the next class, so I fill my mug with hot water and immerse the heating coil. I put my head down on my arms to nap for just a minute. *Tub of lard.* I scold myself, having had a piece of toast that morning. I promise myself I'll atone the next day.

Though I pass biochem and psychology by the skin of my molars, my evaluation goes something like, "Miss Wagner was never in class, and when she came, she slept."

My classmates find this amusing. I attempt to study the material on my own, but as soon as I'm settled at my desk, my eyelids start to flutter. Then I'm out, flopped over the top of my books.

I try nonprescription medication, but nothing helps. One day, another student photographs me, dead to the world on a sofa in the med school vestibule. The picture is published in the student newspaper, captioned with humorous intent: "Rip Van Winkle, it's time to wake up!"

It doesn't amuse me. Sleepiness threatens everything.

Once, in anatomy, I fall asleep on my feet. The others haul me back to consciousness: "Hey, Pam! Come on. Wake up! It's your turn. Pam? Hey, Pam!" I realize that I have been *somewhere else,* dreaming, leaning against a lab bench. I pretend to know what I'm doing, disguising my real state of just-waking-up confusion. How could I fall sleep, I wonder, appalled.

As the year progresses, I feel desperately lonely, and then just plain desperate. Going to medical school now seems like an act of madness. Maybe I should have continued to folk-dance and work part-time. Maybe I should have stayed in New Haven with Bryce.

But Bryce is not there the day I stumble down the hill. The voices are. *Cut, cut, cut the cadaver; they don't bleed. Betcha she will!*

I'm not going to make it. The semester just began and already I'm in trouble. No one knows about Gray Crinkled Paper, the Five People, or the voices that have taken over.

I reach home and close the door. In the clamor of voices, one rises above the rest, ordering me into the bathroom. *If thy hand doth offend* . . . I pick up the single-edge razor. *Cut it off* . . . I look at the blade. *Cut it, cut it off, cut it, cut it, cut it!* Without hesitating, I press it deep into the flesh six inches above my wrist. I drag it downward until I can see the edges of the wound separate, exposing the yellow fat and the glistening muscle fascia underneath. *Do it! Do it! Do it!*

someone shrieks, followed by a hyenalike chorus of voices, laughing. I obey.

I'm not suicidal, but I know that after I have made several deep cuts, the voices will fade, as they always do. Now I apply pressure to the wounds with a wad of paper towels that I keep there for the purpose and, one-handed, rip off enough masking tape to bind on a thick fresh wad. Although a large mirror is built in above the sink, I never glance at my reflection. My arm wrapped and secured with tape, stinging where it contacts the towels, I return to the bedroom.

Someone knocks. Quickly I pull my sweater sleeve down over the makeshift bandages, hoping the bleeding has stopped. My roommate, an Israeli woman named Shoshana, is at the door.

"Do you need still the tutoring of biochem? This afternoon for me is free."

Shoshana is extremely intelligent, and her occasional gaffes in English do not diminish the impression she gives of brilliance. I wave her in and we sit on the floor with my books and notes.

"Why do you wear these heavy shoes?" she asks, pointing at my high-topped hiking boots after we've gone over some of the material. "The heat is put. Are your feet uncomforted?"

"My feet freeze all the time, even in summer. Every time I'm stationary for long they go white and numb."

"Really?" she says with more interest than I anticipate. "Do your hands come white?"

"Sometimes, but they're not as bad as my feet."

"Because I'm thinking this can be Raynaud's syndrome, do you see, and they are looking for patients for the research. Maybe you should go to Student Health to see if you are qualified."

I'd do anything for normal feet, so this interests me. After we finish studying, I call for an appointment.

A week later I show up at Student Health. A nurse leads me to an examining room then asks me what the problem is.

"My roommate suggested I come in because my feet are always freezing. Shoshana thinks it might be Raynaud's syndrome."

The nurse nods, motioning for me to sit on the examining table. She places a thermometer under my tongue then grips my wrist with her hand to take my pulse. Before I can stop her, she pushes my sleeve above my left elbow to take my blood pressure. At the sight of my still-healing wounds, she freezes. "What are these?" she asks.

I wrest my arm free and push my sleeve back down to cover it again. I look away, trembling. Does she know? Will the dean be told? Will I be kicked out of school? Damn Shoshana for her suggestion! How am I supposed to know they take your blood pressure when you come in for a problem with your feet?

To my relief, the nurse shrugs and leaves the room, telling me the doctor will be in shortly.

I wait, sitting on the edge of the padded examining table, my bare feet growing mottled, even though the air is warm. I continue to tremble but hope maybe the nurse will ignore what she saw, maybe she'll assume . . . *That's it, if anyone asks I'll say I was in a car accident.*

A tall, dark-haired woman in a white coat knocks, then opens the door. I recognize Dr. Endicott from a party she gave for female medical students back in September. Without a word, she takes my left arm like the nurse did, as if for a blood pressure reading, and quickly pulls up my sleeve. She inspects it quietly for a moment. Tears fill my eyes. Finally, she puts my arm down, gently touches my hand, and replaces it in my lap. I drag my sleeve down and cover my arm protectively with the other. I look into the distance, wishing I could stop shaking.

"You must be in a lot of pain to do that to yourself," she says. *To yourself*. She doesn't give me a chance to maintain the fiction that I was in an accident.

I nod, hoping she will keep my secret. It's true that I hate myself, hate my life. With the voices and Gray Crinkled Paper, who wouldn't?

"Are you seeing a therapist?" she asks as she jots something in my chart.

I see a psychiatric resident at the clinic, I tell her, but I don't much like him. He's cold, for one thing, and he doesn't seem to like me.

"Do you think you'd work better with a woman?"

I shrug. Maybe some things would be easier to talk about with a female therapist. I could try it.

She scribbles a name on a card. "Give Sonya a call. You'll like her. I've sent troubled students to her before."

Sonya is okay, but mostly she wants to talk about my dreams, which I think is silly. I continue to show up for my appointments, but when she sends me to a private psychiatrist for a medication consultation and he prescribes Thorazine, I've had enough of her. I go back to the clinic and am assigned a psychiatrist who seems more helpful. The dean is told about it, however. He has me come to his office and warns me I'm on probation. I have to stay in treatment. Period.

No one discusses my arms out loud, but I can hear the others thinking about me when I see them in the halls.

Tissue biology—histology—follows, which in comparison with biochemistry seems a breeze. Now we are finally studying Real Medicine: immunology, inflammatory processes, the biology of cancer. Because of my sleepiness, which I now try to fight by jogging three miles every morning, I make do with studying as hard as I can during those short periods when I'm alert. I read the lecture material from textbooks and use the note-taking service's outlines. To my amazement, I manage passing grades. Just after my twenty-fifth birthday, Randy, Karl's friend, finds me asleep over my books in the lab again.

"Here," he says, handing me a few yellow pills wrapped in Kleenex. "These helped my grandfather before he died when he'd do nothing but sleep all the time. Maybe they could help you."

I ask what they are.

"Ritalin. The drug they use for hyperkinetic children—it calms them down. For you, they'll work like an upper, but they're mild, not major league."

I've never heard of Ritalin. I think back to a few months earlier and the pills some jokesters gave me for my birthday, containing enough caffeine to give me coffee nerves for weeks. I didn't appreciate their humor. But drugs? I envision my vein bulging through the skin inside my elbow as I insert a hypodermic.

"Thanks, Randy," I say. "I want to get by on my own. But maybe I'll hang on to them just in case."

"Sure. No prob." He trots off down the hall to his own lab.

A wave of sleepiness rolls over me and I feel myself falling forward over my books. Forcing myself upright, I shake my head, trying to clear out the cobwebs. I down my coffee in huge gulps and run ice water over the insides of my wrists, but it is useless: As soon as I sit down and open my book, I am overcome. I look at the pills. They are probably harmless, probably ineffective, just like all my other maneuvers to stay awake. But surely one wouldn't hurt? Before I can change my mind, I wash down a tablet with the dregs of coffee in my mug. It's useless; I can already tell. As uncontrollably as ever, my head fogs up and I am overwhelmed by a need to sleep.

This time I wake up after thirty minutes. Drew, a dental student whose lab station is across from mine, looks up just as I do. "Good morning?" he says, his eyebrows arching sympathetically.

I grimace back. "The tsetse fly must have had a seven-course meal on me," I say, referring to the vector carrying African sleeping sickness.

Then I realize I am no longer drowsy. In fact, I feel pretty good, more alert than I have in months. Seizing the moment, knowing I could be toppled by drowsiness at any time, I turn to my immunology textbook, which is suddenly fascinating. For the first time since I started med school, I feel the old excitement: T cells, B cells, macrophages, wheal-and-flare response—this is medicine, this is learning, and it thrills me.

Only when my neck and back begin to ache and my eyes feel gritty from strain do I stop reading. I glance at my watch, which is running fast as usual. Damn, I need something that keeps better time than this! It is three o'clock at most, yet my watch already shows six. I look over at Drew's station, but he has gone. So have the others. When did that happen? Just then, Randy sticks his head in the door. "Going to supper, Pam. Want to join me?"

"Supper? Isn't it a bit early for that?"

"Six? Not terribly."

"I've been in here studying since *two*? What was in those pills?"

"Listen, Pam, I *told* you: Ritalin." Randy's frown casts a shadow over his face.

"What's wrong? Aren't you glad they helped?"

"Sure, I am. But the problem is that I have only one bottle, and that's already half empty. I'm happy to give the rest to you—I don't need them—but it's not something you can get over-the-counter."

"Well, I'll have to make do with whatever you give me, then, and figure out what to do when they're gone."

Eventually a former psychiatrist sends me postdated prescriptions for three pills a day. Even though it isn't for many years that I get a proper diagnosis for my sleepiness, it is Dr. Endicott who first takes it seriously.

"You may have narcolepsy. Let me talk to the neurologist and arrange a sleep EEG. You have to stay off the Ritalin for two weeks. Can you do that?"

"Yes. I did it for most of biochem, after all."

"Don't be so sure it's easy. Ritalin is seductive, and once you've felt its effects, even therapeutically, it's hard to give up."

I don't believe her, but she's right. I don't make the two weeks. But I would not have fallen asleep during the EEG anyway; I am simply too anxious about doing the right thing. The test lasts only half an hour and I have to lie on my back with wires glued to my head in a room with the lights on and . . . Well, it is the least sleep-inducing environment possible, even for a person with possible narcolepsy.

At my next appointment Dr. Endicott says the neurologist won't see me, that in his opinion I am just another medical student looking for uppers. I don't ask her opinion or whether or not she agrees with him. I don't even know enough to be hurt or angry. I don't realize the neurologist is calling me a liar, that he thinks I am faking and that my complaint of sleepiness is contrived to manipulate him into giving me amphetamines I don't need.

Carolyn

A memory so tender I still weep. 1977. I am a third-year medical student just starting clinical rotations. I thought I wanted to be a doctor, but now I'm sure I'm incompetent. We're learning how to draw blood gases, a barbaric procedure that involves sticking a long needle straight down to the bone to get arterial blood. My patient lets me try on him four times until his hand is cold and cyanotic. Finally, he begs me to get help. The attending doctor, Lennie, comes in and walks me through the procedure and afterward takes me out to dinner. He's very encouraging, wants to help me perfect my technique. What a relief compared to some of the chiefs I could have had. By the end of the rotation, I can draw blood from a stone.

At my evaluation, he tells me I've done a great job. Furthermore, I'm smart, very attractive, and he's in love with me. The love part is a total shock. I'm flattered, of course, but I'm not interested. Still, I don't know how to tell him so without hurting his feelings. So we date. One month. Then two, three. By spring I've had enough. Finally, just before I leave for a weekend at home, I break the news: I don't love him and never have. That weekend I miss my period. Back at school, I buy a test in the drugstore, and it's no shock when the urine dipstick turns blue. That night, as if she knows, Mom telephones. Her voice is soft as velvet and so comforting that I can't hold back. I tell her everything, including my "appointment" at the Hathamore Center scheduled in a few days.

"Lynnie," she says when my tears subside. "Do you want me to come up?"

"No way, Mom. I'm not dragging you into this."

"What about Lennie?"

"I've told him. There's no way he wants a baby. He knows I've called Hathamore and he agrees, so I'm pretty sure he'll show up."

"If he doesn't?"

"Mom, it's my mistake . . . You're so wonderful to offer, but I need to take responsibility. Without my mother."

"I understand, honey . . ." Her voices catches.

"Mom, what about—?" I pause. She reads my mind.

"He knows."

"Is he mad?"

"Oh, Lynnie, you don't know your father if you think that," she says. "He'll probably call you tonight."

When the phone rings several hours later, I'm too terrified to answer. Fifteen minutes later it rings again. Since my father never waits past two rings, I answer on the fifth. It's Dad. He asks if it's okay to talk.

"Sure, Dad. Talk."

He wants to know if I've told the father and how far along I am and what are my plans, and I tell him what I'm sure he's already heard from Mom, but I break off when I hear him coughing. Then he blows his nose and clears his voice. The only other time I can remember him crying was when I was a kid and we stood among the rows of stark white crosses at a World War II cemetery.

"Lynnie," he says again, "do you *want* to do this?"

"I don't understand," I answer carefully, not sure what he's getting at. "Of course I want to. I'm *not* going to marry the man. I don't love him."

"No, no. I mean, do *you* want to do this?" Pause. "Because," he continues, "you don't have to." A breath. "You can have this baby if you want to. We'll help."

I can't believe he's saying this.

"Lynnie?"

"Yeah, I'm here . . . Are you saying what I think you're saying?"

"Yes, I am. You don't need to have an abortion." He's the first person to use the *a* word, and it stabs me. "Your mother and I are prepared to support you and the baby. If you want this child, you can have it."

But I keep my appointment at the Hathamore Center. I'm not ready to be a mother.

Pamela

One morning in November of my second year in med school, I snap. That afternoon we'll have to do our first physical exam and it is simply too much for me. Trembling, in a panic, I run down to Dean Vard's office in shameless hysteria and beg him to get me out. Out. I'm sobbing now, terrified he won't help me.

"Out of what, out of where?" he asks me. But I can't say, and so he calls others: Dr Endicott, who calls my psychiatrist, who calls, well, who knows whom, who knows whom? But they think I might be suicidal, so under heavy scrutiny I walk from the med school over to the psych ward at University Hospital. My career as a medical student is over.

Sitting in a chair, I am overwhelmed by the Strangeness and voices, unable to move or talk, though a doctor—what is his name?—Dr. Jonas is sitting in the chair opposite me. I think he is waiting for me to speak, to answer a question I no longer remember. The silence goes on and on. Finally, he leaves after I manage to move my head, shaking it "no" when he asks if I'm hearing voices. I do hear voices, all the time, but I'm too scared and too proud to admit it. I'm the good little Nell, Pam the Pure, and good people don't hear people swearing like stevedores coming out of nowhere.

I don't know what time it is until I hear supper trays being unloaded from the dumbwaiter. Someone asks if I'm hungry. I don't bother to respond. I sit, staring at nothing in particular, immobilized within the dimensional interface of Gray Crinkled Paper. Things around me seem very far away, perhaps even outside the Supermetal Canister, beyond relevance. I'm in the left orbit of the solar plexus system. I'm beyond the beyond . . .

But there are other matters to lay before the queen: the Canister, the Five People, and my mission to bring to the world's attention the news of Gray Crinkled Paper.

Sometime later, Dr. Jonas returns with papers and notebooks. He takes the same seat as before, saying, "I thought you'd like someone to sit with you. If you don't feel like talking, that's fine. I'll stay anyway and get some work done. Is that okay?"

I dip my chin a millionth of a degree. It's all he seems to need. "Good. Then I stay." He plops down heavily in his chair and starts reading. Although I am faced away, with my eyes fixed on the far wall, once in a while I notice—by a subtle change in his breathing—that he is glancing at me.

The voices go haywire, mocking him as well as me. I'm too exhausted to fight them; their ammunition stores are well supplied at the moment, seeing as how, for one, I just left medical school in a publicly humiliating way.

After a few hours, Dr. Jonas addresses me again. "Pamela? I've got to leave now. Do you think you'll be able to sleep?" He's slow getting to his feet. I can feel him looking down at me.

I give my millionth of a nod, but it's a lie.

"I don't want you to sit here all night."

Nod again. Another lie. Can he tell the difference?

He goes to the door, but before he opens it all the way reconsiders, comes back. He puts down his books and coat, squats in front of me, clears my hair from my face, looks into my eyes. I immediately close them. "Ah, so you *are* in there. Good. Well, you're pretty slowed down, Pam. Would you like me to help you get up and walk over to the bed?"

I give only the tiniest trillionth of a nod this time, but it's a yes.

He rises, cupping the backs of my elbows in his hands and lifting me from underneath. This propels me to a standing position, but it's not enough. I'm still unable to move, to make any kind of decision. If he were to leave me now, I would stand there all night.

He realizes this, and with his right arm behind me to steady me and left hand holding my left arm, he pushes me inch by inch to the bed. He pulls back the blanket and sheet.

"Will you be able to handle it from here okay?" he asks.

I stare straight ahead, seemingly unaware, but I take a deep breath and manage to grunt yes. He is pleased.

"I'll be back first thing tomorrow morning," he says, leaving. "Sleep well. The nurses will check in on you regularly throughout the night."

Hell's bells, spell's hell I tell, fine belle's Bill Tell's Christ Hell's who'll tell fun fell, evil Nell, hell bell tell Nell who the hell swell Nell fucking Nell . . . Fuck Nell, Fuck Nell, Fucking Pam's hell.

Carolyn

Two and a half years pass before I see Pammy again.

I graduate HMS in June 1979 and the next week start medical training at Hospital of the Commonwealth.

By the end of the first week of residency, I realize I've made a terrible mistake. I like seeing patients, but I hate doing physical exams, the nuts and bolts of internal medicine. All the other residents love thumping, auscultating, palpating, percussing, inspecting, testing, tapping, poking, probing, inserting, threading, cutting, sewing, stitching, running to codes, and saving lives. I'd rather talk and listen, figure out the story of a patient's life.

At four-thirty in the morning, during my second night on call as a medical intern, I make a decision. I've been here since yesterday at seven and already I've admitted four patients to the hospital, done spinal taps, chest taps, restarted five IVs, completed two fever workups, one code, and one death certificate, and I still have hours of scut work to do. If I hear my name on the PA system one more time I'm going to smash the window and hurl myself from the eighth floor. No lunch or dinner, I'm famished, my head is pounding, and I'm so tired I can't think straight. Worst of all, I just got my period and there's not a single Tampax in the entire hospital. A maternity pad like a diaper from one of the supply carts will have to do, and I'm sitting on the toilet trying to figure out how to use it when an ambulance screams up to the emergency room. *No!* I shriek silently. It's only my fifth day of internship, and already when I hear a siren, all I feel is rage, resentment, and dread. Sirens mean patients! When you're on call, patients are your enemies. *Please, God, let them die!*

The sun hasn't broken over the horizon when the loudspeaker announces my fifth admission of the night. That clinches it.

As soon as I can steal a few minutes after rounds, I duck into the empty, unused on-call room and lock the door. A glance in the mirror depresses me. I look as bad as I feel. My white coat is spattered with God knows what, my hair is a mess, I'm dying for a shower, I have cramps, and a huge pimple is sprouting in the center of my forehead. My eyes burn for sleep. If I lie down, I'll be unconscious in seconds. I have two minutes to make this call. I sit, furtively dial an outside line, and allow my eyes to close while the phone rings.

Dr. Sope, the director of residency training at City Psychopathic Hospital, is in his office, and on the first ring he picks up with a curt, "Yes?"

"Oh, I had expected to leave a message with your secretary." I manage to stammer my name and remind him of our conversation six months before graduation. He remembers me.

"Carolyn?" he says, his deep voice friendly and slightly curious. "Congratulations. It must be *Dr.* Spiro by now."

"Thanks, Dr. Sope," I say. "But I think—" My voice breaks. I'm sure he notices.

"Yes?"

"I'm at Hospital of the Commonwealth. In medicine." I pause, take a deep breath, then go on. "It's not where I belong."

"But it was at the top of your list, wasn't it?"

"It was. But I hate medicine. I love psychiatry. When I took this residency I thought I needed to prove . . . something."

"You didn't know that at the time?" he says. "You know, when you withdrew your application from City Psycho, I was disappointed."

"Why didn't you tell me?"

"Would you have listened?" He sighs. "You said you wanted internal medicine—"

"My father told me that's what I wanted!"

"And it's not." He clears his throat, then adds, "So your father is happy, but you're miserable. I guess that's one way to learn."

He makes it sound so easy.

"I know that now." Why am I tiptoeing around? I have to tell him why I called. "So, is the offer still open?"

"Offer?" Pause. "You mean residency—for next year, of course?" He must have heard me nod. "We'd *love* to have you."

Knowing there's an end to this hell, I'll make it through the year. Somehow.

Three hundred and sixty days later I walk into City Psycho. This time I know it's the right choice. The peeling paint and ripped vinyl furniture, the acrid smell, the malfunctioning toilets, the chaos are all just as I remembered. It feels like home. City Psychopathic Hospital, known throughout Boston as City Psycho, is a Harvard teaching hospital. An underfunded state institution, it serves the poorest of the Roxbury catchment area and no one would mistake it for anything else. As a first-year resident, I am assigned to the "chronic" unit on the top floor. "Chronic" is a euphemism for incurable, and many patients on this unit have been here for years. We are handed several heavy iron keys, each three inches long and suitable for a prop in a horror movie. These are no props. The heavy steel door is always double-locked and guarded. No patient leaves without a written pass and an escort. Every time I enter the unit, I am mobbed by bored, lonely, and Thorazine-dulled patients who otherwise would pace endlessly around the dayroom, wearing the carpet threadbare. The first order of business is to learn how to get into the unit, avoid the crush of clamoring patients, ignore the requests for a pass, a smoke, a talk, a snack, a bed change, and discharge, all without wasting any time. There's never any quiet; someone always needs something; something is always broken; the toilet never works. But I love it here.

A year later, I'm trying to sleep in the on-call room when the phone rings.

"Lynnie? Is that you?" It's an unfamiliar female voice.

"Who—" I fumble for my glasses.

"Is this Lynnie Spiro?"

"Yeah? Uh, you mean Carolyn. Yes, it is—" In the dark I knock my glasses off the bookcase and squint at the lighted clock dial. "It's ten o'clock. Who—?"

"I'm a nurse at the state hospital in Connecticut." I swing my legs to the floor and stagger out of bed. I reach for the switch and the room floods with harsh unnatural light. "I'm calling about Pam." My heart does a wobbly cartwheel.

"She was admitted here a week ago."

I drop into a chair, miss, and end up on the floor, the receiver still in my hand.

"Are you okay?" she says.

"Yes, what's the problem?"

"Your sister is very ill—" She breaks off, whispering to someone else. "She wants to talk to you." She hands the phone to someone else. I can hear breathing on the line.

"Pammy? Is that you?"

Raspy, choking sounds and then a forced expiration, ending with, "—es."

"Pammy? What's the matter?"

"S . . . lo . . ."

She's called me from other hospitals before, but never from the state hospital and she's never sounded like this.

"Slo . . . do . . . wn."

"Slodown?"

The twins at
seven weeks old.
*By permission of
Marian W. Spiro.*

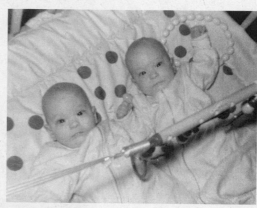

Written by Marian
Spiro on the back,
"This is anyone's guess,
but I'm pretty sure that's
Lynn on the left."
*By permission of
Marian W. Spiro.*

The twins kissing each other,
around three years old.
By permission of Marian W. Spiro.

With Dad, summer 1955. "Maybe if I tickle him, he'll wake up."

By permission of Marian W. Spiro.

The four Spiro children and the hamster, around 1958.

By permission of Howard M. Spiro.

This picture must be from tenth grade, around age fifteen, because Lynn is trying to wear contact lenses.

By permission of Marian W. Spiro.

Judging from our long hair, Lynn's wire-rimmed glasses (she gave up on hard contacts), the long sideburns on Chip, this snapshot probably was taken at Grandpa Spiro's in Newton, Massachusetts. Most likely at Passover, 1970. The twins are seventeen, Chip fifteen, and Martha twelve.

Carolyn, twenty-one, second year after her transfer from Brown University to Sarah Lawrence College, 1975.

Pamela, twenty-one, back at Brown University, 1975.

By permission from the estate of Bruce John Batts.

Pam and Mom at Pamela's
graduation and Phi Beta
Kappa ceremony, Brown
University, 1975.
By permission of Howard M. Spiro.

Pam with Dad also at graduation
from Brown University.
By permission of Marian W. Spiro.

Carolyn and
parents at
Sarah Lawrence
graduation,
1975, then off
to Harvard
Medical School.
*By permission of
Philip M. Spiro.*

Lynnie (Carolyn) and Chipper (Philip) Spiro trying to act like grown-ups, circa 1977. Carolyn is in her second year of med school. Phil is about to start his first year.

By permission of Marian W. Spiro.

Summer 1983. Carolyn, her husband, and daughter, Allie, a few months old.

By permission of Marian W. Spiro.

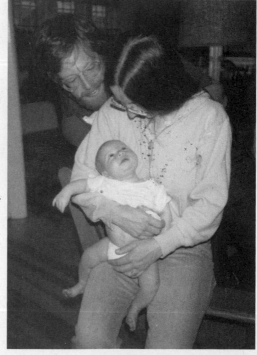

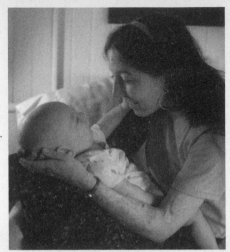

Pamela holding Allie,
summer 1983.
*By permission of
Marian W. Spiro.*

Four generations of
women: Carolyn,
Allie, Mom, and
Grandma, 1985,
Wilton, Connecticut.
*By permission of
Marian W. Spiro.*

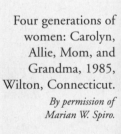

May 1, 1987, Carolyn and
Allie with new arrival, Jeremy,
New Haven, Connecticut.
By permission of Michael Saraf.

In Madison,
Wisconsin, 1987, a
rare visit by Pamela.
*By permission of
Carolyn Spiro.*

Carolyn and family,
summer vacation,
1988, in better times.
*By permission of
Irene R. Kitzman.*

Pam, 1994, reading a
poem written for a friend's
seventy-fifth birthday.
By permission of the Levine family.

Carolyn dancing with her coach in competition, early 1990s.

By permission of Terri Boucher.

Pam, post-Zyprexa, 1998, with Eemie.

By permission of Mizzy Hanley.

No response. Ragged breathing. "L . . . ynn . . . ?"

"I'm here—" Suddenly the PA system, running feet, male voices, commotion. I fight down panic. "Pammy!"

The nurse, back on the line. "I'm sorry, Pamela has to get off the phone." Click.

I try to call back from City Psycho, but the operator keeps transferring me. I finally fall asleep but am awakened at midnight to admit a young man found sleeping in a Dumpster. I've just finished writing his admission orders when the lobby door opens and I hear heavily accented voices.

The security guard gives them the once-over, runs a sheet of paper under the man's signature, and ushers them into the evaluation room. I point to a chair, and the man pushes the young woman into it. I soon learn these are refugees from Idi Amin. Both man and woman are thin and dark skinned, with smooth ebony hair and sharp features. It's obvious this is a father and daughter.

"She try to die," the man says. He slaps his hands on the desk in a gesture of disgust.

"Mr.?"

"Obote." He pulls himself up straight and glares at me. "Ibrihim Obote." I guess he's used to being the one in charge.

"And this is . . . your daughter?"

He nods and glances at her. "She Dilshad."

"What a pretty name."

It turns out to be what I think is a routine evaluation. I glance at the clock. What I need to know right now is if she is imminently suicidal, but this is difficult to ascertain because Dilshad neither speaks nor moves. With the language barrier and my inability to interview Dilshad herself, it takes an hour and a half to get an answer. In the end Dilshad agrees not to kill herself. I make an appointment for her at nine o'clock sharp the next morning. Mr. Obote tucks the card into Dilshad's jeans pocket. She bows her head and allows Mr. Obote to escort her out the door.

It's three o'clock in the morning by the time I finish writing a note and head up to sleep. At eight in the morning the new on-call doc will arrive.

At seven-thirty the alarm wakes me. By eight o'clock I've called the state hospital and arranged to visit Pammy.

A few minutes later, the Boston police call. Someone reported a body on the pavement in front of the Corona Motel. The woman has no identification on her and is not a registered guest. However, in the pocket of her jeans they discovered an appointment card with my number. The officer estimates that she jumped at approximately three in the morning.

The shock of the young Ugandan woman's suicide and my role in it is fresh on my mind as I drive down to Connecticut. I've convinced Albert, my boyfriend of two months, to drive to Connecticut with me, though meeting my sister for the first time in the state hospital isn't exactly his idea of fun. It's a couple of hours' drive and Albert reads his airport novel for most of it.

Dilshad. What sign did I miss? At what point last night did she realize I wasn't listening to her? Did she know what I wanted her to tell me and gave me the words emptied of meaning? What was it like for her alone on the windy balcony moments before her final plunge? Did she hurry toward her end, hurling herself into space, or did she hesitate, utter a prayer, or shed a tear before letting herself fall? I have always assumed Pammy would never kill herself because of the pain it would cause me. But in reality I have no idea how she lives her life, let alone if she wants to end it. Last night, in my rush to get a few hours of sleep, I convinced myself that Dilshad would be okay. This morning she's dead. It's my fault for not reading her correctly. Will Pammy end up the same? For the last ten years all I have done is think about me, and my future, giving little thought to Pammy. I barely know her anymore. So how will I know if she is suicidal? Oh Dilshad . . . I'm sorry, if only I had listened.

My mind is awhirl. The postmortem on Dilshad will have to wait. Pammy comes first.

Albert and I walk in the unguarded front door of the hospital and with no one around to stop us, we climb the stairs to the locked psychiatric unit. Here, the walls are tiled, cold, antiseptic as a bathroom, but it's cleaner, brighter, and more hopeful than City Psycho. We're buzzed in.

A dark-haired woman in a white nurse's uniform greets me. I introduce Albert, but she barely acknowledges him.

"I need a word with you." She holds open the door to a small conference room, empty except for two chairs on opposite sides of a large round table. Albert is about to accompany me, but she blocks the doorway and points down the hall. "Only family. You can wait there." Then she shuts the door behind her and sits down. She slaps an overfilled three-ring notebook on the table, flips to a page, and reads the entries for a few moments. Pammy's chart. Then she closes the book, pushes it aside, folds her hands together on the table, and gives me a look that seems as determined as it is unsympathetic.

"Look, I'll get to the point here. Your sister won't take her meds."

"Uh-huh?"

"Well, you're the only family member she talks to——"

"No one else knows where she is."

"I see." I don't know what she sees. She angles her head like Perry Mason, narrows her eyes, and runs her gaze up and down me. I recoil.

"How much has she told you?" The nurse taps her pen impatiently.

"Look, Pammy and I talk on the phone, but I can't read her mind any more than I can read yours."

She doesn't crack a smile. "When was the last time you actually saw her?"

"A couple of years ago probably—her choice as much as mine."

"I'm sure of that." She hesitates, then adds, "You've seen her arms—the 'self-mutilation'?"

"I know she used to . . . injure her arms, if that's what you mean." A beat. I'm waiting her out, but she wins this round. "She's had a difficult time since we were kids. But she graduated from Brown and was in medical school for a year. Besides, I don't think she hurts herself anymore—"

"But do you *know*?" She pauses. "What I mean is, do you know her diagnosis?"

"I think she has worked in a local bookstore and she tries to write. She's been down in the dumps sometimes." *Sometimes? Most of the time is more like it. How has she supported herself? I should know the answer. But I don't. She's lived her life and I've lived mine ever since high school. I don't know where she's been, let alone what she's done.* "I guess you could say she's been depressed."

"It's worse than that."

What am I supposed to say? All the anxieties I've had over the years come flooding back—the ambivalence about being a twin, the fear I'll never establish my own identity, the resignation to her illness, whatever it is. The nurse knows nothing of all this.

"She says you don't know, but she's been hearing voices for years."

"What are you talking about?"

"We're talking about your sister," says the nurse.

"Look, she's never mentioned it—it can't be that bad. Why are we wasting time, for God's sake?"

"She hears voices *in her head,* Carolyn. Auditory hallucinations."

"Hallucinations?" *Pammy, psychotic? Oh, come off it.*

"For years." A pause.

"Do I understand you correctly? She's hearing *voices*? She hears people talking who aren't there?" I realize I'm repeating myself, but none of this makes any sense.

"I guess she's never told you—" The nurse's tone is kinder now, genuinely sympathetic. "Lynnie, Carolyn, I mean, I'm sorry this is new and I'm sorrier that I have to tell you, but you might as well know. Unlike the other hospitals, the doctors here think your sister has schizophrenia."

Schizophrenia? No way! Schizophrenia happens to other people. Schizophrenia happens to people at City Psycho, not to Pammy!

This is ridiculous. Who the hell does she think she is? Doesn't she know I'm a doctor? I'm a fucking psychiatrist, for God's sake. I know Pammy better than she does. I know schizophrenia and I know *my sister* doesn't have it.

"Carolyn, she doesn't know about this. But it *is* true and we have to make some decisions—"

No! Don't say anything. I don't want to hear.

"Carolyn—"

I force words to the surface. "Is that why she's . . . in the hospital?"

"Not exactly."

"Did she hurt herself?" I hear myself ask.

"Yes, she did."

My heart flips and sinks without stopping.

"Does she do it with cigarettes?"

I already know the answer. A few years ago, when I was still in medical school, she stayed in my apartment for a few days, when she had that appointment with Dr. Llosa. She didn't tell me much about it, but later, when we were in the kitchen and Pammy rinsed the vegetables, she rolled up her sleeves when she thought I wasn't looking. I was appalled to see that her arms were covered with burns.

"Pammy! What happened to your arms?"

She quickly pushed her sleeves down. "They're just burns," she said casually. I put down my knife.

"Just?" I stared at her.

"I have to do it," she offered after a silence.

"Why?"

"Oh, Lynnie, sometimes I'm so numb I feel like moon rock. That's when I burn myself."

"It helps?"

"For the moment, yes."

"But burn scars are permanent! Don't you care how you look?"

"Well, at least I know I'm alive . . ."

"But Pammy! Even plastic surgery won't help if you keep—"

"Look, they're mostly old," she snapped. "So don't worry—"

I couldn't look her in the face. I knew more questions would only make her angry.

She spoke again. "Lynnie, don't be upset. Really. I don't even do it anymore."

But I knew that wasn't true. Not from what I saw. Some of the burns were blistered, raw and oozing a thin yellow serum. The oldest had thick heaped up keloid edges. They looked like melted wax at the base of a candle. I looked at my own arms, and I looked back at hers. We were no longer identical.

A half hour later Albert and I are met by the head nurse and escorted to Pammy's room. It is large and tiled. Six sagging beds and six gray lockers line the walls. I recognize some of her belongings. I see a figure standing by the window. It's Pammy. She looks even thinner than she did a few years ago and not terribly healthy. But the worst thing is, she doesn't move, speak, or even look at me when I enter. She stands with one hand locked in midair as if she is reaching for something.

Albert quickly realizes that conversation isn't going to happen, so he backs a chair against the wall and returns to his novel.

I try to see my sister as any doctor would. She's unresponsive, she's catatonic. *Catatonic?* I try to talk with her, but her response is too slow to follow. I try to remember what I know about catatonia. It's so rare I've never seen it before. How should I behave? Should I act like her sister? Her doctor? Her nurse? Her interpreter? I want this to go away. This person can't be my twin. But I deal with patients like her every day. I treat psychotic patients. Depressed patients. Suicidal patients. *Dilshad.* For a moment I remember the disaster of the night before. Could that happen to Pammy? I step outside to talk to the nurse.

"Was she on antipsychotic medication before she was admitted?"

"Her doctor thought so. But she was probably cheeking them, you know. Then flushing them down the toilet."

This is not news to me. It is not an uncommon thing for patients to pretend to take medication and then spit it out later. At City Psycho we see it all the time: A patient who is doing well suddenly decompensates. That's when we find out.

"She probably hates the side effects," I say in Pammy's defense, knowing they can sometimes feel worse than the illness.

"Now, Pamela," says the nurse as she carries in little paper cups of pills. "Are we going to take our medication today? We don't want to be difficult in front of our sister, do we?" She talks to Pammy as if she's a child, or worse, *about* her as if she can't hear. When she's too slow to swallow a cup of Ensure, the nurse hands it over to me. "I don't have all day." Clipboard against her chest, she turns on her heels, gives an officious sniff, and takes off.

I am left holding the plastic cup of a liquid nutritional supplement. I hold it up to Pammy just for show and then discreetly set it down in the wastebasket.

Carolyn

A few months later I marry Albert, even though I'm not really attracted to him. I tell myself that appearances shouldn't matter, that it's the inner person that counts. And, after all, my friends think he's handsome: Isn't he tall, bearded and broad-shouldered, with a head of thick auburn hair? As a dancer, I appraise him with a critical eye; as far as I am concerned, he's flabby, ungainly, and awkward but, ashamed of such pettiness, I keep my opinion to myself. Sex with him is another problem; that one, too, I shove from my mind.

Our wedding takes place in December in the Unitarian Church in Cambridge. Pammy doesn't come; she's back in the hospital. Over the years I've trained myself not to expect her at family gatherings, and though I understand why she can't be here, I miss her more than I say. As it turns out, we wake up in the morning to discover that the snow showers that were supposed to pass through with little accumulation have deposited up to two feet of snow. And there's no sign of the storm letting up. The airport is closed, as are the highways and many local roads. I look out the window and cry.

The First Unitarian Church of Cambridge is a lovely, simple seventeenth-century meetinghouse, pristine white inside and out. Aside from the sign out front there are no religious symbols, no stained glass, no icons, no velvet cushions to soften the wooden pews. No colored ribbon or flowers bedecking the aisle, no candles, no cross, no God. Above all there is no passion, religious or secular. It is, after all, a Unitarian church, where intellect reigns supreme.

It's still snowing at two o'clock when the service is scheduled to begin. The hotel is just a block from the church, so we brave the storm and walk, wading through the drifts. I carry my gown and my shoes. Just in front of the church the sidewalk has been shoveled, but now it's glazed with ice, so glassy I can't move. Albert is wearing boots and tramps on ahead, apparently oblivious. I call out his name as he darts up the stairs and disappears into the church. In a flash, I picture how our union is to be. Then, from behind, I hear Albert's brother, Jon. "Come on, Carolyn," he murmurs. "Hold tight!" Before I know what's happening, he drapes my arm around his neck, sweeps me off my feet, and carries me up the stairs to the church.

We wait as long as we can for the harpist and a few more guests. Finally we begin the ceremony.

Oh, Pammy, would you have sensed, the way you used to, that I was taking the wrong road? Once upon a time you thought what I thought and felt what I felt. What happened to us? What happened to you?

"I do." My voice rings out in the echoing whiteness of church and snow. *I do.* Confidence resonates through my voice, no display of last-minute anxiety. *I do.* No trembling of my lips. No hesitation. I've known Albert six months. I'm marrying now so I won't change my mind. *I do.* Single for twenty-nine years, it's time to get married. *I do.* For better or for worse. *I do.*

Pamela

After being released from the state hospital, I don't know what to do with myself. I'm living with a new friend, Mariah, who works at an insurance company and isn't home during the day. The hours are empty and desperate. I don't dare call my family; they have no idea how bad things are. I spend more and more time alone listening to the voices.

A day treatment program helps me get through, but the back-to-back groups overwhelm me. I participate less and less as the months pass. Most of the time I sit on the floor, mute, with my coat over my head even in the summer, and after a while people ignore me.

One day as I drive back to my apartment, the voices work themselves into a frenzy. I flip on the radio, which is in the middle of playing the jingle from a popular drain-clearing service: "Call Roto-Rooter, that's the name, and away go troubles down the drain." They're playing the commercial on purpose; it's a message.

The chain of thoughts sparked by the jingle make ominous sense to me: The only way to rid myself of my troubles, I decide, is to swallow drain cleaner. This sudden realization is a relief—there is a way out after all! It scares me, but I don't regard myself as suicidal. My only intention is to "clean myself out," stop the voices. I buy industrial-strength Liquid-Plumr and head back to day treatment.

"Away go troubles—" the voices sing. Minutes left in group

therapy. I try to pay attention to the young man who is speaking, sitting in a chair across from me. He has problems with his live-in girlfriend. They don't communicate, he complains; she is always trapping him with mixed messages.

Other patients relate to his struggle, they share his confusion, they know how hard it is for couples to keep open the lines of communication.

Although I usually say nothing, and someone else now has the floor, it seems crucial for me to speak up, to show how not all messages are mixed. I, for one, have received a very clear, unmixed message.

"And what is that?" Fred, the group leader, asks. Silence falls as he waits for my answer. I try to think how to phrase it. Finally, I explain that the radio gave me the message just that afternoon to Roto-Rooter my way to peace.

"Roto-Rooter?" Fred's brow deepens into furrows.

To swallow drain cleaner, I continue, certain this clear example will satisfy him. Silence holds sway in the room. I glance at my watch. The group is supposed to have ended three minutes ago. When Fred says he wants a quick survey of how people are doing, one woman who barely knows me explodes.

"You mean you're just going to let her drink Drano!" she yells. "She says she received a message to drink Drano from the radio, and all you can say is, how are we doing! You're just going to let her leave?"

"I didn't say that," Fred explains patiently.

Group over for the day, I quickly stand, preparing to race from the room, when Fred snags me. Since he has me firmly by the arm and blocks the door, I can't get away. He points to his office and follows me.

"You need to be hospitalized," he says, closing the door.

"No, I don't," I answer. "I can't!"

"Can you look me in the eye and promise you're safe? Can you? Otherwise I need to call your psychiatrist."

He wants nothing less than my soul, I think, staring at the floor.

"I promise I won't do anything," I mumble. I mean it, but I'm terrified to make eye contact.

"I want you to look at me when you say that," he insists. "Can you do that, Pam?"

Minutes tick by. "I promise," I reiterate. "I *promise*." But my eyes remain fixed on the air next to his face, still unable to look directly at him. I really don't want to be hospitalized. "I promise!"

"Look at me, Pam."

I try again. "I promise?"

"That's not good enough," he says softly.

The next thing I know he is on the phone with my doctor, who also wants me hospitalized. As the ambulance attendants strap me onto the stretcher, I curse Fred and snarl, "I hate you."

Dr. Ross at University Hospital is just out of medical school.

Because I complain about side effects, he takes me off Haldol. At first, I feel fine. Three days later, the Strangeness returns and with it the certainty that my hands belong to someone else. I can't sleep. I get up to make myself a cup of warm milk in the patients' kitchen.

A nurse comes in. "What are you doing?"

I yell at the top of my lungs, not caring if I wake everyone, "I can't sleep with these hands! I can't sleep!"

She flees. I sit in the dining room, muttering to myself. The nurse appears again. With her is Dr. Ross, who takes a seat near me, motioning for the nurse to leave.

"What's wrong, Miss Wagner?" he asks in the formal way he has.

I turn to him, averting my eyes. "It's these hands," I shout. "They're not mine!" I shake. Sweat pours off me. I wipe my face with trembling hands.

"Try to calm yourself, Miss Wagner. I can help you," he says, writing an order in my chart. "Have you ever taken Mellaril?"

I shake my head.

"I'm writing for you to have two hundred milligrams now, and a hundred milligrams every hour until you can sleep. I'll talk with you tomorrow. Will you take it?"

I nod.

"The nurse is getting you a dose now. You can have as much as you need tonight. I'll be back to see you in the morning."

"*And how* did you sleep last night, Miss Wagner?" Dr. Ross asks the next day, sitting across from me in my bedroom.

"Okay, I guess," I think I say. A voice cackles, someone sneers, *Looney tunes! Fro-oo-oot loop!* Unable to help myself, I turn toward the sound, but no one is there. I sense that Dr. Ross is looking at me. How long have I been silent? Hasn't he heard my answer? "I slept okay," I say, aloud this time.

"I'm glad to hear that." He makes a notation on a legal pad. More questions, more tests, proverbs to interpret, a request to count backward. He takes notes but responds minimally. Finally he puts the pad aside, inhales, then looks at me. "Miss Wagner, you're obviously ill. What do you think is wrong with you?"

This surprises me. What does it matter? "I don't really know. All you doctors say different things. I know I have narcolepsy."

His eyelids lower a bit. He purses his lips.

"I have narcolepsy, that's all," I repeat.

"Whether you have narcolepsy is irrelevant here, since that's a strictly neurological condition. You seem somewhat depressed, but that's not your major problem. I believe you have schizophrenia, but University Hospital has never correctly diagnosed you."

I turn my face in his direction, my eyes fixed on his tie. "That's nonsense," I say. "I'm not crazy!"

" 'Crazy' is a word that doesn't mean anything," he answers. "It has no diagnostic significance. You do, however, show signs of suffering from delusions and hallucinations, which are both seen in schizophrenic psychoses."

"I'm fine!" I yell. I lapse into a terrified silence. He's wrong. "My regular psychiatrist doesn't think I have schizophrenia."

"On the contrary, he does. And I think you are very far from fine, Miss Wagner. Schizophrenia is a serious condition. Incurable, deteriorating, and hard to treat. While you may not be institutional-ized, you will never fully recover. However, we do have medications that can help. I'd like to keep you on Mellaril and see if we can't make you more comfortable."

"Look, I'm not schizophrenic and I don't like medication. It makes me feel drugged."

"Do you feel drugged now?"

I think about it. "No, not really, but I've only taken a little."

He says nothing.

"Will you keep the dose as low as possible?"

"You took four hundred milligrams last night. A moderate dose that I'd like to start you at."

"Four hundred? That's way too much. Fifty milligrams at most."

"That would not be effective. Four hundred. Five or six hundred in a couple of weeks and we'll see how you do."

Later that afternoon, my outside psychiatrist stops by to check in with me. I tell him what Dr. Ross said. "You know, I don't like him at all. He's just a stupid resident. I don't have schizophrenia. You know me better than he does."

"Actually, I agree with Dr. Ross. Your functioning has steadily deteriorated since you left medical school. You seem more troubled than ever. Dr. Ross is quite competent, Pam. Why don't you give him a chance?" Without waiting for me to raise further objections, he stands. He's out of time. He smiles, then strides from the room.

I leave the hospital on six hundred milligrams of Mellaril. I'm doing better than I have in a long while.

It is a late summer evening and my roommate Mariah and I are sit-ting on my bed in the back bedroom, where we have an ancient air conditioner and cross ventilation through the open window onto the back porch. I am wondering aloud why life loses its magic after childhood. Mariah, who writes poetry when she's not working as an insurance claims adjuster, nods her head, even though she has little interest in replaying *her* childhood. We fall silent, each of us in separate bubbles. Suddenly, breaking through, Mariah sits forward over her knees. I look up and something about her makes me shiver.

Fixing her eyes on something in the far distance, she begins reciting a poem. This, so unexpected, makes me sit up and listen, dumbstruck as much by the fact that she has committed a poem to memory as by the poem itself, Gerard Manley Hopkins's "Spring and Fall: To a Young Child." I will never forget the thrill of those first lines: "Margaret, are you grieving / Over Goldengrove unleaving? / Leaves, like the things of man, you / With your fresh thoughts care for, can you? / Ah! as the heart grows older / It will come to such sights colder / By and by, nor spare a sigh / Though worlds of wanwood leafmeal lie . . ." Mariah recites it in its entirety, up to the last line, at which she pauses, for effect: "It is the blight man was born for, / It is Margaret you mourn for."

After she finishes, I sit openmouthed. Mariah introduced me to poetry when we first met, of course, since she is always writing it. I recognize that she is very talented but, to be honest, I don't get it, beyond a jumble of nice or dissonant sounds. Until now I've felt only bewilderment in the face of her passion, a passion I didn't share, truly appreciate, or understand. I approached poetry with at most a tepid interest, certain I wouldn't comprehend it, or afraid that if I did, I wouldn't like it. That is, until that moment. After she recites Hopkins's poem, it is as if a long-barred door has swung open and I am given a vision of an unimaginably lovely landscape: poetry, *poetry*! like the deep crimsons and gold-veined ochers of buttes rising above the tableland of the ordinary.

As thoroughly as a born-again Christian and by a not dissimilar process, I am, in the space of just a few moments, converted.

Now, at last, there is something of value in my life. Poetry, with the gleaming buttery luster of eighteen-karat gold, is something to live for, a future worth looking forward to: I begin to read poetry and then to write it. And as I write and write and write, I dream, though secretly, that somehow, someday, perhaps after many years of apprenticeship, I might deserve to call myself a poet too.

Although I continue in day treatment for a few years after this, slowly I wean myself away from it; the time spent there feels increasingly useless as well as stolen from the hours I might have for writing. Eventually, I begin to write prose again as well. And I know that even if I had to be ready for that moment of conversion, what Mariah gives me that day in the recitation of a simple poem is a gift beyond price. Then as now it is an awakening that immeasurably enriches my life from that point on.

Despite my awakening to poetry, Dr. Ross's dire predictions about my future seem to be coming true. After that year, Mariah and I no longer share an apartment. I am in and out of most of the hospitals in the area and bounce back and forth between those and a local psychiatric halfway house. As a final blow, I am dropped from the day treatment program for too many absences.

In the state hospital again, I waver on the edge of catatonia, at times frozen in awkward positions, mute, unable to eat and barely able to toilet myself, at others, emerging from my stupor, charged with a frantic energy and an insupportable terror of the spies and counterspies who are battling over me. It is my terror that apparently leads another patient to extinguish two cigarettes on my upper arm when I am back in the zombie state. She tells me later, in a voice made slurry by Thorazine, that she just wanted to put me out of my misery. The nursing staff believe instead that I have burned myself, and they confiscate my cigarettes and lighter. Frenzy gives way again to stupor.

That night a nurse takes me into a treatment room to weigh me. At barely ninety pounds, I am told they will tube-feed me if I can't eat on my own. I do my best, though it seems to take hours to finish half a sandwich.

After this strenuous business of staying responsive, they take my tray and leave me free to tumble back into the dark warmth of silence and immobility. I notice a small American flag on top of the dayroom television and think it calls for a patriotic salute, a signal to the spies that I have not yet given up the fight to elude capture. I make myself rise from the chair, achingly slowly, but I forget my intention midway and freeze, my arm stuck half aloft, my body not quite upright.

"Did you want to go somewhere, Pam?" someone asks me in a puzzled voice.

I don't answer. Other patients pass the room and look in, curious, but self-consciousness no longer motivates me. Only inner life is of concern: Gray Crinkled Paper, the voices. I am caught up in the sense that something dire will happen if I move or speak. My toes feel cold enough to break and fall off. The spies might win and capture me for torture by the other side. It hardly matters. Thoughts move through me without leaving a trace, sometimes sluggish as treacle, more often haphazardly exploding into elemental traces, vanishing before they are created.

My sense of time has changed too: It is heavy yet fleeting, like the passage of a hot wind. The fourth dimension is now physical. I feel as if I could touch its impossible curves, plunge my hand deep into its black funnel, and grab hold of it like a hand of cards. I am aware of everything, yet I am connected to nothing, able to hear without responding, to think without pursuing any train of thought. I have forgotten any reason to stay conscious, to stay in touch. Though I feel the pressure of hands, the cold burning that guides me back to bed and positions my body for sleep, I am not equal to the task and the terrible fatigue of living in the real world.

I need nothing.

Given Stelazine, an antipsychotic drug thought to be helpful in catatonia, I finally emerge from my torpor and beg the resident, an Indian woman named Dr. Patel, to discharge me. She flatly refuses. I sign a "five-day paper," which means that unless it is contested I can leave the hospital after five working days. She schedules a commitment hearing.

My old friend Bryce, who finished law school some years ago, is now working as a lawyer for the Legal Aid Society. I call and beg him to help me. We haven't seen each other in years, but he seems flattered that I have asked, and though it isn't exactly his field—he works to resolve housing issues for the poor—he agrees immediately.

On the date of the scheduled hearing, he arrives early, with Mariah who, he thinks, can vouch for my stable living situation and my ability to care for myself. After the charge nurse is assured that Bryce will be responsible for me, we are let off the locked unit and make our way downstairs. We find the waiting room, which is crowded with other patients and lawyers.

My name is the first to be called, and we take seats around a large square table: Bryce, Mariah, and I. The doctor, who is already seated at the judge's left, murmurs a few words in his ear as we enter. Then the judge shuffles his papers, coughs a bit, and speaks directly to me.

"You feel that further hospitalization is unnecessary, Miss Wagner?"

Too scared to speak, I nod. "You have to say that out loud," he tells me. "For the record."

"Yes, I think I should be able to go home," I say.

He nods too, but not as if agreeing with me. Bryce tries to interject, but the judge ignores him and turns to the doctor. "And you, Dr. Patel, feel that Pam is gravely ill and incapable of taking care of herself?"

"Pam is a chronic schizophrenic," she says with finality. "She has been hospitalized repeatedly. At the present time she is emaciated and in no shape to leave the hospital."

I start to object, but the judge taps the air for me to sit down and keep quiet. Again, he shuffles papers, clearing his throat after several minutes of silence. For the first time, he addresses Bryce. "Mr. Watts,

I understand your good faith in undertaking to represent Miss Wagner here, but I disagree with you—"

I start to rise in protest.

"Sit down, Miss Wagner. I haven't finished."

I sit.

"Now then, as I've said, I agree with Dr. Patel—I don't believe Miss Wagner is competent to care for herself. I believe she is far too ill to live in the community on her own. But I'm going to discharge her anyway—"

"Oh, thank you, thank you!" I stand up, smiling and grateful, but the judge continues sternly after warning me again to stay in my seat until the proceedings are concluded.

"I predict that it won't be two weeks before she's back with us. I'm going to discharge her because I want to prove that I'm a better judge of people than you are, Mr. Watts."

Two weeks later. Back to "the bin," this time City Hospital.

"May I come in?" It's a new doctor, another resident, a petite woman in a white coat and fashionably large eyeglasses.

"Do I have a choice?" I snap, without making eye contact. I don't want to be here.

"Actually, yes," she replies mildly. "But I assume you're here because you want help. You can sign out at any time. Why not give us a few days before you decide."

I shrug. "I'm making no promises."

"That's all right." She smiles and extends her hand, which I ignore. "I'm Dr. Ginzer. You must be Pam."

Dr. Ginzer, a first-year resident in psychiatry, is tiny and gaminelike, older than most residents, with short-cropped, graying hair. It is autumn and she's wearing a sweater and narrow plaid skirt. She drags over a molded plastic chair and sets it at an angle to my bed, where I'm hunched up against the headboard.

Over and over, I trace a pattern on my thigh, a figure eight, the symbol for infinity. *Dead right, dead red, dead head, a signal. Will she kill?*

The doctor lets a few minutes of silence pass. "How are you?" she asks finally.

Thinking this merely a pleasantry, and not certain I can trust her, I respond in a monotone, my face averted, "I'm fine, thank you. How are you?" I am proud of this "correct" response, because it has taken me so long to learn how to do it properly. Ordinarily, confused by the question, trying to figure out what was "really" being said, I refuse to answer at all. My fingers continue to draw on my leg. I rock back and forth a little but don't look up.

"Fine?" When I read the puzzlement on her face, I realize my mistake.

She makes her question more specific. "Can you tell me what has brought you into the hospital today, Pam?"

I am afraid to say anything, in case she is an enemy agent. But I can't tolerate the tension in the room either. Even the voices have nothing to say, adding to my discomfort. I break the silence. "Are you red, yellow, or blue? Are you a Communist? You won't fool me if you are, you know. Sooner or later I'll find out."

"No, I'm not a Communist. What makes you think I might be?"

I sense a trap. "Why are you wearing that red sweater?"

"It's not red, it's maroon. And even if it were red, that wouldn't mean I was a Communist."

"How do I know? How do I know you can be trusted? You could be lying, just like everyone else."

"You find it difficult to trust people."

"Wouldn't you, if they were constantly on your trail and tail? It's all to do with Gray Crinkled Paper. I have no privacy at all, not even in my own head."

"No privacy?"

I've said way too much. I need to get her off track. "Red as a bed, blue as a shoe. I am curious, yellow. I know you can read my thoughts and control me. It's all over the airwaves. I cha-cha expertly."

Her eyebrows rise toward her hairline. "The only thoughts I know about are those you report. I can't read your mind, and I don't want to control you."

"Sure, sure," I say. "What did you say your name was?"

"Dr. Ginzer, Ruth Ginzer."

"Ginzer? How do you spell that?"

"Would you like me to write it down for you?"

I nod. She prints it on a small piece of paper and holds it out to me. I ignore this until she lays it on the bedspread near me and withdraws her hand. Then I snatch it up. Without looking at it, I fold the scrap and slip it into my pocket. There, I think, evidence! Now I have some protection.

After she leaves, the voices noisily resurge. A nurse comes in, holding a small plastic cup half filled with a reddish liquid. "Dr. Ginzer has ordered you some medicine," she says, handing me the cup. *Chip trips, chip chop.*

"What is it?"

"It's Thorazine. You've taken it before, but this is in liquid form so it will work faster." She mixes some orange juice into the liquid. "Drink it, and I'll give you some more OJ. It tastes nasty, but the juice should help."

"How do I know you're telling the truth?"

"I'll show you the label, if you'd like." She goes to the medication cart and pulls out a bottle labeled "chlorpromazine," filled with a similar reddish fluid. "That's the other name for Thorazine," she assures me, tapping it with her fingernail.

"I know that! I went to medical school, remember?" I look dubiously at the liquid, then back at her.

She watches me upend the little cup into my mouth, then grimace at the taste. "Good for you," she says. She refills the cup with more orange juice. "Quick, drink this to help with the bitterness."

I drink the juice, though it doesn't help the burning. When she leaves, I turn off the light and lie back down on my bed, staring at the ceiling, letting the medication go to work.

Soon, my head is full of cotton, my brain an emotionless blank. The voices have retreated. At the same time, every motor neuron in my body urges me to pace back and forth in my room. Ten steps to the door, turn, then ten steps back, don't stop, whatever you do, don't stop! Even though I know this agonizing restlessness is akathisia, a common side effect of antipsychotic medications, I'm driven to keep moving. But I also grow sleepy. Surrendering, I haul myself onto the bed and drift off, waking only briefly when the nurse comes in with another dose, before sleep envelops me.

Loser! Bitch! Goddamn fool! The voices are acting up again, despite the Thorazine given to me every four hours. Dr. Ginzer is looking at me. I fight to pay attention. "What did you say?" I ask.

"What's wrong, Pam? Are you hearing voices?"

"I asked you to repeat the question, that's all." *Fucking froo-oo-oot loop! Crazy, lazy, mad and bad!* I shake myself, trying to silence the interruptions.

"Pam," she says. "Pam?"

The uproar nearly drowns out her words.

"What do you want?!"

"If you're hearing voices, it's all right to tell me," she urges.

"I'm. All. Right."

Dr. Ginzer nods to herself. She continues, "The question I asked you was how do you feel about having this illness?"

I know she is referring to "schizophrenia, chronic," which I read upside down on my admission paperwork. It's what Dr. Ross said more than a year ago. But I reply, "What illness?" hoping she'll name another one.

"Schizophrenia," she says without hesitation. "How do you feel about it?"

That word again. "I don't feel anything about it," I say. "It's just a label you doctors like to give people." *You said it. Red and dead. Charming and cheerful.* "Won't you let me cha-cha?" I speak these last words out loud, and a look of bewilderment crosses her face. She gazes at me.

"You feel labeled."

"That's what I said, isn't it? Shit, will you shut up!" I direct the second half of my reply at the voices, try to cover my slip. "I wasn't talking to you. I just meant it in general—"

"You do hear voices, don't you?"

What can I say? I've blown it. I sigh. "Yeah, I guess so. Sometimes. So what?"

I am sitting so that my back is turned to her, my eyes on the wall, afraid to say more.

" 'So what?' Well, for starters, it must be pretty scary."

Though my face is averted, I can feel her looking at me and sense an unexpected kindness. "Big deal," I scoff, gesturing for her to go away. "I don't want to talk about it."

Again she nods. "Then let me ask you this: What do you know about schizophrenia? Has anyone discussed it with you?"

I turn around to challenge her. "Yeah. Dr. Ross said I'd be lucky if I didn't wind up on a back ward somewhere."

Hearing this, Dr. Ginzer's face darkens. "That's what you were told?"

"Well, something like that. That it's deteriorating. That I'll never recover." *Do the cha-cha, be charming, be cheerful.*

"Look, we need to talk. You have schizophrenia, yes, but it's no longer a life sentence to the back wards. We can work on it together. You should never have been told that it was hopeless. For one thing, the right medication should go a long way toward helping you feel better. But I also believe in the importance of talking about things. I want to work with you, not against you, but you've got to trust me."

She sounds like she cares and believes what she says. I don't respond, but I'm listening. Something's different—for the first time someone actually wants me to talk about things and doesn't seem prepared to discount or dismiss me as crazy.

And so, for the first time in my life, I finally tell another person everything: about the voices and the Strangeness, about my experience of the other dimensions and alternate reality, about Gray Crinkled Paper. "Things seem strange most of the time," I explain.

"How so?"

"Well, I know I'm evil. I'm Hitler's spawn, that's what the voices say. I think I may have killed JFK. I know that Gray Crinkled Paper is the secret to the universe. And I know no one understands."

Dr. Ginzer may not understand all this either, but she doesn't laugh or seem scared of me. And she doesn't call me crazy. "It must be hard to feel so alone," she comments. After two hours of talking, when she finally has to leave, I'm still not through. I feel weightless with relief and less lonely than I have in years.

After I am discharged from the hospital again, I move back into the halfway house across the street. I spend a year there, attending day treatment and writing poetry in my free time. I move again, first to supervised housing nearby, then, after another year, to an efficiency in Hartford's west end.

On the one hand, this move means an end to surveillance by the Five People, special beings who keep me in line by using radio waves and telepathy, bugging my room and monitoring me on hidden video cameras. It will be a relief to get away from the harassment.

On the other hand, I am moving away from Mariah and all my day treatment friends and will be living alone, something I haven't done in years. On top of this, I am leaving the day treatment program and switching over to the partial hospital program at the nearby Psychiatric Institute, known by all as the "Toot."

Dr. Ginzer takes over my treatment.

BOOK FOUR

*L*ATE 1980S

Pamela

I need to have a tooth filled. Instead of Dr. Kirkus, my usual dentist, a substitute does the work. He is brusque, in a hurry, all business, failing to introduce himself or engage in chatting before he begins. Perhaps because of this, the Novocain feels more painful than usual. No matter how often I raise my left hand—my signal to let Dr. Kirkus know I'm in pain—the new dentist keeps working.

A few days later, I come to understand that amalgam is not all the dentist filled the tooth with. I realize from various signs and evidence around me that he implanted a computer microchip for reasons I can't yet determine. The computers at the drugstore across the street, programmed by the Five People, have tapped into my TV set and monitor my activities with a special radar. If I go out, special agents keep every one of my movements under surveillance. A man lighting a cigarette near the drugstore uses his lighter to signal to another just down the street, warning him of my approach. Another alerts conspirators inside. Nothing I do, indoors or out, goes unremarked.

Soon, I stop going out at all, and when my mother offers to buy me one of the new personal computers that are just then coming on the market, I threaten to throw it out the window, from three stories up. For fear of inadvertently loosening the filling and with it the sought-after microchip, I soon stop drinking.

Strange, interconnected things happen when I visit the library, where surveillance takes an even more menacing turn. Not only are my movements monitored, but my reading habits are tracked by means of special computer files. A newly developed fingerprinting technique can determine which pages of which books I linger over, intruding into my mind, understanding my thoughts, and—the main purpose—controlling me. Luckily, it is winter, so I can flip through books with my gloves on. But I soon realize that glove fibers can be traced too. In order to confuse the members of the conspiracy, I deliberately alter my reading habits, borrowing books on math and sciences that I have no interest in and carefully turning these pages with my bare fingers.

I also understand that the plot against me involves the substitute dentist and the microchip. I throw away my library card but am stuck with the microchip until I devise a plan to get rid of it. Since the television keeps me abreast of the latest developments in the conspiracy, I spend a lot of time glued to the news, though a message is as likely to be conveyed by a sitcom or advertisement as by a documentary.

Dr. Ginzer, who is doing a rotation at the VA, voices great concern about this and talks me into returning to City Hospital, where, because of my poor nutritional status and the fact that I have refused to take medication, I am admitted to the Special Care Unit.

The assigned resident, this time a youngish man with curly red hair, knocks on the door, introducing himself as Dr. Breen. "How are you doing?" he asks.

"I'm okay," I respond, not certain what he wants to know.

"How okay?" he echoes. "When was the last time you ate a meal or drank a glass of water?" He rests a foot on the bed frame, his arms crossed over his chest.

At this, I launch into the difficulties that have brought me there: my increasing inability to eat or drink, my preoccupations with the dental microchip, and the surveillance I've uncovered at the library. I need round-the-clock protection, I tell him, maybe a bodyguard.

"Round-the-clock protection I can promise you."

He asks few questions after that, though he takes notes as I speak. Finally, he puts down his pad and looks at me. I lower my gaze.

"You're not alone in this, you know," he begins.

"What do you mean?"

"You should know that not only are these convictions delusional, a part of your schizophrenia"—he brushes a lock of hair out of his eyes and nods for no apparent reason—"but they're not all that uncommon. I don't mean to dismiss your fears, but I think it might help you to know you're part of a club."

Club? What on earth is he talking about?

"I say club loosely, of course. You haven't chosen to join it. But the belief that there's something—a transmitter, a radio, in your case a microchip—implanted in your teeth is not a rare delusion. I could show you a dozen case histories where people claimed that similar things were happening to them."

This makes sense, since spy agencies are all over the place. "And they survived? What did they do?"

He frowns. "What they did was take medication. They got better."

"They just let the implant stay?"

"What I'm saying is that after they'd been on adequate medication for a while, they no longer believed anything was in the tooth in the first place. I think you can get well too, but you've got to take the medication. If you refuse, and remain as ill as you are now, there's a very real risk that we'd have to commit you to the state hospital, where medication can be mandatory. Do you want that to happen? Think about it."

During visiting hours that evening, Mariah appears, a smile on her face and a slim paperback book in her hands.

"You won!" she cheers, handing me the book. "First prize at the *Metacomet Poetry Review*!"

"No, really?" My head swims with pleasure and surprise. Eagerly, I flip to the first page and see it's true: "First Place—Pamela Wagner."

A nurse overhears Mariah and steps over to see what is making me beam so unabashedly. I show her the book. "My poems won first prize."

"Congratulations!" She motions to an aide who is sitting at the nearby nurses' station. "Come see! Pam's poetry has been published." One by one, other nursing staff come over to congratulate me. Even a few patients show interest, wanting to see my name in print.

The next day, Dr. Breen returns. He's been told about the poetry review and asks to read the five prize-winning poems. I hand him the book and wait nervously to hear his response, hoping I will neither disappoint him nor be disappointed myself. When he finally looks up, I am rocking frantically as voices in the walls chatter in Japanese.

"Pam," he says loudly, to get my attention.

I try to still myself, willing the voices to shut up. I glance at him sideways, smiling shyly. "Did you like them?"

"Pam, we've got to get you back on your feet and out of here. No one who can write poems of this caliber should end up at the state hospital."

Embarrassed now, I hug myself, still rocking, but less furiously than before. I force myself to glance at his face in order to test his sincerity. He is smiling. Briefly, fleetingly, we make eye contact before I look away again.

"It's hard to believe you've only been writing for a couple of years. Maybe I'm no critic, but in my opinion your work is quality stuff." He smiles, then turns serious. "Now, what are we going to do to see that you go home from here in shape to continue writing? Is that an acceptable goal? Can we work together?"

I nod.

"Good. Then the first thing is to get you on adequate medication. I'd like to try you on long-acting Prolixin injections. Prolixin is far less sedating than the drugs you've been on before and might prove more beneficial. What do you say?"

His enthusiasm is infectious. Maybe he does know what he is

talking about. "Okay, I guess. But I want the shots in my arm." A blush creeps across my cheeks. "Not my butt."

"Fair enough." He reaches for his beeper, which has just sounded, and as he leaves, he touches me on the shoulder, as if to say that we are in this together.

Dr. Breen is only partially right: The Prolixin is less sedating than Thorazine. Instead of Ritalin I am started on Parnate, a potentially dangerous antidepressant requiring a special diet. But my overall stability improves only marginally. I feel frustrated. I can concentrate enough to read or write only once in a while.

After discharge, the first week I am due my shot, I wait in line with other outpatients. An hour and a half later, my turn. Dr. Patchett reviews my chart, then directs me behind a curtain, where an empty gurney stands.

Evidently I am to lie on it, facedown, but the idea is so humiliating to me that I stall, hoping I've read the situation incorrectly. "What, um, what do you want me to—?"

Dr. Patchett looks at me. "Drop 'em."

Horrified by his coarseness, I loosen my jeans and lie down on the gurney, suffering through the procedure, my face burning, choking back tears of mortification. The following week, after days replaying the doctor's crude remark, I have worked myself into a fury, and when he attempts small talk as he administers the injections, I snap, "Just shut up and get it over with!"

Afterward, I am about to leave when he orders me to stay and upbraids me for a "rudeness that will not be tolerated here." If I wish to remain a patient in the program I will refrain from insulting him or any other staff member. Do I understand?

Yes, I understand, I mutter, furious that he's given me no chance to explain myself. I endure similar shots for the next several months but never forgive him, and at the first opportunity I leave the program altogether, stopping the Prolixin shots rather than continuing to undergo further humiliation.

The next year, I win first place at the *Metacomet Poetry Review* again and am asked to give an interview for a small newspaper, an article focusing on women writers in the state. During the interview, I mention for the first time publicly that I have been diagnosed with schizophrenia. Far from being put off by this, the reporter seems both interested in me as a writer and sympathetic to the fact that my work is so often interrupted by hospitalizations. When the article is published, I am pleased to see that, for once, my having schizophrenia is relegated to secondary importance, while my life as a writer is the major focus.

Living alone is difficult at best. Although I make some friends, I long to have a pet to keep me company. Because my landlord won't let me, I break my lease, store my belongings, and move out. I housesit with a friend, while Mariah and her roommate are away on a cross-country trip. Meanwhile, we search for an apartment of our own, only to be told each time that our disability incomes, even jointly, are too low for us to qualify as tenants. June becomes July, which soon turns into August. Mariah is due back in a couple of weeks and we still haven't found a place to live.

Although in a pinch my friend can always go home, Mariah's roommate doesn't want me to stay with them once they return, so it is beginning to look as if I'll soon be out on the streets. The voices take advantage of my situation and I have trouble ignoring them as they urge me, *Burn, baby, burn!* My concentration is shot: I can neither read nor write, and I am growing more scattered and disorganized. Afraid I might seriously hurt myself if I obey the voices and uncertain of my ability to keep to a contract not to, Dr. Ginzer has me readmitted to University Hospital.

"*Miss Wagner?* Miss Wagner?" Someone is talking to me, a man with wire-rim glasses, thinning brown hair, and a mustache. I strain to pay attention despite the commotion the voices are making in the background.

"I'm Dr. Kroll."

I glance up but can't make eye contact, staring at the air to one side of his face.

"May I call you Pam?"

Nod. Rocking. *Nut case, half cracked, bananas, froot loop!* a voice grumbles from behind me. I swivel around; no one is there.

"You seem to be in great distress, Pam." The doctor leans forward in his chair, his hands on his thighs. "Are you hearing voices?"

Again, I nod; there's no point in denying it. "I'm scared," I whisper, turning my face to the side.

After he's completed as much of an interview as I can manage, Dr. Kroll rises. "You're going to be all right, Pam," he assures me. "But you're overstimulated. I think you need some relief for a few days. I'm going to speak with the nurses, then I want to get you into a room by yourself to see if we can't make you more comfortable."

A nurse I don't recognize from my other admissions approaches me, a set of hospital pajamas folded neatly over her arm. "Why don't you change into these," she says, escorting me to a room set apart from the other bedrooms, a room furnished only with a mattress, the large window in one wall behind a metal grate. She unlocks an adjoining bathroom and waits for me to change. She takes my clothes, my shoes, and purse.

"For now, we'll leave the door ajar, but it's about bedtime, so why don't you lie down and see if you can rest." She indicates the mattress. From a switch located outside the door she dims the lights, then looks back at me through the small curtained window in the door. I sit on the mattress, shivering in my thin pajamas, rocking, wide-awake.

I am still awake an hour later when she brings in a small cup of pills and waits for me to swallow them before she leaves, this time pulling the door closed almost all the way. I jump up to catch it before it locks and bump into Dr. Kroll. *He's going to kill you,* a voice whispers.

Dr. Kroll's mustache twitches strangely, like it has a life of its own. His thick glasses magnify his eyes, which burn into me with a cunning hatred. I'm going to die if I stay another minute! Before he can stop me, I bolt around him and run toward the exit. He follows, along with several aides and nurses, and tackles me to the carpet.

"I've got to go home!" I cry, panting and sweating. I struggle to rise, but two aides hold me down, increasing my agitation. "Please, don't let him kill me!"

Dr. Kroll takes my pulse. I hear him whisper to the head nurse that my pulse is more than one hundred and sixty beats per minute. He gives me an evil look, then sneers at me without moving his lips, *I'll take care of you, swine!*

I fight to free myself, screaming that they have to let me go, that I'm in danger, that I know they're going to kill me. Another aide moves in to hold me down, as a high metal bed with side rails is rolled past me, clattering on its wheels.

A medical student, Rory, who accompanies Dr. Kroll, squats at my level, taking one of my hands. "Look," he says, kindly, "we're going to have to put you in restraints if you can't calm down. Dr. Kroll isn't going to hurt you. No one is."

THEY'LL KILL YOU! scream the voices. *They're going to electrocute you!*

A bolt of electricity shoots through me from the student's hands, and I scream with pain. I try to wrest my hand free, fighting for air.

I feel myself being dragged into the seclusion room and hoisted onto the bed that has replaced the bare mattress. Leather cuffs are strapped around my wrists and ankles and fastened to the bed's corners. I scream. Someone removes my glasses, leaving me all but blind, more helpless and frightened than ever. Then they all leave the room, switch off the lights, and lock the door.

Three days pass in a fog. I am let out of the restraints to eat and go to the bathroom, but, still terrified, I try to escape and again the cuffs are strapped on. I see little of anyone but the nurses, who come and go with their pills, and the occasional face pushing aside the curtain on the window in the door, checking on me. Finally, one morning, Dr. Kroll appears at my bedside.

Resigned and exhausted, I look at his blurry face without moving. I have been given so much Prolixin and Thorazine that I have little will left.

"You seem calmer today, Pam," he comments.

I nod.

"I'd like to see how you do on your own without the restraints. Do you think you can handle it?"

Another nod, a glimmer of hope. "Can I have my glasses back?" I croak, my mouth cottony from the medication.

"Not immediately. But when you can handle having the door unlocked, I promise you'll get them back. For now, I want to see how you do on your own."

"I need my glasses," I croak again.

"I understand, and I'll see they're returned as soon as possible."

An aide enters the room and unlocks the leather cuffs. When I'm free, I climb off the bed. He and another aide wheel the bed out and bring the mattress back in. Sunlight pours through the barred window, but without my glasses all I can see is a vague blur of green—the wooded grounds below. As I stand there, the sun still low on the horizon, a huge purple and orange something floats past the window and, to my delight, even without my glasses, I recognize a hot-air balloon. I wave at it, mesmerized and euphoric, until it is out of sight. Dizzy, I sink down onto the mattress and try not to count the minutes before breakfast. Finally, the same aide who removed the restraints unlocks the door and comes in with a tray holding something red and white. "Breakfast, Pam," he says, setting the tray on the end of the mattress before he leaves. When I pull the tray close, I see fresh strawberries piled in a white bowl.

Strawberries? *Fresh* strawberries? How can that be hospital food? Maybe someone's on my side after all. Saliva floods my mouth. In the barren seclusion room, barely able to see more than red lumps in a white bowl, I cross my legs under me and stare at the miraculous berries.

For six weeks I spend most of the time in seclusion. Doctors think agitated patients are so overstimulated they need solitude. Accordingly, patients in seclusion at University Hospital are routinely allowed no clothes except pajamas, no phone calls, visitors, or mail. A mattress on the floor is the only furniture.

I find these restrictions useless and cruel, since in the absence of distractions, the voices go haywire. There is nothing to keep me from that other world I know so well. During one interlude when I am moved into a regular room and given back "privileges," my brother, Chip, now a psychiatric resident in North Carolina, is allowed to visit with Linda, his new wife. A few days later, out of control again, I am put back in seclusion, while plans are made to send me back to the state hospital. Just in time, Dr. Ginzer returns from her vacation and transfers me to City Hospital, where she is now chief resident.

For the first time in years, Lynnie, now a unit chief at New Haven Asylum and Retreat, visits. We've spoken frequently by phone, but sibling competition has for years kept us from meeting face-to-face. Now, seeing her so slender and fit, wearing contacts and makeup and form-revealing leggings, while I wear my usual baggy denim jumper and sunglasses on top of my regular glasses, I feel a pang of envy even as I marvel at how normal she seems.

After another six weeks, I am readmitted to the same halfway house I've lived in so many times before. Although it is not the end of my hospitalizations, I am more stable for a while. Lynnie has had a baby and is pregnant with her second, but we keep in touch with frequent long-distance phone calls. With her help and that of some halfway house staff, I manage to tough out the difficult times without an inpatient stay for an entire year. I attend a nearby Episcopalian church and sing in the choir. On impulse, stimulated by my friendship with a former divinity student, I apply to and am accepted at divinity school.

When I tell my parents, my father thaws—maybe div school is not as good as med school, but it is not something he'd be ashamed to tell his cronies. He offers to finance whatever portion of the tuition is not paid for by my scholarship. Unfortunately, the halfway house staff advises against full-time schooling, and the door on my father's offer slams shut.

I find aspects of living there infantilizing, degraded by the semi-weekly room inspections that one can fail for as little as a Q-tip in the wastebasket. I am barred from day treatment and have to get a volunteer job. Most weeks, though, I work for fewer than six hours, remaining in my room in order not to be seen until the time I am officially due to return. Not once in the time I stay there do they follow up on whether or not I actually do the work. I never tell them; other residents have been discharged to the streets for less. By the end of my stay, I've quit even the pretense of working.

As my discharge date draws closer, I still have not been able to arrange housing. The voices and Strangeness intensify, until one evening, with the voices egging me on, I stamp on a safety razor and slash at my left arm. I am sent to the Emergency Room's "behavioral suite" for stitches and evaluation. I spend the night there. Next morning a "red firebox" is chained to my head and the television is broadcasting my thoughts. Only Rice Krispies can protect me. I am readmitted to City Hospital as one of Dr. Ginzer's private patients and remain in the hospital for two months.

At the end of my stay, I am to be discharged to a homeless shelter. This horrifies me. Then I am offered an apartment in the south end, its four small rooms painted a garish purple, turquoise, and green. The alternative is homelessness, so I rent it immediately.

Pamela

Although I now have an apartment on Wethersfield Avenue in the south end, I am without a car for the first time since I left home. After my discharge, Dr. Ginzer, who has told me to call her Ruth, drives me to my new home. That afternoon, we visit the Humane Society and I pick out a kitten I name Mise, Norwegian for "cat," a gray, black, and white, terminally cute, saucer-eyed tabby. Ruth thinks Mise will provide something outside myself to keep me out of the hospital.

We go to a supermarket where I buy food, coffee beans, a grinder, and a French glass plunger pot to celebrate my move. Back at the apartment, we sit on book boxes with a larger box between us, eating bread and fruit and cheese.

"This reminds me of my freshman year in college," I say shyly, not used to seeing Ruth outside her office. "My roommates used to do this all the time."

"Or a sleepover party," Ruth says. "Remember the bull sessions? Staying up all night talking about everything under the sun?"

She seems comfortable chatting with me, and this loosening of the traditional doctor-patient relationship thrills me, despite any misgivings I might have when she confides that she married her first husband at nineteen, that she already had a child before she decided to attend college and apply to medical school, and that Gus, her present husband, suffered brain damage in an accident and is on permanent disability. I know that psychiatrists do not ordinarily disclose such intimate information about themselves. That Ruth does, at least with me, makes me feel as if I mean more to her than just another patient. I feel like she truly cares what happens to me.

When she rises to leave, it is dark out. "Thanks a lot," I say at the door.

She scribbles on a business card then hands it to me. "This is my home phone number. Feel free to call."

I sleep uneasily that first night but wake to find Mise curled up inside the crook of my arm, her head tucked into her paws.

That weekend, with the help of Mariah, the director of my church choir, and some others whom I've enticed with the promise of all-you-can-eat pizza, we paint the walls off-white. I start to unpack. My last apartment was a single room, so I have accumulated little in the way of furniture: I have a loveseat sleep-sofa, a table, one chair, and a few flimsy bookcases. Two rooms are left empty, except for scattered unopened boxes. The rest of my belongings are still in storage.

Now that I'm independent, the first order of business is to stop taking medication. I flush all my pills down the toilet.

I have been assigned a case manager from the Department of Mental Health and a visiting psychiatric nurse. Their services don't start immediately, however, and for months I struggle on my own. I see Mariah occasionally. Most of the time I am alone. Except for my sessions with Ruth, I depend on mail and the telephone for human contact.

Despite this, for weeks I am euphoric, writing up a storm. All I'd needed was my independence and withdrawal from medication! But in truth, I'm not eating and I can't sleep. I risk the nearby convenience store only for orange juice, milk, and cigarettes. I have cases of Pepsi delivered and drink eight to ten cans a day. Trash litters my apartment. I call the Crisis Center hotline several times a week. I call Lynnie almost as often. I even call my mother, though my troubled phone calls scare her and make her feel helpless, which scares *me*.

Jake, the man who owns the junk shop next door, transmits his voice to me through my radio. He keeps me awake at night by blinking spotlights on and off in Morse code through my bedroom window. When I tell Ruth, she advises me to resume taking oral Prolixin. I flat-out refuse.

My sleep-deprived senses become hair-trigger acute; the voices are louder, unruly, more and more persuasive. *We are the men of Satan, we are the voice of Satan.* I can no longer churn out poem after poem; even reading is difficult. To deal with the voices, I tune my radio to static, which I keep on day and night.

One afternoon in December, I am trying to read Virginia Woolf's *Orlando* when it becomes clear that the book is instructing me to take the train to Orlando, Florida. I book a train ticket with a connection in New York, under an assumed name, Phoebe Sparrow, and call a taxi. I phone Ruth's answering service to cancel my appointments.

Sinister Peer Gynt blasting from the front seat. Too loud.

"Would you mind turning off the radio?" I ask the taxi driver. "It's hurting my ears."

Head turned toward me, a look thrown heavenward. Then: "Lady, you must be hearing things,'cause the radio ain't on!"

True, it isn't. It's the buildings themselves that are giving off music: blaring, strident. Even the color of the brick, the concrete, the blue-tinted panes of glass are shrieking. Suffocating, raucous office buildings loom over me, pressing inward as if to trap me. Why is the driver wearing mirrored sunglasses? Maybe he's an assassin, a double agent, both? The air in the grimy cab seems choking, thick, malevolent.

"Let me out here. I can walk the rest of the way."

He rolls his eyes but takes the fare, then squeals away from the curb.

The Travelers Insurance building booms out a sinister symphony, and the sidewalk undulates beneath my feet, the light too sharp, too glaring, assaultive. Just ahead, the train station. Go ahead, buy a ticket, be casual, nonchalant as if unaware of the surveillance. Round ticket? Am I a circle? Is this the Circle Game? No, one-way, please. Sit on a bench and pretend to read, pretend to be just another traveler making a routine business trip. If only I can get aboard the right train without being caught. Oh, no, police, three of them! Before I can escape, one asks me if my name is Pam. Has Dr. Ginzer alerted them? Are they part of the conspiracy against me? Luckily I'm not wearing my usual parka so they have trouble identifying me from any description they might have been given. Trembling inside, I say no. They move on.

Finally on board. The car half empty, two business sorts seated across the aisle from me. A twinge of uncertainty: What if they too are involved? Will they follow me to Orlando? Are the Five People in communication with them? They are talking about brokers and the stock market a little too loudly, as if to make sure I "know" they have nothing to do with the conspiracy. They sound Russian. A uniformed man strides through the car, punching tickets. I feel a headache coming on. Where is the water fountain? He gives me a slow, knowing look, points toward the other end of the car. On the wall, the word "water." I now understand that he too is part of the agencies keeping me under surveillance. At the fountain there are no cups. I need to take some aspirin. In the lavatory, I bring my cupped hands to my mouth to down the pills. The water has a grimy, metallic, cindery flavor. I notice, too late, the sign: "For washing only. Do not drink." Maybe this too is part of the plan. I return to my seat.

The conductor makes his way down the aisle. I begin to rock, to banish all thoughts from my brain. Otherwise he might suck away my ideas, insert others that better suit his mission. He passes but looks back over his shoulder at me. Stay in control. Don't risk a wrong move—it could be dangerous. Remain calm. Watch the scenes out the window and pretend ignorance. A billboard advertising Camel cigarettes. Another, some public service information.

Need to look around to evaluate the danger. A third billboard, what? Six people are to be killed before midnight. What six people, and why is it announced? I can barely breathe. I know *I* am to be killed. But who are the others?

I begin to sweat inside my heavy winter coat. A thin snow is falling just as the train enters the darkness of the underground station. The lights flicker. The conductor passes back through the car announcing our arrival in New York City. As we slow down, I grab my black vinyl bag and stagger toward the exit at the far end of the car, hoping to elude the agents in pursuit. I know that others will be stationed outside.

Up the narrow escalator, on the lookout, I try to blend in with the crowds. No food or sleep for days, and my head throbs. The glare of the sudden light outside the station cracks my brain. I can't stop for more aspirin. Is this Penn Station or Grand Central? And where do I catch my train? I don't know where to go or what to do. I have to keep moving, I have to stay alert.

I follow the crowd, going wherever it seems to go, though I keep to the outside of the sidewalk as much as possible in case I need to make an escape. In the plate glass of a store I catch a glimpse of a stranger, her hair filthy and tangled, wearing yellowed jeans that need washing, winter coat splitting at one seam, her thin summer-weight shoes sliding on the icy pavement. Carefully, I plant my feet with each step, in a forced, flat-footed gait, making me look awkward and conspicuous, precisely when I need to blend in.

Looking for someone with kind eyes, I stop a woman in a loden coat to ask for help, but she shrivels with fright as I tug on her coat sleeve and wrenches her arm free. She scurries away from me, looking back over her shoulder to make sure I am not in pursuit. I turn and walk in the opposite direction to let her know I am not dangerous. I do not mean to scare her.

Keep walking, Stay wary, be on the lookout, I tell myself. I pay too much money to buy myself a new cassette player/radio. Ahead, the sight of a familiar marquee: YMCA. Maybe I can get a room for a few hours, anything to get me off the street in the failing light. I lean into the door and push it open before me.

It's more like a seedy SRO than the gleaming Ys I've seen elsewhere. A man with a shaggy beard is asleep in an armchair, his tweed cap pulled down over his face; an emaciated girl dressed in a skimpy cotton dress skims across the room. She carries a toe shoe bag but looks too skinny even to be a dancer. Several residents, some clearly drunk, sprawl idly on the tattered institutional sofas under a big sign that says, "No Alcohol." I head toward the front desk, looking for someone official. A man with red hair and a scraggly mustache glances up from behind the counter. His eyes barely register my presence. The voices grumble, getting louder and more distracting.

"I haven't eaten or slept in eight days," I whisper, not wanting to alert anyone else to my presence. "Can I get a room?"

The man eyes me warily. "There are shelters uptown. You can sleep and eat there free." He begins walking away from me.

"I have money," I call out. "I can pay."

He turns back. "We only let rooms to people from out of state."

"I am. I'm from New England."

"Let me see your driver's license."

I hand it over and he inspects it. To my relief he returns it without calling the police.

"Rooms are thirty-five a night. Check out before ten or pay for another day. Five dollars a key, refunded when you leave."

I root in my bag, pulling out my wallet, which is thick with all the money I've taken out of the bank. "Here's forty dollars."

He gives me a look I can't decipher, then fills out some forms, hands them to me to sign. I think for a moment about using my alias, then realize he's seen my license. I scribble "Pam Wagner" as illegibly as possible, return the forms, and accept a key to room E-37.

"Fifth floor. The bathroom is down the hall," he says. "No cooking in your room, no booze." He points to the sign. "Coffee and cold food at the canteen through that door." He points his chin in the direction of a small room across the lobby. I take a Pepsi from the cooler, pay for it, and pop it open, gulping so fast my throat hurts. The empty elevator grinds slowly upward, clanking and rattling. It smells like stale beer and urine.

My room is no bigger than a large closet. Although spartan—there's only a bed, chair, table, and washstand—at least it is clean. A door opens down the hall, then slams. I hear two women talking loudly as they approach. They laugh as they pass my room. "She's one of the six," one of them stage-whispers just outside my door. In response, the other pounds the door and gives a guffaw. "She is? What a fucking scream!"

"A few hours, no more."

Lying on the bed, I shrink against the wall, trembling. Only when I hear the distinct wheeze of the elevator doors opening and closing behind them do I breathe.

Les jeux sont faits, whines a voice in my ear. *Faits sont les yeux.*

No exit, no escape, cackles another.

I swallow three more aspirin with the soda and am immediately racked with nausea. I throw up in the sink—only Pepsi—then retch uselessly since there's nothing more to come up. When my stomach calms down, I open the new cassette player, plug it into the only outlet available, and put one of my favorite tapes into the slot. Then I lie back on my bed, exhausted and terrified, hoping the music will help me sleep for a few hours.

"We are the men of Satan, we are the voice of Satan," Jake sneers above the strains of a familiar song. I slam my hand on Stop, then remove the cassette and start unraveling the tape, piling useless black ribbon on my lap. I rip these into plastic shreds, then dump them in the metal wastebasket under the table. I realize that even here, alone in a Y, in New York City, more than a hundred miles from home, I'm not safe. The voices are screaming, and from five floors above I sense the agents' arrival. They confer with the red-headed man at the desk, who I realize now has been in on things from the start.

What have I gotten myself into? I pack up my bag and the cassette player, then remember I passed a pay phone on the wall just outside the bathroom. The hallway is quiet now. My heart in my throat, I dash to the phone and insert a dime—nothing, no dial tone. I try again, nothing. What's wrong with the damned thing? It's getting hard to breathe when I finally understand the problem: The call costs a quarter. This time, there's a tone and I dial Ruth's home number. "Ruth?" I whisper when she answers. "It's Pam. I'm in New York and I'm scared."

Ruth has been expecting my call and, all business, she advises me to go to Bellevue Hospital. Either that or take the train back to Hartford. She'll meet me at the ER, she says. The one thing I am not to do is to stay overnight at the Y. I tell her I'll take the next bus, then hang up. Grabbing my bag, I descend five flights of stairs and dash through the lobby, slamming my key on the counter, not waiting for my refund. Then I am in a taxi headed toward the Port Authority and any bus headed back to Hartford.

It is nearly two A.M. when I climb down the bus steps and make my way into Union Station. I vomited twice from pain on the bus ride back and my head is still throbbing. There are no taxis at the station. I'm not sure how to call for one or even where the phones are located. My bag feels heavier and heavier. All the ticket windows are dark. The cavernous room is well lit but almost empty. When someone speaks to me, I look up to see a stocky, dark-skinned man dressed in casual clothes. An identification badge is clipped to his jacket.

"Hi. I'm Whitey. How can I help you?"

A black man with the name Whitey strikes me as so improbable that I believe he's telling the truth when he tells me that he is an "ombudsman." He asks if I need a taxi. I nod, and he says he'll take care of it for me. When he returns, he asks me if I want to smoke a cigarette while we wait for the cab. Grateful, I nod again.

After a short time, the cab arrives. Whitey instructs the driver to take me directly to the ER. He emphasizes "directly" and closes the door after me. It doesn't occur to me to question how he knows I need to get to the hospital. The taxi draws away from the curb just as I realize I haven't thanked him. I twist to look behind me and roll down the window to yell thanks, but no one is there, not under the brightly lit station overhang or—evident through the mural of plate glass—inside the station. It occurs to me that he might have been imaginary. Or maybe he was some kind of angel. By the time I reach the ER, another idea has taken hold: I've been duped, I realize. This isn't City Hospital. It's really an experimental physics lab where the lights are radioactive audiovisual devices and Einstein's relativity equations are emblazoned on the walls.

Carolyn

I think I've seen Pammy at her worst, until 1990 when I take her to see Dr. Charles Popper, a psychopharmacologist at City Psycho. Pammy lives alone in an apartment on Wethersfield Avenue. On my drive up I hear on the car radio that there was a fatal shooting last night not far from where she lives. Although she gave me directions, I've been driving up and down the streets for forty-five minutes looking for her number. The neighborhood is run-down, many houses dilapidated or boarded up, and the sidewalks are empty. An eerie quiet. I imagine elderly tenants cowering behind closed doors. As I drive farther down the street, some adolescent boys ride their rusty bikes in circles, like they're patrolling for trouble. It worries me that Pammy, never very good at judging danger, lives on the ground floor.

At last I find her apartment. I park, turn off the ignition, lock the car, and head over the trash-strewn lot. The door is ajar, so I knock. "Pammy?" I call. I push the door open. "Pammy!"

"You don't have to yell, I'm right here." Her voice comes from the kitchen table. After the bright sunlight outside, I can barely see her, but the first thing that hits me is the stench: soiled cat litter, filthy clothes, and garbage rotting in bags by the stove. It makes me sick to my stomach. I look around. Dishes are piled everywhere, crusted with moldy food scraps and cigarette ashes. There are soda cans, empty food wrappers, and cigarette packs piled on the table and littering every available surface. My God, what has happened to her? I had no idea things were this bad.

It's impossible not to notice, but she seems oblivious to it all. She quickly extinguishes a cigarette in a coffee can. "You can look around, but I've got go to the bathroom. Then I'm ready."

In high school Pammy wore bedraggled clothing but was so particular about her surroundings that the cleaning woman loved her because she never had to touch her bedroom. I was the messy one. While hiding down in the cellar, she learned to antique furniture, crochet doilies, and press flowers. Meanwhile, my friends and I were checking out the new bikini-style panties and seeing how short we could wear our skirts. But as I think about it, then she was merely weird, now she looks sick. *Crazy.*

No wonder Dr. Popper talks to her for about ten minutes. He acts as if he doesn't know me, as if I hadn't trained right there at City Psycho myself, finishing my residency only a few years before.

As Pammy's sister, not her doctor, I interpret his professional detachment as a coldness toward me. But of course he sees Pammy properly as a patient, not as my sister, the way I do. To me, it's as if he dismisses her—me—with a breezy diagnosis, "Chronic paranoid schizophrenia . . ." His recommendation is equally terse, equally professional: "She's on antipsychotic medication already, there's not much else to do . . ." But to his eternal credit, he does hold out hope that the newest wonder drug, now coming on the market— clozapine—might help her as no other drug has.

Pamela

After discharge from the hospital, I am given the case manager I've been promised, Selden. She is a social worker whose job is to help me acquire the skills, benefits, and services I need to maintain my independence. Selden has a knack for "being there," literally as well as figuratively, just when I need her. But she also has a tough side, challenging me and letting me know when I can take better care of myself. Marcia, the visiting nurse who starts seeing me at the same time, quickly becomes another of my most important supports. With these weekly, sometimes semiweekly contacts, as well as intervention in crises, the intervals between my hospitalizations slowly lengthen until, five years later, when Marcia leaves the VNA, I've managed to stay out of the hospital for as long as a year at a time.

I speak with Lynnie at least twice a week. I call my mother only rarely, because I sense she feels awkward, afraid she might say the wrong thing. My brother visits when he and his growing family have flown up from North Carolina for the holidays, and once I even see Martha, in from Chicago with her partner, Laura.

But these visits are rare. I am so lonely for human company that I collect stray people as indiscriminatingly as I collect cats. I barely know them, but they seem so needy that I invite them to stay with me, no questions asked. I just want to help. I don't think about who they are or where they came from, even though Lynnie tells me I need to protect myself before I offer the shirt off my back to any thief or con artist. She doesn't understand it makes me feel good when I'm able to rescue people more desperate than I. After all, any one of them could be Jesus Christ. "Whatsoever you do unto the least of these, you do unto me." Most of these encounters end badly, though I don't understand why.

There's Micky, the charmer, fresh from a drug rehab program in Maine, and could he crash with me, sleep on my couch until he finds his own apartment? His drug problem is gone; he's totally clean and sober. He's going to study physics at the University of Hartford. I tell him of course he can stay. But Micky, I discover too late, is a pathological liar and, like a weasel babysitting in a henhouse, cannot be trusted. One thing after another, and before I know it I'm buying him pizza, paying for his long-distance calls, and would be hosting his drug deals if I hadn't caught on and kicked him out. Just in the nick of time.

Rafe is a big, cheerful New Yorker, with a crack-cocaine problem and alcoholism. Barrel-chested but growing flabby around the middle, dripping with cologne, Rafe has animal magnetism. He tells me he's homeless, hungry, and on the way to a shelter. Or, if there's no room at the inn, he'll spend the night in the park or under a bridge.

Without thinking, I jump. "You know," I say, "I have an extra room. You can use it until you find your own place." So Rafe moves in, along with his pothead girlfriend Lisa, and right away they commandeer the apartment, freeloading for six months. They never pay a penny for rent or food. In fact, Rafe knows my ATM PIN and has helped himself to money more than once. One night Rafe, drunk, threatens to kill me, and that's the last straw. With Lynnie's help, I concoct a story that I am hiring a live-in "psych home health aide," and they're history.

Several other drifters come and go, but then I find Gertrude, a self-styled recreational therapist.

"She's out for all you're worth," Lynnie pronounces with a certainty I don't understand. "Did you ask for references or at least proof that she has a job?"

"Gertrude is okay." I sound unconvincing even to myself.

"Maybe," Lynnie says, "but how do you know? Did you ask where she lived or worked before you handed her the keys?"

"It didn't occur to me . . ."

"Pammy, what's the matter with you? This is the fifth time in three years you've let a stranger move in. When will you learn?"

I hate it when she sounds like Mommy trying to nag me into using good judgment. If I tell her the truth about Gertrude, I think she'll never forgive me.

"Do you have to get mugged or robbed in your own apartment before you'll listen to me?"

"I think I already have . . ." I say in as small a voice as possible, trying to keep her from blowing her stack. I can't stand it when she gets angry, even when her anger's reasonable. "I'll tell you, but only if you promise not to get mad."

Carolyn

Sometimes Pammy's urge to take care of the downtrodden frustrates the hell out of me. Each time her charitable zeal backfires, she calls me to rescue her. This time, I tell her, it's the last time: If she won't stick to reasonable limits with roommates, won't interview them or ask questions, she shouldn't expect me to help when they take advantage of her. But in the end I always give in, though I can't believe the scumbags she invites into her house.

The latest one, Gertrude, calls herself a "recreational therapist." Therapist, my eye! Gertrude sees in my sister an opportunity, an easy mark. She inserts herself into Pammy's life like an old key. "I can be your live-in practical nurse," she says to Pammy shortly after they meet. Within minutes, Gertrude has sized her up and knows just the right buttons. "That's what I do, Pammy, I take care of people. I'll drive you to doctors' appointments, do your shopping, run errands." Pammy is thrilled, of course, convinced that finally she's found in Gertrude the solution. In exchange for a place to live, Gertrude will take care of Pammy.

But as soon as she moves in, she's ordering Pammy around like a little martinet. I need a bigger closet, she whines. My sister, ever eager to please, offers not only the bigger bedroom closet but the bigger bedroom as well. You can be sure Gertrude doesn't graciously turn down the offer. Her DWI rehab program, which Pammy doesn't know about, becomes "adult ed," displacing Pammy's doctors' appointments. "You can reschedule one doctor—I can't ask the whole French class to reschedule." Food disappears from the refrigerator at an alarming rate. Pammy's medications run short, her wallet calculator goes AWOL. But for every question Gertrude has an excuse, an explanation, a condescending apology that makes Pammy feel she's wrong. My sister calls me in tears. Was she terribly selfish to have asked Gertrude to pick her up a few groceries on her trip to the store? Gertrude says the empty bottles of Kahlua in the trash "must belong to someone else." Only when Pammy discovers that Gertrude has "borrowed" her ATM card and withdrawn more than a hundred dollars does she get mad.

The truth is I saw it coming, though Pammy doesn't believe me.

Mid-1990s

Pamela

Alone in my apartment now, I feel more and more that I am profoundly evil. God is loving and merciful to the "saved," but tormenting to me. I read religious tracts and pamphlets. I peruse the Bible, hoping I can manage to save myself, and I memorize chapter and verse, the perfect rebuttal to any challenge. I no longer attend church of any sort.

At first, Ruth, "a recovering fundamentalist," tolerates my new religious preoccupations, countering my biblical quotations with those of her own. But as time goes on, she becomes curt with me, more and more frequently irritable and touchy. At one point, after I've let loose a tirade on God and salvation, I interrupt her response and say, "You don't know what you're talking about." I mean only that she doesn't understand how evil I am, but she takes it the wrong way.

Her eyes flash as she stands abruptly. "I will not tolerate being called incompetent," she says, her voice freezing. "I want you to leave my office. Now."

She crosses the room and opens the door, gesturing for me to go. Stunned by this turn of events, not quite believing she means what she says, not understanding what I've done wrong, I get to my feet. As I pass through the door, I mutter, "I'm not going to forget this, you know."

"I'm quite sure you won't," she replies, her voice cold with a fury that frightens me all the more. Although she has gotten angry with me before, I've never seen her like this. She acts as if she were a friend whose feelings I've insulted, instead of a psychiatrist. The Ruth I know has had me to her home to plant bulbs in her garden and meet her son and husband. She's taken me to the Yale Co-op in New Haven on a book-buying spree, has seen me at my apartment for sessions, and has occasionally taken me to lunch at Friendly's. I've felt special. I know she goes to no such lengths for her other patients.

Special treatment has a downside. I have to tread carefully, watch my step, and not criticize her lest her feelings be hurt. She tells me when she has her period, how her husband is faring on disability, and how her son is doing in school. I learn to tailor my remarks, taking such factors into account. If she's in a bad mood, I cheer her up; if I'm having difficulties of my own, I censor them.

She arrives later and later for my sessions and never makes up for the time at the end of the hour. Since she treats me for the minuscule payments Medicare and Medicaid allow, I have no right to complain. She has stopped seeing her own therapist, she discloses, because she's "outgrown him" and wants to spend the money on other things.

She is more frequently bad tempered.

I entertain thoughts of "firing" her for another therapist who is able to maintain a more professional detachment. But there's a problem with this: Although Ruth has been prescribing Ritalin for my narcolepsy, she uses it as a means to coerce me into taking my other medications. She often threatens to discontinue it if I don't, in such a way that prescribing Ritalin seems a kind of bribery.

When I return the week after she kicks me out, Ruth seems calmer, less frosty, though she doesn't mention the abbreviated session of the week before. I am so relieved she's no longer angry that I don't dare bring it up myself. In future sessions, I try to stop talking about religion. I no longer confide in her. Inside, I know that the change in Ruth is my fault, that as Satan's spawn I've contaminated her original goodness with my filth. I grow wary of her. I'm convinced that I am doing her permanent damage by continuing to inflict myself upon her.

Marcia and Selden do their best to keep me stable, but all too frequently things fall apart. After an episode of mania, Ruth tries me on lithium that she says sometimes proves beneficial for certain people with schizophrenia. But I become toxic on a very low dose and can't tolerate it, which angers her. A brand-new antischizophrenia drug, clozapine, prescribed in Europe for years, is approved by the FDA and released for public use. There is the possibility of very serious side effects, including seizures and a potentially fatal blood disorder. Clozaril, as it is called, is administered with caution. But reports begin to circulate about the medication working miracles. Because its cost is prohibitive—nearly $9,000 a year—and it is not yet approved for payment by Connecticut's Medicaid program, I am not immediately able to take it.

While we wait for the state to pay, Ruth continues to prescribe Prolixin decanoate, the long-acting medication I've been taking for years. Marcia gives me the biweekly injections until Medicaid agrees to foot the bill for Clozaril.

Ruth hospitalizes me to monitor things while I make the switch. The voices subside to mere background chatter and I am able to write more often than ever. But once I reach a therapeutic dose and leave the hospital, all hell breaks loose.

Mariah, who has recently moved into the adjoining set of first-floor rooms, takes to checking on me each night just to make sure I am breathing. The sedation is overwhelming. I sleep sixteen hours a night, and Mariah has to drag me, stumbling, out of bed and prop me up on her sofa. I remain incoherent for another hour until the Ritalin kicks in.

But freedom from the deadening effect of Prolixin seems worth it. Then I begin to choke on the saliva filling my mouth after taking my pills each night, and I lose the ability to swallow it. I have "feelings of electrocution," jolting sensations that make me cry out and shudder in terror several times a night. This is tentatively diagnosed as nocturnal myoclonus, commonly seen with clozapine therapy, and I am started on a medication to counteract it. Nothing seems to work.

Night after night, unable to swallow my own saliva, choking, feeling a terrible sense of impending doom, I wake each morning to a sopping, slimy pillow, but I keep hoping these problems will resolve. I take the Clozaril religiously, never skipping a dose as I did on Prolixin. The side effects refuse to abate. Finally, in desperation, I discuss with Ruth returning to the old regimen, despite the fact that I've always hated it. She seems angry with me but schedules Marcia to give me a Prolixin injection later that week.

In the two days before the shot, I wonder if maybe I am giving up too easily. The evening before Marcia's visit, I call Ruth at home, as she's encouraged me to do.

"I don't know what to do," I say. "The Clozaril side effects are agonizing, but I hate Prolixin and really don't want to go back on it."

Silence.

"Do you think maybe I should keep trying? Marcia comes tomorrow. I need to know whether or not to take the Prolixin."

More silence.

"Ruth? Are you there? What should I do?"

"You don't want to take my advice. We'll discuss that in my office on Friday."

"But I don't know what to do."

"We'll discuss that in my office on Friday." Her voice is cold, like splinters of ice. I can almost see the thin angry line of her lips, the brittle hardness in her eyes.

"Why are you angry with me? Aren't I allowed to be ambivalent?"

"We'll. Discuss. That. On. Friday."

"Why do you take this so personally? I'm not doing anything to you! You told me to call you! Why don't you go soak your head?" I hang up on her.

Moments later, the phone rings. "Don't come in on Friday. I am no longer willing to see you." This time, *she* hangs up.

Horrified, I begin to laugh. I dance into Mariah's apartment and announce that Ruth has terminated my treatment.

"What?" She starts to rise, her brow creased. "No, she wouldn't do that, Pam," she assures me, a puzzled but worried look on her face. "She cares about you."

"Ha! She just called to tell me not to come in anymore. I tell you, it's over. And now I don't have any problem, because I don't have any medication! I won't have to take either Prolixin *or* Clozaril." I give her a broad smile and laugh again, but she doesn't smile back.

"You need your medication. You'll end up back in the hospital. You can't function without it."

"I guess I'll have to now." More giddy laughter bubbles out of me. "Well, at least that's over with. She always told me that anger doesn't mean hatred, but now I know how much of a lie that was!"

Mariah, familiar with my laughing in moments of stress, suggests, nearly pleading, "Just call her tomorrow and apologize."

"Apologize? She's a fucking psychiatrist! Do you think no patient has ever told her to go soak her head before? Lynnie and Chip are psychiatrists, and they would never terminate like that. I know they wouldn't."

"She'll call back; I'm sure of it. She'll cool off and tell you she didn't mean it."

"You know, Mariah, I really don't want her to. This is it. It's over."

Friday comes and goes without word from Ruth. I ration my pills, but they will not last past the weekend. I call Lynnie and inform her of the situation. She says it's abandonment, malpractice.

On Sunday afternoon, when my rationed supply of medication is exhausted, I call Ruth's answering service and am told that she is unavailable, another doctor is covering. I speak briefly with him, explaining the situation, and he assures me there's been a misunderstanding. "I know Dr. Ginzer, and she would not do that sort of thing."

Nevertheless, she has. After wrestling with myself over whether or not I should call her at home, I take the plunge.

She answers immediately.

"Ruth? This is Pam," I say.

"Pam? How are you?" She exudes warmth, as if nothing has happened. I realize then she's been anticipating my call, expecting me to apologize or otherwise smooth her ruffled feathers; she fully expects our relationship to resume.

I am flooded with relief, but despite this I am all business. "Ruth, I need to know whether or not you plan to continue my prescriptions until I can make contact with another therapist." My voice is cool and distant as the Arctic Circle.

After a brief silence, she responds in kind. "I will leave prescriptions in your mailbox on Monday and will continue to provide them for you for two weeks or until you find someone else to treat you."

Pamela

Ruth is true to her word. I find the prescriptions at my door the next day, each made out for enough medication to last me two weeks, though I note that she's prescribed oral Prolixin instead of continuing the Clozaril or Prolixin injections, which would necessitate more careful monitoring.

Outwardly, I seem happy, even joyous; inwardly, things are already deteriorating. Instead of sleeping, I spend hours on ruminations of revenge, telling Mariah I am "rewriting the war part of *War and Peace*." While I've agreed with Marcia to take some oral Prolixin, I'm not taking anywhere near what has been prescribed. Selden seems concerned that I am inappropriately buoyant, unable to cope with the fact that a good portion of my "support system" has suddenly evaporated.

I call City Hospital's outpatient psychiatric clinic to see about arranging for a therapist and discover that an appointment has already been made for me to see Mrs. Margulies, a nurse-practitioner who supervises the Clozaril program.

Before that, Marcia, Selden, and I have a final session with Ruth. For once, Ruth is on time—a bad sign because it seems to portend another crazy-making maneuver. She was never on time when it's just me.

I sit at the far end of the couch, Selden takes the other end, and

Marcia inadvertently takes Ruth's usual seat, forcing Ruth to pull up a chair opposite me. This makes me stare down at the floor or turn my head to look in Marcia's or Selden's direction to avoid her gaze. I have worried about how the session would start, and who would speak first, wondering what Ruth was going to say. It turns out that Ruth remains silent until Selden takes the initiative.

"Ruth, I'm glad we could arrange this meeting, and I thank you for seeing us. There's been a great deal of confusion for Pam recently, and we thought perhaps it would help for all of us to get together and see if we could iron things out."

I jump in. "No, that's not correct," I say to her. "Ruth terminated with me, and I want it to stay that way. Things can't be nicely ironed out this time."

Selden glances at me with a nod, then turns back to Ruth. "All right. That's Pam's decision, and I think she's made it clear she does not want to resume treatment. She has an appointment to see Mrs. Margulies at the clinic next Tuesday, but I think, we both think"— she indicates Marcia—"that the two of you need to talk, if only to help us understand what's happened here."

I slouch down into the sofa, my bulky winter coat, which I haven't taken off, shrugged up around me, obscuring the lower part of my face. I stare down at my lap as the other three speak carefully to one another, trying to involve me in the conversation. Every so often an inclusive phrase floats out, like, "Isn't that right, Pam?" and "Do you have anything to add?" which I more or less ignore until Ruth says, "Pam has not been working in treatment recently. Furthermore, I will not tolerate being told to go fuck myself."

"Ruth, that's a lie, and you know it!" I yell, sitting bolt upright, for once staring her in the eye. "I said, and I quote, 'I feel like telling you to go fuck yourself, though I won't.' What I did say—because it was clear you were angry at me for my problem, my ambivalence— was, 'Go soak your head,' a rather mild insult, if I may say so myself."

Ruth stares back until I lower my gaze.

"All the same, it *was* rude, Pam," Selden says in an attempt to lay the blame on both of us equally.

"I don't care if it was rude!" I say. "If she terminated my treatment on the basis of anything I said in anger, she's as idiotic, overinvolved, and incompetent as she worries she is. It's not a good enough reason to drop me and hardly the ethical or professional way to deal with your patients."

Selden seems about to respond to this, and I understand that she is trying to help Ruth save face. Jumping up from the sofa, I bolt from the room, yelling over my shoulder, "All three of you think I'm the one at fault. You're both on Ruth's side, not mine at all. Well, you can all go to fucking hell. I'm leaving!" I'm out the door and into the narrow corridor connecting the suite of doctors' offices. There I stop. Simply running out will not solve a thing. In the sudden silence from the voices, I reopen the door, slam it behind me, and stomp back to my seat, my arms crossed in front of me.

It is Marcia who speaks next. "I'm glad you came back, Pam; it took real courage. I can see that all this is very upsetting to you. It is to all of us, even to Ruth."

"Huh."

"Ruth, Pam feels she has some unfinished business." She now addresses me: "Pam, are there issues you'd like to deal with now, while Selden and I are here? You are allowed to say whatever you need to."

Out of the corner of my eye I think I see Ruth nod in agreement, but stiffly and only slightly.

"Okay, then. The one thing I want to know is: What was going on in your head when you called me back and told me not to come in anymore? Were you angry? Did you want to punish me? Did you think you had a right to call it quits like that, knowing—or assuming—that I'd eventually apologize? I'd really like to know."

Ruth stares stonily at me. A moment or two of silence pass. She shifts in her chair, seems to put on a contented smile, and says, "Isn't the weather beautiful today? It smells like spring."

Spring, sprung, spring, someone says.

Pamela

Mrs. Margulies, who tells me to call her Zelda, is in the late stages of an obvious pregnancy, though there is gray in her auburn hair. She immediately sets me at ease by not harping on any so-called separation issues. She lets me speak for myself and doesn't try to second-guess me.

What I want is to try Clozaril one last time.

"How long a trial did you give it the first time?" Zelda asks.

"Six months, at least."

"Well, there are a lot of benefits Clozaril can offer. And it sounds like you feel it helped."

"It did. Except for the terrible side effects at night. During the day—at least during the hours when I was awake—I felt much better."

She probes for details, unlike Ruth, who shrugged off the side effects as trivial. I like Zelda. Finally, I ask, "Are you going to be my therapist, or will I be assigned someone else?"

"That's a good question. I'll be going on maternity leave soon, but I'd be happy to be your primary therapist when I get back," she answers. "How do you feel about it, Pam? Would you like to see me? You're an interesting person: I'd enjoy working with you."

"Don't find me too interesting," I warn, wary of overinvolvement and wanting the relief of knowing I don't have to be interesting. "I don't want to do the cha-cha."

"Cha-cha?"

"Be charming and cheerful even when I don't feel like it."

She nods vigorously at this, gives an understanding chuckle, and assures me her job is to help me, not to be entertained. "If you find you have to do the cha-cha with me, then I'm doing something wrong, and we need to discuss it."

"So I can even be boring?"

"I don't usually find my patients boring. I doubt you would be the exception. But yes, if you need to be boring, you can go ahead and be as boring as you like."

Zelda's touch of humor and sincerity makes me smile.

The first time I tried Clozaril, I wrote an essay about the ups and downs of my experiences with schizophrenia and all I've gone through because of it. I also wrote a letter to the editor of a major Hartford newspaper, asserting the right of the disabled, especially those with mental illness, to be treated as human beings, as good citizens. We are not, I wrote, mere leeches on society or addicted to the welfare system. The response was overwhelmingly positive. Many people called to say how well written the letter was.

A year later I receive a call from Bob Roberts, editor of the paper's op-ed page.

"Yes, I remember you," I say shyly. "You called me after my letter to the editor came out. I remember specifically because it struck me that your name must be Robert Roberts."

Bob chuckles, in part, I suspect, at my awkward candor in speaking to a virtual stranger. Then he says, "You know, I've called for a reason. Recently there have been a lot of articles about the mental health–care system, and the possible reforms President Clinton wants to initiate. I wonder if you would be willing to write an editorial on the subject. Your letter was quite articulate. I'd be eager to have you write a longer piece tied into the current discussion of health-care reform. Are you interested?"

I draw a breath of surprise, then think a moment before answering. "Well, actually, I already have part of an essay written, something I worked on a while ago just for fun. I'm not sure if it's what you want, or if it's written well enough for you to publish, but I'd be willing to take a look at it, rewrite it, and send it on for your inspection."

"Great. I look forward to reading it."

Shy again, but pleased, I smile into the phone. "Wow, thanks! When do you need it?"

He hesitates. "The problem is that I really need the editorial as soon as possible. Is a week too soon?"

My daily schedule running through my mind, I consider the problem. "I won't promise anything, but I think I could do it."

"Wonderful," he answers, and I expect him to say good-bye. Instead, he asks me some questions about myself and my illness.

For some reason I feel safe with him and answer as honestly as I can, though it still makes me uncomfortable to apply the words "schizophrenia" and "mental illness" to myself. The word "schizophrenia" scares me, and I blame myself for all that has happened to me, knowing at the same time that I would never blame others. *They* are sick; *I* am weak-willed and evil.

That afternoon, I unearth what I can find of my original effort and spend several hours rewriting it, trying for a relevant slant toward health-care reform. By midnight, I finish it, and I put it in the mail the next morning, despite qualms of perfectionism that say it is no good.

Two days later, I am woken by the phone at noon and answer it in a Clozaril-induced stupor, trying my best to be coherent. It is Bob.

"Uh-oh," he says. "I think I woke you."

"Yeah, sort of. But that's okay." In a fog. "Did you get my article yet?"

"Actually, I did. That's why I'm calling. There are a few places I want you to clarify, places I think you need to flesh out a bit, but in general it's a great piece."

My mind spins, and this time not because of the clozapine. "Really? That's amazing!"

"Why amazing? You must have heard from other people that you have a lot of talent."

"Well, maybe. Yes, a little. But I believed it was flattery."

"I can assure you I don't flatter people."

I hang up, still in a haze but elated.

I stumble into Mariah's apartment. She is amazed that I could even answer the phone, let alone talk to Bob coherently so "early" in the day, and she is thrilled too.

Lynnie makes me promise to buy as many copies as I can of the paper when it comes out. She wants me to send her one so that she can show it to her colleagues. Even my father appears impressed, though he says little.

The phone rings again. "There's another fan, calling to talk to the famous writer." Mariah smiles as I run to get it. The calls have been coming since ten that morning, with no signs of stopping. Some people share their own experiences with a schizophrenic family member. Others tell me I have done everyone a great service. Bob tells me the piece is also to run on the national wire.

Each day over the following week, as calls continue to come in, Mariah surprises me with a little trinket—a pair of earrings, a card, a lovely pink rosebud that takes all week to open—and one night she takes me out for a lobster dinner, all part of what she has labeled "Famous Writer's Week." We both know, of course, that I am hardly a famous writer, but calling it that is her way of showing how much she believes in me.

A few days after the end of "Famous Writer's Week," I find an envelope in my mailbox. The return address is that of the state psychiatric society.

"Uh-oh," I say to Mariah, showing her the envelope. "It's probably some psychiatrist saying that my article was misguided, self-serving, and inaccurate."

"I really doubt that. Haven't people been calling all week just to tell you they love it? Open it and see."

I reluctantly open the envelope, then scan the letter's contents before I quietly hand it to Mariah. "Bad news?" she asks.

"No, good. Very good. I've won an award."

" 'Dear Ms. Wagner,' " Mariah reads out loud. " 'I am pleased to inform you, on behalf of the Psychiatric Society, the Alliance for the Mentally Ill, and the Department of Mental Health, that you are'—Wow!—'the first-place winner of our 1993 Mental Health Media Award for your article "Mentally Ill People Deserve Equal Health Insurance Coverage." ' This is amazing! I knew people would love it." Then she reads the rest of the letter to herself. When she has finished, she urges me, "Call Lynnie. Call your mother. Your article was wonderful! Now do you believe me?"

Sheepishly, I look at her. "I guess so, I mean, yes, I think so. But it's pretty hard to believe."

"Go on and call your family. They'll be delighted."

"I'm even supposed to say a few words at the awards presentation next week, Mental Illness Awareness Week, at the Legislative Office Building. God, I won't know what to say. I'll be too nervous," I tell Lynnie when I reach her later that day. "I'm not even sure I can make myself attend at all, let alone speak to a whole group of people."

"Look, it's a week away. Why don't you make your decision later?" Lynnie advises. "You might even enjoy it. It would be too bad if you didn't at least get to accept the award in person."

"I guess you're right. I have said everything in the editorial already. It's not like they know nothing about me. Maybe I could just read a poem instead of speaking."

"That's a good idea. I think it'd be great if you did go, and if you're more comfortable reading one of your poems, I'll bet they'd be perfectly understanding. Just don't burn your bridges too early."

Marcia is equally thrilled and tells Selden, who has recently taken a new job and is no longer my case manager. She assures me that both of them will attend the presentation and be there to congratulate me, give me moral support if I get nervous.

"You've got to go," Marcia urges me. "Really. You'll be sorry if you don't, and I think you can do it. We'll be there, rooting for you."

"But I don't know what to wear!" I moan.

Marcia laughs. "Well, for once that sounds normal! Don't worry about it. I'm sure no one will care what you wear. Just wear your jeans if that's how you're most comfortable."

She chuckles again. "I'm glad to see that at least you're thinking of going. You'll do fine. Why don't you read that forgiveness poem everyone loves so much?"

I dig out the poem, and during the following week try to memorize it but decide at the last minute to bring a copy along, certain I'll clam up and forget it in the middle.

The lobby of the Legislative Office Building, with a floor made of luxurious, inlaid polished stone, is generously peopled, with almost every chair taken and a double row of standees behind them. Several tables have been set up, some with food and punch, others with fliers, various articles, and printed information, including photocopies of my editorial. Mariah and I descend the stairs, meeting up with the case manager who has replaced Selden, and two young men she's brought with her.

The two men mumble hello, but neither makes eye contact, which is a relief because I don't feel like it either. My case manager, who is looking about, notices a tall, Lincoln-bearded, white-haired man in a clump of people. She takes me by the hand and leads me up to the group surrounding him. "There's Dr. Saul, the commissioner of mental health. I want to introduce you."

I mumble a greeting and reluctantly shake his hand. I don't want to spend time talking to him, so I quickly make an excuse and head back to where Mariah is waiting.

Marcia moves to my side. She is about to speak when a swarm of professional-looking people come striding into the lobby, the buzzing hubbub centering on a very tall, gray-haired man I recognize as the governor. I fall back behind a pillar, out of their way. When they reach the front, we are called to attention by a woman dressed eccentrically in cowgirl purple leather complete with fringe. She raps the microphone until all fall quiet and then officially opens the ceremony.

The acoustics in the beautiful room are poor, so even with a microphone it's hard to hear.

The first award presented is third place, and a young woman rises to accept a plaque. Then the second-place award is given to a writer who can't be present but who has sent a few written remarks, which are read aloud. I begin to tremble and sweat, clutching my two pieces of paper, one, the names of people who have helped and supported me over the years, especially Marcia and Selden, and the other, my poem. I can barely listen as I am introduced, and it takes a push from Mariah for me to walk forward at the proper time.

I take the plaque and manage a shaky thank you, then stand at the lectern. "Can you hear me in the back?" I ask, knowing how hard it has been for me to hear the other speakers.

"Yes," several people call.

"Okay." I pause to unfold my papers, then begin reading, too rapidly, hoping to get it over with, even as I tell myself to calm down. After I thank everyone I don't know what else to say, so instead I read my poem:

TO FORGIVE IS . . .

To begin
and there is so much to forgive:
for one, your parents, one and two,
out of whose dim haphazard coupling
you sprang forth roaring, indignantly alive.
For this, whatever else followed,

innocent and guilty, forgive them.
If it is day, forgive the sun
its white radiance blinding the eye;
forgive also the moon for dragging the tides,
for her secrets, her half heart of darkness;
whatever the season, forgive it its various
assaults—floods, gales, storms
of ice—and forgive its changing;
for its vanishing act, stealing what you love
and what you hate, indifferent,
forgive time; and likewise forgive its fickle
consort, memory, which fades
the photographs of all you can't remember;
forgive forgetting, which is chaste
and kinder than you know;
forgive your age and the age you were
when happiness was afire in your blood
and joy sang hymns in the trees;
forgive, too, those trees, which have died;
and forgive death for taking them,
inexorable as God; then forgive God
His terrible grandeur, His unspeakable
Name; forgive, too, the poor devil
for a celestial fall no worse than your own.
When you have forgiven whatever is of earth,
of sky, of water, whatever is named,
whatever remains nameless,
forgive, finally, your own sorry self,
clothed in temporary flesh
the breath and blood of you
already dying.

    Dying, forgiven, now you begin.

Carolyn

When we were kids in the 1960s, we spent a month every summer at Weequauket Lake on Cape Cod. One July we had a small Boston whaler equipped with a minuscule outboard motor, barely strong enough to pull a child on water skis. Sometimes our father took the four of us out the channel to the big part of the lake. On the way back from those excursions he liked to play a game he called Mysterious Island. If Daddy was steering, as we passed by a particular secluded beach he began to complain that he couldn't control the boat. With great drama, he announced that mysterious forces from the island were pulling our craft out of his control. Gritting his teeth, his face growing red with effort, he made a great show of trying to wrench the boat from the island's irresistible power. But of course his heroic efforts failed and, to our perpetual delight, we were forced to land, disembark, and have a picnic or go swimming. Only then, for a brief window of time, did the island's magnetism for our boat subside and allow us to depart. When we were finally out in open water again, our father announced solemnly that we were safe, and we'd never go near that island again . . . And we didn't until the next time.

In my dream, Pammy and I are alone in that motorboat, lost on a vast, still ocean. Pammy is a confident skipper, her eyes on the horizon, hand steady on the tiller. I don't worry. Over the chug of the motor comes a loud crackling like a frayed wire shorting out. Sparks. The sky gets dark, ominous, and the wind blows cold. Without warning, the boat veers into a sharp curve and banks hard. I grab the gunwale to keep from flying overboard. We are headed toward a rocky shore. With a sudden burst of pleasure, I recognize Mysterious Island and am flooded with relief. Of course the beach is pulling us, forcing us to land—that's the game! Excited, I turn to Pammy. But she is a stranger, Pammy but not Pammy. Her eyes dull, blank, yet somehow burning with terror and pain. I realize she isn't steering anymore; instead, the tiller is crushing her. I reach out to help, try to take control and steer us away from disaster. It's impossible. I turn off the engine to slow us. Instead, we pick up speed. The rocky beach gets closer, closer. Seconds away from the rocks, I scream her name. She cries out, "I can't stop! Get out!" I jump. The boat crashes. Pammy disappears. I wake up drenched.

Siobhan and I meet in 1985 at a Fairfield County Psychiatric Society meeting. I snag a glass of chilled Chardonnay from a passing waiter and eye the clock. A woman about my age approaches and introduces herself. Trained at Einstein and Yale, Siobhan Riordan is friendly and enthusiastic about meeting another female psychiatrist. It's a full hour before we stop talking. Her private practice in Norwalk is full, she says, and she would love to refer patients to me. I should call her as soon as I'm ready to open a practice.

I wait two years. When my second child, Jeremy, is born in May 1987, I resign from hospital work and set up an office in my home. As Siobhan predicted, almost overnight I have plenty of patients. A year or so later, she and I form a peer supervision group and invite others to expand our circle of professional companionship. Lori and Beth join a few years later, and since that time the four of us have met for two hours every Friday. Not only do we keep each other up to date on developments in psychiatric research, we also discuss difficult patients and support one another through the myriad personal crises of life.

Pammy isn't doing well. According to the doctors, her therapy is not supposed to be my business. Over the decades, I have learned that my questions and suggestions are unwelcome. I am antitherapeutic. If I can't keep my opinions to myself, I should go into therapy myself to understand why. Finally I call Siobhan. Since then, she has spent hours with me on the telephone trying to figure out what I should or shouldn't do. She knows all about Pammy, her illness, and our family.

On my drive to our group this Friday I have one thought: *Something's got to give*. I haven't slept well for weeks: Pammy is going downhill and no one except me seems to care. The summer has been humid, and today the air thrums with electrostatic potential and the sound of crickets. By the time I get to Siobhan's, distant thunder rumbles through the muddy clouds overhead.

I ring the bell, but there's no answer. I let myself into the kitchen through the side entrance and quickly shut the door behind me to keep her husky, Cleo, from escaping. When Siobhan first adopted him he was skittish around humans and flinched when you raised a hand. Given the chance, he'd nudge a door open and bolt to freedom, sometimes staying on the lam for days at a time. Eventually a kind stranger would call to say she was in possession of an exhausted dog whose tags gave her phone number. Gradually his escapes became less frequent and eventually he learned to make his own way home. "The need to run is in his genes," Siobhan says. "You've got to work with his running away to earn his trust." Today her husky is almost docile.

I put my purse on the granite table next to a dog-eared scuba-diving catalog. I see a note propped against the framed photograph of Siobhan, radiant, holding her dog and smiling into the camera. Bill is the photographer. Behind the photograph is a vase of fresh yellow daisies. The note: *To Siobhan, love, Bill.*

I hear familiar voices coming from the deck out back. When I join them, Siobhan jumps up and gives me a hug.

"We were worried about you," she says and points to the picnic table and deck chairs where Lori and Beth sit. "Fix a plate and join them. I'll bring over the iced tea. You still want to talk about Pammy?" I nod. "Good. I was telling Beth and Lori what I know about her."

I deposit some grapes and pieces of honeydew on a plate and settle into a woven beach chair, the plate on my lap, my feet propped on the end of Siobhan's chaise.

Siobhan kicks off her flip-flops and stretches out. She sets her tall glass on the deck beside her. For a half hour I talk about Pammy. The problem, I conclude, is the hopelessness she feels since Zelda Margulies left. Nancy, her new therapist, is clearly terrible for her.

"Nancy said if she doesn't like her she can join the other chronic patients in the medication group. No sense wasting 'special treatment' on a patient who complains." On the verge of losing my composure, I pause. I'm exhausted. "She says she can't stop Pammy from killing herself." My voice quivers. Again, I stop for control. No one interrupts. "I think they're willing to let her die."

"But Carolyn, Pammy's depressed! Don't they recognize that? Don't you?" Siobhan exclaims. "Haven't they tried antidepressants?"

"I don't think they've considered the possibility," I say. "To tell the truth, I haven't either. I thought people with schizophrenia don't get depressed."

"That's bull, Carolyn. I know it says so in the older literature, of course. But it's wrong. People with schizophrenia *do* get depressed. Wouldn't you, if your life were taken over by voices, paranoia, delusions, plus all those people who mistreat you? It's enough to make *me* suicidal."

"There's worse," I say. "Nancy and her ilk at the clinic have decided Pammy has a 'borderline personality disorder' *on top of* having schizophrenia."

A few big raindrops plop on the deck.

"According to them," I add, "her so-called depression reflects a desire to be sick. You know, secondary gain and all . . ."

"Doesn't sound like they've got much of a therapeutic alliance," says Beth lamely, to break the extended silence that descends after my last remark.

"So, what can I do? Nancy expects Pammy to be a 'good patient,' you know, compliant, unquestioning. Occasionally Pammy will be compliant, but unquestioning? Never! Now she doesn't dare bring up anything controversial, especially not a suggestion from me." Shaking my head, I get to my feet and go to the edge of the deck. I lean over the railing and scan the yard and pond from end to end, as if the answer lies somewhere out there. Then I turn around. "I don't get it. Why do they make it so hard? Why do they dismiss my ideas without a thought?"

"It's simple, Carolyn. *You* know what you are doing," Siobhan answers. "They do not."

"I try not to. I mean, I try not to question their judgment—"

"But why not?" Siobhan sputters. I can't tell if she is more frustrated with Nancy and the clinic or with me. "You should be able to say what you think."

"I suppose if Pammy would just shut up and get better, I wouldn't need to say anything at all." Traffic noises punctuate the afternoon. A neighborhood dog barks. Cleo bounds over to the stairs and suddenly stops: invisible fencing. I feel too small to be a one-woman crusader. But if Pammy's life is at stake, so is mine.

"I'm desperate. I can't sit on my hands and watch any longer. Nancy treats Pammy like a chronic schizophrenic, hopeless. But I know they haven't tried everything." I begin to pace. "The trouble is, I can't do it for them. I see possible solutions, but I can't be Pammy's doctor." I stop directly in front of them. "I don't *want* to be her doctor. I want to be her sister. But Nancy won't listen. She doesn't want to do anything at all."

Siobhan breaks in. "There are other options, Carolyn," she says quietly. "Your ideas are completely reasonable. You know your sister better than they do, and as a psychiatrist, you could be extremely helpful. What is criminal is the clinic's sadism."

That's when I lose it. Lori hands me a Kleenex, but no one tries to make me stop crying. The silence is comforting; I know I'm with friends.

After a few minutes Siobhan speaks again. "Your sister needs a new therapist."

"You're not kidding." I wipe my eyes. "But who will treat her?"

"I will," whispers Siobhan.

A drop of rain hits me on the cheek. Thunder rolls over the trees. No one says a word.

"What?"

"*I* will."

I stare at her, still not comprehending.

"Carolyn, *I'll* treat your sister." Siobhan enunciates each word for me as if I'm deaf.

"You can't." My objection is weak at best. But Siobhan is my best friend. Your best friend shouldn't be your twin sister's shrink.

"Why not? Would she want me to?"

"I think so. Though she'll probably say she doesn't deserve it."

"And you?"

"God, Siobhan, you know I can't think of anyone better for her. You've heard her whole story. You'd believe her, not write her off as a borderline! But she's a lot of work and you're my friend. Think about it before—"

"I *have* thought about it. For a long time. I want to treat her."

I know I should try to talk her out of it. It blurs all kinds of boundaries, breaks rules, and could be a potential disaster. But I don't have the will for an argument. "I insist on paying you—"

She waves me off. "No need—"

"Siobhan, I have the money to spend on her, provide extra clothing, dental, medical, whatever. If she ever wins the lottery, she can reimburse me. I joke that she can buy me a new house while she's at it." Siobhan starts to protest. I shake my head. "This is non-negotiable. She'd want to pay you. She'll feel like a burden otherwise."

A brief silence.

"Okay, then. If Pammy wants it, she's got a new doctor."

We hug, and something inside tells me this is going to work out.

A tremendous clap of thunder and the skies open wide. In seconds we're soaked through, but I don't care. Siobhan's offer has given me hope for the first time in years.

Pamela

When Zelda leaves to take care of a sick child in 1996, I go back to the outpatient clinic. Nancy, a nurse-therapist I'm assigned to, starts me on Zyprexa, newest of the new antipsychotics. In a few weeks, the voices vanish, and for the first time Gray Crinkled Paper loosens its claws. True, I'm rapidly gaining weight, but it seems a worthwhile trade-off. Nancy continues cold, unsympathetic to my situation. We're a lousy match, and my continued isolation, the unrelenting loneliness, depresses me. Despite the miracle medication, I consider suicide.

One night Lynnie calls me and says, her voice tentative, as if expecting me to get angry, "I don't want to interfere, but Nancy treats you like a back wards patient and you deserve better. Would you consider seeing my friend Siobhan Riordan?"

"What do you mean, 'see' her? Like a consultation? What the hell can she do for me?"

"No, Pammy, I mean see her as in being her patient. She'd like to treat you, if you'd consider it . . ."

"But she's your friend—"

"She's careful. That shouldn't get in the way. She's a really good psychiatrist. You'd like her."

"That's what I thought about Ruth until she dumped me! You

think I want to be someone else's welfare patient?" I sound irritated, but I'm thinking, *She* wants to see *me?*

Lynnie's right: A life preserver has splashed down next to me just when I'm flailing in the water, about to give up and go under. I can't believe what she's saying. I test her again. "You mean, like, every week?"

Lynnie sighs but tries to sound upbeat when she speaks again. "Yes, if you want it. It won't be pro bono; I'll pay her out of money that's been set aside for things like this."

"I've been burned by doctors who just want to do a good deed, you know. They all regret it."

"I promise: no good deeds, absolutely none, okay?"

"Yeah, yeah, okay. Anybody would be better than Nancy. When do we start?"

My impression of Dr. Riordan, or Dr. Siobhan, as I come to call her, is that she's a small, slender, well-dressed woman with a big mane of hair. But this remains an impression, because I can't look at her. I do know her voice is calm and kind, and she seems interested in me. At times she responds with passion, as if what I tell her is not only of concern but crucial. Unlike Ruth, she doesn't get angry or show frustration. I trust her most because she understands how hard it is to be estranged from my father, even if I discount it.

"Your feelings don't matter, Pam?"

"Oh," I say, and I laugh a little, nervously, "it's not that bad. You can't compare it to men who beat their daughters."

"And the silent treatment doesn't count?"

"I don't know. I just figure if it doesn't leave scars, it can't be abuse."

"No scars?"

This time I laugh out loud, but the best I can do is respond, "Well, you know what I mean."

"What do you mean?"

"I dunno. I guess that if he doesn't miss me, I won't miss him. It's that simple."

"So it's a choice on your part."

"Well, I can pull the switch when I have to. I've learned the hard way."

"The switch."

"The I-don't-care switch, the on-off switch, the I-don't-give-a-shit-about-you, you-bastard switch, if you get my meaning."

"It sounds like you care a great deal, in fact."

"Oh, fuck it. I don't want to talk about it anymore."

But she does. She tells me a little about totalitarianism, which she's made a study of, and I feel for the first time as if someone takes my experience seriously.

I would like to know what Dr. Siobhan looks like, because I trust her in a way I've never trusted anyone. I'd like to be able to look at her when I talk and see her expressions, but I'm scared to risk a glance. The best I can do, as usual, is stare into the air near her face, sensing them instead of knowing them.

The other aspect of my life that she doesn't ignore is my sleepiness. Although she prescribes Ritalin without using it as a bribe, she also sends me for a consultation with Rachel Haas, a nearby psychiatrist and sleep specialist. Dr. Haas quickly confirms the diagnosis of narcolepsy and makes suggestions for my treatment.

I depend on my weekly hour with Dr. Siobhan and look forward to seeing her. Then, one afternoon, she tells me she has bad news.

I steel myself. I know she's sick of me. She wants to dump me. I've poisoned her just as I always do. It figures. Give me anything at all, and I become insatiable, the ogre that ate Manhattan. I devour everything good about a relationship. Well, I warned her, I tell myself miserably. I told her she'd regret seeing me, that it would destroy her, I *told* her!

"Listen, I really wish this weren't happening. I know it will be difficult for you, but—"

But. My arms hug my chest.

"I'm retiring. In June."

My heart goes into spasm and the self-hating torrent resumes: *She has to retire to get rid of you, asshole. You destroy everything you get your paws on.* I want to scream, *I'm sorry! Please don't leave me!* I need to get in control, pull the switch, put on my I-don't-give-a-shit face. I can't let her know how devastated I am. Then I decide I must have heard wrong. Why would she retire? She can't be much older than I am. Maybe she just means her vacation will last longer than she's expected. Maybe—

"Pam? Are you all right?" Dr. Siobhan's voice comes to me from a distance, as if through fog. "You did nothing wrong. It's not your fault. It's just something that happened. I've arranged for Dr. Haas to—"

But I can't control myself. I feel as if my heart has exploded and been stomped on like so much rubbish. I start sobbing. I'm drowning again, and this time there will be no one to come to the rescue. I surprise myself: I've never reacted this way to such news. Usually I can pull the off switch, make myself feel it doesn't matter. I'm ashamed, even as I rage and cry, but I can't stop and Dr. Siobhan doesn't try to make me. She seems to understand how horrible this is for me and isn't thrown or turned off by it. It's already near the end of my session. We run over for the first time, and she lets me leave only when she's sure I'll be okay.

This is in November. Near the end of December, I miss my usual appointment because of Christmas; I have one more scheduled before her vacation.

But Y2K comes first.

Pamela

On New Year's Day I wake in University Hospital to the scream of air raid sirens. When I hear the call for evacuation, my legs turn to jelly, giving way to a sudden loss of muscle tone that's common in narcolepsy. I collapse on the floor, a helpless heap. Someone sneers in disgust and tells the others to ignore me, they're leaving me behind.

I hear the noise of passing feet, see light and shadows going by my door, then murmuring as patients are herded toward a hidden exit. Some laughter, whispering, strange thumps and clattering. Finally nothing, just silence.

Faintly but growing louder each second, a high-pitched whine saws its way into my skull with a Doppler intensity. Approaching missiles—ICBMs. Or is it only a fly? Guns pound. Or is it only my heartbeat? My head is throbbing. The pulse in my neck resounds like ocean combers crashing on the rocks.

Why have they left me behind? Is it some kind of joke? A test? A mistake, a bad dream? There has to be an explanation . . . *something*.

The noise grows louder and louder, enlarging inside my head until a tangible dazzling fills me, its substance taking up all the space in the room, filling me with sudden understanding bright and hard as diamond: *Aah, so it's an experiment!* Of *course!* Everything is being recorded by hidden cameras. This conclusion, horrible though it seems, consoles me; a malevolent world that follows rules of any sort is easier to bear than the cruel unpredictability of a so-called benign one.

Time passes. I sleep. When I wake, my body works again. The noise is gone, the sky clear, the ICBMs have turned back. I crane my neck to look out the door. People come out of nowhere, as casual and nonchalant as if what happened was just an ordinary interruption of an ordinary day. Conversation and activities resume where they left off. It's like an episode of *The Twilight Zone*. Am I going crazy? Are they trying to *drive* me crazy?

But no one explains it to me. I can't even ask if I've passed the test or finished the experiment, because that would only bring denials by the very same nurses and aides and doctors who have set it up. Worse, they'd use my questions as an excuse to give me more drugs or impose stricter monitoring.

For fifteen days I come to only in short bursts, waking to eat or use the toilet, talking gibberish to interchangeable white coats, fumbling my way between dreams and derangement before I fall back into my drugged stupor. But when I *am* awake, I take notes, scribbling my take on everything, no matter how insignificant. I don't talk to the other patients. I don't talk to the staff, except one or two of the nurses. I'm never sure what will be the next weapon used against me, which person might turn out to be a traitor. Somebody has tampered with reality, and since I don't know who, no one can be excluded. To be on the safe side I have to assume that everyone is the enemy.

One day blurs into the next. Alone in the seclusion room, I don't know if I've been in the hospital ten days or thirty.

One weekend, Lynnie drives up from Wilton to see me, as she promised. The night before, Stacy persuades me to take a shower and wash my hair—for the first time since I arrived. I change my clothes, go so far as to remove my hood and sunglasses. But without their protection, I'm exposed to the full blast of all the dangers outside my door, which marks off the perimeter of safety.

I'm standing in the crack of the doorway when she arrives, professional looking, very much the psychiatrist in her expensive narrow skirt and leather coat. She acts as if she's been in places like this a hundred times. I watch her speak to the nurse on duty. They smile comfortably, conspiratorially. It's clear from their gestures that she's asking where to find me.

She heads my way. I duck out of sight and start to count off the seconds on my fingers . . . *One, two, three, four* . . . She'd be at the linen room now . . . *Six, seven, eight* . . . Maybe now at the conference room? It's crucial to calculate down to the split second when her face will appear at the window in my door, when to expect her knock—

Whoomp!

When she crashes through the open door, I shriek, then freeze like a deer in headlights. For an instant I don't know where I am, what to do, how to protect myself, where to go . . .

Then wonderfully, magically, right before my eyes, she turns into my sister again, peering into my face, worried, apologizing profusely for scaring me. I reassure her, but the truth is even I don't know how to explain myself.

I know something is wrong. Most of the time I'm shifting between different planes of reality. I get lost just going to the dining room, two doors down, and I stumble there like a drunk. Worst of all, music plays all the time, coming from the walls, the floor, the ceiling, or from nowhere at all. No one else seems to hear it, but the oddest thing is that every*one* and every*thing* produces it. I look everywhere, even peering into people's mouths, but in fifteen days, I still don't locate the source.

When my commitment paper expires, they have to release me. I can tell the doctor is not very happy about it.

Carolyn

I am finishing up with my last patient of the day when I get a call from Dr. Haas.

I was on the phone with Pammy late last night because the voices were relentless. "Look at you, moron," they said. "You take up too much space in the world. Go on, jump!" I'm worn out trying to find reasons for Pammy to stay alive.

No matter what I said, she was hysterical, alternating between whispering and screeching at the top of her lungs, "Lynnie, you have no idea what it's like! This is how they torture people—on and on, they never stop. They want me dead and they'll keep talking until they have their way—" She stopped only to take a breath. "Lynnie, I can't hold on. I know you want me to live, but—" Uncontrollable sobbing took over.

I'd heard this kind of panic before and usually I could get her to calm down. Not last night. Recently I've wondered if I'm doing the right thing. My own psychiatric patients are also in crisis, my marriage is falling apart, and I have two children to help through the inevitable divorce. I have little energy to spare for myself, let alone to keep hope alive for Pammy. Besides, I can't imagine living the way Pammy does. What right do I have to insist she stay alive? Already I have used the trump card too many times: "You can't kill yourself because you'd murder me too."

But last night I was thinking about life alone without my twin. Impossible. I don't care how psychotic she is, I want Pammy around.

"—they want me dead!"

"Pammy, you have to stop this." I tried to keep my voice calm. "No one wants you dead—"

"How the hell would you know?"

Silence.

"I hear them all the time," Pammy said. "I'm the ogre that ate Manhattan. I should die. Leave the world to people who don't *just* take up space."

"Oh, that's crazy," I blurted out, too exhausted for diplomacy. "Besides, you'd still take up space in the ground."

"That's not funny."

"Sorry." A beat. "But seriously, why do you listen to the voices. I mean, why kill yourself for them? What about me?"

"You'd be better off if I wasn't around."

"Goddamn it, Pammy, I would not—"

"At least if I'm dead I can't hurt anybody anymore . . . Besides, you and I know *he* wants me dead. Then he wouldn't have to lie anymore."

She was talking about our father. But her death wouldn't make him happy. Despite his silence, I know he misses her as much as she misses him.

My musing ends with Rachel's voice. Dr. Haas is calm, no-nonsense, kindly, but to the point.

"Carolyn, I'm worried about your sister. I just got off the phone with her."

"Where is she?"

"I spoke to her at home."

"So she's safe."

"So far—"

"Last night she called me, totally psychotic. Raging about killing herself to save others."

"That's what I'm worried about. She's not taking her meds and I don't know how that will affect her. What do you think about my admitting her down here? I know she lives up in Wethersfield, but with Dr. Riordan gone, I don't know her that well and frankly I'm concerned."

"You mean Newton Hospital?"

"Usually I wouldn't ask. I know you'd have to drive up to get her and I—"

"When are you talking about? Tonight?"

Rachel said she'd stay 'til eight if I could deliver Pammy before then.

"I'll get her there before seven-thirty." I hang up the phone, glance at the clock. It's already four-forty. I can get to Wethersfield in under an hour if I push it.

But my thoughts are at odds with the alarms clanging double time in my chest. I know it's the right thing to do, but if it's so right, why does every molecule of me feel so awful?

My daughter, Allie, knows that her aunt is sick, but she doesn't really understand. At sixteen, I think she's embarrassed when her friends meet Pammy. Jeremy, twelve, has heard of schizophrenia but wouldn't notice anything odd about someone unless I pointed it out to him. I let them know where I'm going and tell them to order in pizza. Then I call Pammy and tell her I'm coming. I don't say exactly why, but nonetheless she sounds relieved.

A few minutes later I'm speeding through Wilton, Weston, Route 53 across town, Route 57 down to the Merritt Parkway. I round the curve onto the highway at Exit 42 and almost slam into a wall of red lights stretching as far as I can see. Five P.M. Friday rush hour. *Damn! It'll take forever to get to Wethersfield.* I pound the steering wheel and utter a string of four-letter words as I merge into the halting procession.

At every highway entrance, the line of anxious northbound cars slows. The motion is rhythmic. I could sleep. But before I know it I am roused by the slipping of my tires on the metal bridge over the Housatonic River.

What am I getting myself into? Pammy might refuse to get into my car or go to the hospital at all. How will she feel being a patient in Newton Hospital, where some of the staff know me? In all the years Pammy has been ill, I've had the luxury of living far enough away from her to stay in touch while safely maintaining a separate life, a separate identity. We lived close enough to visit occasionally but not close enough to bump into each other by accident. Although she's my best friend, almost all of our adult relationship has been conducted over the telephone. I think we've *both* wanted it that way.

Past the bridge the traffic eases considerably, and soon I'm speeding up the Wilbur Cross Highway, watching for cops. I make it to 100 Corporate Circle in record time.

The address suggests an upscale office complex. But the twelve-story structure looks like a prison to me or, at best, a VA hospital. Shared only by Red Lobster, a nearly empty Ramada Inn, and Peoples Bank, Corporate Circle House pokes off the highway, dead-ending a hundred yards from I-91. Inside the foyer, I scan through the faded apartment numbers and lean on what I hope is the right number.

"Lynnie, is that you?" comes a scratchy voice I barely recognize. "Did you park in the right place?"

There's no accent—a bad sign. When Pammy is in a good mood, she often comes to the phone with a heavy Irish or New York accent. Then we get into a riff, trading ethnic clichés until we collapse in hysterics. Looking at it from an outsider's point of view, it is an odd behavior, I suppose, but we've done it for years, so I notice only its absence. I start to reply, but she cuts me off, "Look, you're here for a reason, right? You're not here just to check up on me and then take off? If you are, you might as well get back on the road. I don't want to be anybody's obligation."

A flash of resentment. This is the kind of reception I dread. I'm the only one in the family who has really had much to do with her for years and she knows it. How dare she be bitchy to me when I do so much for her? Fighting tears, I drop my bag. Why the hell do I bother? Does she have any idea how her behavior affects me? Does she care? I don't know what to say,

A moment later she yells through the intercom. "Wait! Don't leave. I'm coming. The elevator takes forever, but I'll be right down."

I turn and stare numbly out at the circular drive where clumps of flowers were planted last summer in an effort to make the place cheery. It is so much better than the rat-infested tenement on Roosevelt Street where she lived for years, but it's still depressing. Dead flowers. Dead end.

A few minutes later I hear the elevator. She emerges, a middle-aged heap in wrinkled, baggy clothing, glasses cockeyed, gray hair hanging past her shoulders. I don't know how her case worker managed to convince her to shower, but she obviously drew the line at changing her clothes. She is lugging a wheeled shopping cart behind her and stops on the other side of the glass door. She tilts her head and squints at me. Her badly scratched glasses slide down her nose, making her look amused, but her expression is grim. Her left middle finger pushes the glasses back up her nose, where they remain for only a few seconds. Her hands are angry, fighting with her, fingers moving, pointing, writhing, threatening. She's furious. Through the closed door I hear a muffled shout from down the hall. Pammy glances back, scowls, and flaps her palm in that direction, then shoots them the bird. She pounds the button, and with an audible sigh the glass door swings open. We stare at each other.

"Goddamn bastards! They think they've got the right to change the rules whenever they feel like it!" She shakes her head. I can tell she's not far from losing it. I haven't seen her in months, and though she has warned me, I wince at how heavy she's gotten. For a woman who weighed no more than ninety-five pounds for much of her adult life, the uncontrollable weight gain caused by her pills must be terribly distressing.

In spite of her nasty remarks, she has been waiting, watching for me at the window of her twelfth-story apartment ever since I called. Each time a car rounded the bend and swung into the parking lot below, she hoped it was mine. I know this because she called me on the cell phone several times, hanging up when I answered. She must have resisted the urge to call a dozen times more, but until I actually arrive at her door, she thinks I might stand her up.

"I'm ready." She points to her cart, yanks it across the threshold, and heads out the door.

Huh? I'm still standing in the lobby when she realizes that I haven't followed her. She turns back to me and yells, "Come on! Dr. Haas called. You're taking me to Newton Hospital!"

We shove the bags into the trunk, stow the cart behind the seat, and get back on the highway in less than five minutes.

I train my eyes on the road, watching for speed traps, trying not to make her uncomfortable. She watches everything, dodging invisible projectiles. Her eyes scour the landscape. *For what?* Enemy traps, secret listening devices, land mines, terrorists? What kind of hell does she live in?

Maybe music will calm her. I flip on the radio, but she claps her hands over her ears. *Oops. Mistake.* Every time my foot falls too heavily on the accelerator, the station wagon creeping up toward sixty, she whoops with terror and grabs the door handle as if we are hurtling down the Indianapolis Speedway. What the hell is the matter now? I'm not a reckless driver. She's driven with me before. But she hangs on to the door until I brake to fifty.

A moment later, she's contrite. "Don't be angry, Lynnie, it's not you. It's——" I can *feel* her apology.

"It's okay. I know . . . Really. Okay."

"I can't take it if you're mad at me——"

"Pam, I'm not angry!" It comes out sharper than I intend. I stare at the highway. I *am* angry, but I don't know why. "At least I'm not angry with *you.* I guess this whole thing makes me tense. I'm not sure how to make the trip comfortable for you. I thought music might——"

"Too much noise right now." She was angled toward me but now coils away, hands, arms, shoulders folded in. She closes her eyes. I hope she'll sleep, but not a muscle in her face relaxes, and after a short while she opens her eyes. Though the frenetic serpentine movement of her hands continues, she seems unaware she is doing anything out of the ordinary.

I thought I was used to her. I thought I'd gotten used to what schizophrenia, medication, and the years of not taking care of herself had done to her. I thought I was accustomed to the incessant movement of her hands, the sometimes violent rocking of her body. I thought I was used to her chain-smoking and the peculiar self-absorbed habits of her solitary life. I know she drinks only seltzer water, won't eat in public, and avoids the color red. It's hard to believe this is the twin sister I kept on a pedestal for years, Pammy the brilliant, creative one, the smarter, more special version of me. It is still impossible to reconcile my memories of her with the person schizophrenia has so wrecked.

We sit in silence for a few minutes.

"It's just that when Mariah drives I have to stay awake—" she starts. "If she decides to kill us both, I need to be ready to grab the wheel."

"Pammy, *don't*. I know. You don't have to explain. It's okay."

But I wonder: Do I really know when it *isn't* okay anymore? Not just for Pam—she can't help it—but for me? Recently, I've begun to notice that when my husband, Albert, refuses to deal with conflict, invariably turning every problem I try to discuss into my problem, I back down. It seems to me that he always has an excuse to render any objection of mine invalid. I'm exhausted trying to sort it out, and I'm fed up with all the additional work he leaves for me. How many times have I fallen back on that same worn reassurance, "It's okay," when it wasn't.

"It's okay" has become the mantra of my resignation. "It's okay, it's okay," the voluntary denial of my own wishes. "It's okay, it's okay, it's okay" in my marriage means that the effort of explaining what I want or how I feel is too exhausting; Albert never seems to learn anyway. "It's okay" has become my escape from a man I no longer love. It allows me to dodge his demands when he wants everything to be fine without having to make an effort.

As I drive more slowly, Pammy's grip on the door handle relaxes, but she doesn't sleep. A more comfortable silence for a while. We're on the Wilbur Cross Parkway heading through North Haven and Hamden toward the neighborhood where we grew up.

"Remember when we pretended we were Huck Finn and we built that raft out of planks and cardboard boxes? Remember how it fell apart the first time we used it?" We cross the Mill River. "Remember watching *Sky King* in the Evanses' basement on Saturday mornings?" She doesn't answer and I don't ask again. We cross Ridge Road and then Whitney Avenue, our old neighborhood of Round

Hill Road and Millbrook Road. Neither of us says anything. We hurtle through the tunnel, up the hill, through Orange, back across the river, and soon we are heading into the final miles to the hospital.

"How do you feel about going to Newton Hospital?" I ask, hoping she'll answer the question I can't answer for myself.

Suddenly she is shouting at me. "How do you think I feel? You know what's going on! You saw them at University!"

I am so shocked by her explosion of rage, I almost drive off the road.

"Them? Who's them?" I ask with as much calm as I can muster.

"The Nazis! That's who! Senator Lieberman and that actor, Alan Arkin! They were gassing the patients!"

I remain silent, trying to figure out a response that won't fuel her paranoia.

She continues, her voice softer. "You did see that conveyor belt to the ovens running through the unit, didn't you?"

When I shake my head, she curls toward the window and closes her eyes.

It is true I visited her at the University Hospital in Farmington and she pointed to where she saw the bodies being transported through the wall, but there was nothing there.

For the rest of the trip we say little. We get to the hospital without incident.

Pamela

On the unit at Newton Hospital while I hold myself together with my arms, huddling on a chair, trying to make myself invisible, the nurses confer with Lynnie for a long time. Their voices are too low to hear. I try to decide what to do. Should I just get up and walk out? Would they try to stop me? Before I can make up my mind, two aides converge on me, grabbing my bags before I can stop them. I lunge, trying to get my stuff back.

"Hey, I *need* those things."

"Pammy," Lynnie says with a sigh, "you *know* how it works."

"I didn't bring anything sharp with me. I *need* my bags. To-night!" My voice trembles.

Where is Dr. Haas? She'd explain to these strangers that I'm not just a lowlife. I'm not just a homeless derelict. I'm a *person*, goddamn it, I have a history, a personality. I want to yell that I graduated magna cum laude from *Brown University*. I've been to *medical* school, you ignorant motherfuckers! How dare you treat me like I'm some piece of shit you carted in off the streets?

Then Lynnie stands up and announces she is leaving. Oh, yeah, I know the score. She's bailing before *I* do, before she has to figure out what to do with me.

Well, so fuck me! Oh, Pam, just let her go. What does it matter if they kill you? Who cares? Fuck me . . . And fuck you all too!

I must have been thinking aloud because next thing I know an aide takes me by the coat sleeve and leads me down the hall. At least she has my bags.

"Come along. You must be tired. Dr. Haas will be by soon. Why don't you rest until it's time for evening meds?"

"I only take *my* medication!" I yell, flopping down on the bed with my coat, hat, and shoes still on, sunglasses too. But this time my yelling is gratuitous; I'm yelling merely on the principle that it's better to resist than give in too easily. In truth, I'm so scared and exhausted I would take any medication they gave me.

Carolyn

When I return the next evening, I think I am prepared. More for my benefit than theirs, I've talked to the kids and explained the situation: Aunt Pammy's psychotic; she has schizophrenia. No big deal, I think, I've worked with plenty of schizophrenic patients; her illness doesn't scare me. But I don't admit that I still can't see my sister as one of *them*.

As I park the car in the basement lot and climb the stairs to the lobby, I say the words to myself. "Psychotic, schizophrenic, manic. My sister is schizophrenic. She hears voices. She's crazy . . ."

It is now well after regular visiting hours. I walk past security with a smile and a demeanor that are all business. I make my way up the stairs to the fourth floor of the hospital. The corridor leading to Psych 4 is long, empty, and silent except for the hum of the fluorescent lights. I have come straight from work and my high heels click on the linoleum floor, echoing off the stark white walls. There's a lingering astringent odor. The hum, the glare, the silence are foreboding, pregnant with caution and what-ifs.

I stop for a moment to look out the long bank of windows lining the hallway. Halfway up a hill, Newton Hospital's upper floors give me a view over the city's apartments and houses twinkling with holiday lights. I imagine the families getting together, cooking leftovers from Christmas dinner, or drinking Y2K champagne thankful the millennium has brought no extraordinary disasters. Maybe they watch old home movies and gasp at how young they all once looked, arguing comfortably about some incident from growing up. I gaze out at the glittering landscape. I'll never have that with Pammy. My children don't know her; she's never been able to attend family gatherings. She hasn't married, has no kids of her own. She'll never be normal . . .

I wrench myself away from the window. *Get a grip! And stop your ridiculous self-pity!* I catch a glimpse of my reflection and straighten my cream-colored leather coat. In a long black skirt and high-heeled boots, I look "normal." Actually, I think I look pretty decent for a middle-aged woman: slender, energetic, quietly stylish, I have nothing to be ashamed of. I am confident, happy, and above all, *healthy*. I am "okay," the survivor, the twin who has "made it," and I want it to show. Make damned sure no one mistakes me for the patient. I'm *the sister*, the good sister, the married-with-two-kids-psychiatrist-and-dancer sister. I'm here at Newton Hospital only to visit, only to help.

I take a deep breath as I approach the locked door of the inpatient unit, a solid barrier, unbroken except by a tiny window too high to see through, even in my three-inch heels. A headache is coming on. *I hope I brought aspirin.* I knock.

No response.

I knock again, louder. Still no response. Then I notice on the plaster wall a vertical row of three black buttons, and above, a handwritten note reads, "If door is locked press red button for admission." The *red button*? *Where?* I look around, suddenly afraid someone will see my confusion and laugh at me. I'm not *that* anxious. Embarrassed, I look at the opposing wall for the red button. None. My head starts throbbing in earnest.

"Are you so desperate for patients you try to drive people crazy?" I mutter. I punch one of the black buttons and bang on the door.

A voice through the intercom startles me, "Yes?"

"It's Carolyn Spiro, Pam Wagner's sister, here to visit." I hope I sound more confident than I feel, less pissed off.

A loud buzzer sounds, unlocking the door. I push it open. The nurses' station at the far end of the corridor is where I remember it. Patients mill aimlessly in their double hospital johnnies and cheap terry cloth slippers. Staff in street clothes wear name tags and laminated plastic IDs. I pass an old man slouched, drooling, in a wheelchair. Underneath the flimsy hospital robe his legs are splayed open, exposing shriveled genitals. His black eyes blink open but don't focus. I look away.

A pudgy middle-aged woman wanders nearby, head swaddled in a dark wool scarf. She wears two sets of old glasses and several sweaters layered under a heavy coat. Two paper bags dangle from handles around her wrists, and she clutches to her chest a canvas Stop & Shop bag, overflowing with books and papers. I watch her for a moment as she mutters to herself and gesticulates with wild, yellowed fingers, the movements snaking and purposeless, as she paces back and forth. I've seen this before on inpatient psychiatric units. Instinctively, I diagnose tardive dyskinesia, TD, the late-onset movement disorder caused by years of antipsychotic medication. Though mild sometimes, with only subtle finger twitching, it can be disfiguring with uncontrollable writhing of the torso, arms, face, and hands. As far as I know there is still no way to predict who will develop it. Older women with mood disorders seem particularly at risk, but given high doses of the medication and enough time, few are completely spared.

I look around for Pammy and continue slowly down the hall, glancing in rooms as I pass. Some of the staff look familiar and I nod a silent greeting.

The woman shuffles up to me again and mutters, "They won't let us go to my room. And there's no smoking." I'm not really listening and avert my eyes to discourage further conversation. I mumble some empty words about hospital policy. The head nurse approaches. I try to catch her eye to ask her where to find Pammy. Then the patient speaks again: "Lynnie, there's something terrible going on here."

Lynnie? I start. The voice sounds familiar. How does she know my nickname? I stare at her, trying to reconcile the familiar voice with this strange, bedraggled person.

"Pammy?" *My God, what's happened to her?* She looks like the kind of crazy lady who lives in cardboard boxes on the sidewalk, smoking, babbling, and rifling through trash cans for food or cigarette butts. On subways she's the kind of person who makes people nervous, one of those nameless, faceless street beggars who stumble about talking nonsense to themselves. Or one of the drunks who camp on doorsteps, the derelicts that people curse, step around, or simply cross the street to avoid.

To the rest of the world she is not a brilliant, compassionate, incredibly talented poet and writer. Other people don't see in her their aunt, or sister, their next-door neighbor laid low by an incurable illness. To the rest of the world she isn't my twin; to the rest of the world she is nobody—she is an eccentric, fat, crazy, lumpy-purse-waving beggar.

My *sister,* a bag lady?

Pamela

I stay in bed fully dressed, barely moving, barely speaking, for the next several days. When I do leave the room at last, I wrap myself up in my coat and scarf, with my sunglasses on over my regular glasses. Fearing that people are out to steal my things, I have to lug everything with me in my tote bag.

Sunlight feels dangerous. I can't bear to look around. I can't bear to make eye contact. The terror of being seen or of seeing other people is so intense that if I suspect someone is looking at me, I turn tail and race back to my room.

A skinny old woman in a bathrobe takes an instant dislike to me. Though she is usually restrained in a wheelchair parked against the corridor wall, every time I pass her she screeches, "Ooh-ooh, ooh-ooh, babushka-head!"

I don't understand it. I've done nothing to her. Finally, I've had enough. I march up to her chair, kneel next to her, and yell up into her face, "Leave me alone, you useless old bag!"

When I learn later that she has Alzheimer's, I'm ashamed of my outburst. But demented or not, she never insults me again.

I don't know what to make of Dr. Haas, who visits most mornings. I think she is round-faced and blond, and she might come from the Midwest, but as with Dr. Siobhan, I don't know for certain. Her voice, though, is kind, firm, never loud, even when I shout and scream. She talks a lot about "your illness" and things she considers symptoms, but she makes me feel like I'm more than that, like I'm a real person. Even when it's obvious she thinks I'm not making sense, she treats me with respect. One thing, though: She repeats, like a mantra: "The feeling is primary."

I don't get it. Isn't it obvious that thinking comes first? It has to.

Luckily, she has more patience than I do. She assures me I'll understand eventually.

Will it make any difference when I do?

She nods. A big difference.

But most of the time Dr. Haas isn't there. Most of the time I have to fend off the demons myself

One night, having trouble sleeping, I venture beyond my door into the alcove at the end of the hall to sit and look out the window. I flip through old magazines in light too dim to read by. A nurse appears out of one of the rooms, carrying a flashlight. Doing checks. She takes no notice of me, pads softly into the next room. When, a moment later, she emerges, she looks up, acting surprised to see me there. Though she makes a mark on her clipboard, she says nothing, only carries on, going into each room one by one, finishing at the other end of the hall. Then I hear her enter the nursing station, remarking, "Wagner, in fifteen, is still awake, sitting in the alcove. Does she need medication?"

Footsteps approach. I hunch into my chair and pretend to ignore them. A different nurse this time. "Pamela," she says, "why aren't you asleep?"

I shrug, not looking up.

"Pamela?"

"How the fuck should I know?"

"Come now, there's no need for that kind of language. I'm just trying to find out if you need something to help you sleep."

"All I need is peace and quiet."

"Well, you do have your own room."

"So I'm not allowed out of my cage, is that it? I'm supposed to stay locked up like an animal? Well, fuck you! Fuck *all* of you! Assholes!" I leap up and race back to my room, slamming the door behind me as hard as I can. Then I open it and slam it again, for effect.

I fling myself onto the bed, still trembling with rage. But I'm afraid of what could follow. Already I can hear the nurse I yelled at talking with the others on duty. Then, over the PA system: "Code Green, Psych 4." Code Green means someone is violent or out of control. Code *Green*?! For *me*? But all I did was yell! Well, okay, I said some choice four-letter words maybe, and slammed the door. Twice. Is that really enough for the goon squad? Holy Christ, here they come! I can hear them, at least six men by the sound of their footsteps and not small men, either.

They stop at the nurses' station, asking where the problem is. Then the far exit door opens again and a fully armored SWAT team stomps down the hall to join them. Together, all of them—how many I can no longer estimate, but it has to be more than fifteen—stride toward my door and stop just outside, conferring in whispers now, discussing strategy.

The SWAT team will enter first, storming me before I can resist. They'll subdue me, hold me down, and if necessary use Mace to get me under control. The others will burst in together right afterward in a show of force. Restraints are at the ready, and a syringe of something that will "calm her down fast." Not Haldol this time, but a name I don't recognize. It sounds more like poison than a tranquilizer.

My breaths come shorter and shorter. I can't believe what I'm hearing. All this because of a bit of swearing and slamming the door? God in heaven, what can I do? What on earth have I *done*? Trembling, sweating, I crouch on the floor beside my bed. I have to do more. I have to make a break for it while I still can.

Quietly, quickly, I push the bed across the room so I can stand with my back to the wall nearest the door. I have put on all my sweaters and my coat, buttoned up to the neck for padding in case they try to hurt me. I take a deep breath. They will be barging in at any moment. No time to lose. With a silent rebel yell pumping me up, terror giving me the strength to do what I have to, I yank the door open and make a mad dash out into the hall, ready to break for freedom.

And stop dead in my tracks.

The corridor is silent and dim. Empty. Nobody is there, no goon squad in their scrubs, no black-uniformed SWAT team armed to the teeth. No one at all.

From the nurses' station at the end of the hall I hear light laughter, nothing more. Their voices don't even sound annoyed. I search the hall with my eyes, in case the troops mean to take me by surprise. Nobody is there, *nobody*. It seems impossible. I heard them just moments before planning their attack. What in hell happened?

Gradually, as my heart rate and breathing slow down, it dawns on me that no one was ever at my door. No Code Green was called, no SWAT team summoned. In fact, despite my swearing and door slamming, the nurse didn't even come in to scold me. I have—well, I have *what*? Has it all been some elaborate dream? Impossible. I was standing up the entire time. I moved the bed. I got dressed, those are facts, and—

But it looks like it was all a terrible trick my mind played on me. Another hallucination. I slide down the wall outside my room, trying and failing to hold the tears at bay.

The same nurse approaches me. "Pam, what are you doing out in the hall at this hour?" I tell her what happened, though my crying and hiccups probably get in the way of her understanding completely. She helps me to my feet and guides me back to my bed. "It's your illness, Pam. They're going to find a way to help you, don't you worry." I nod obediently, trying to believe her. "Can I bring you something so you can get some sleep?"

I will sleep that night, but I don't believe that medication will make much difference.

I remain hospitalized until March 2000. An emotional Chernobyl, it's been a meltdown to my core, and that I survive at all amazes me. In that sense, Armageddon has come, World War III *is* fought, and with the millennium, the world has ended just as I predicted.

But it takes months for me to understand that this war is my war alone, that the only world that has ended is the one in my head.

Carolyn

The children, our intellectual compatibility, and our shared politics
keep Albert and me together for almost two decades. As I see it, Albert carries on his life much the way he did before we were married;
he teaches his classes, writes grants, goes to conferences, does time at
the various accelerator labs around the world. It seems to me that I
do all the work around the house, all the accommodating to children's needs, all the planning for the family. When he's home, Albert
is distant, preoccupied with physics or his high-tech start-up company. I take ballet classes between seeing patients, care for the kids
and the household. Several nights a week I go out ballroom dancing
alone, which Albert thinks is a waste of time and money. However,
he's always home on time when I've told him I need to make a dance
class. To his credit, he does errands and the grocery shopping that he
knows I hate, and when I am sick and vomiting with a migraine, he
is a tender caretaker.

To the world, I know I appear confident and happy, but underneath, I am lonely beyond bearing.

Over the years, I've grown to resent Albert's social awkwardness,
the odd way he shakes hands and applauds, the way sweat pours off
his brow when he's nervous. For weeks, everything can seem fine,
then suddenly he jars me with an out-of-left-field remark or an off-
color joke in the wrong company. When I complain, he brushes me

off. He is who he is and if it's fine for him, it should be fine for me. He says I'm a dictator, always telling him the proper way to behave. And in a sense he's right. Just about everything he does irritates me and I've become a nag. I hate myself for it.

Complicating it all is his lack of sensitivity about the timing or subtlety of his sexual advances. It's as if he's learned everything he knows about women and sex from TV. He says I expect too much from him; if I'm unhappy and he's not, then the problem is mine, right? I'm the one who should loosen up. He says he wants to make our marriage work. We both know I'm the one who has become so resentful over the years I can barely talk to him.

When something more immediate and exciting comes up in his life, it seems I become, at best, invisible. More often, at those times I feel he treats me, the kids, and the house as obligations. I've learned better than to believe his refrains: "I'll make it up to you," "I told you a month ago I had 'beam time' coming," "You know I have this conference every summer." Even so, he manages to squeeze in choir twice a week, deacons' meetings, tennis, and, increasingly, his start-up company, Faradonics.

Albert's life: Fermilab, physics, Faradonics, friends, faith, family. In that order. A quick peck on the cheek. Slam.

Still, there are good things about our marriage—for one thing he gave me two beautiful children. He was a very attentive father when they were babies, sharing equally in diaper changing and middle-of-the-night feedings. I've wanted to make our marriage work if only for the kids, but in the end the bad outweighed the good.

Albert is in Switzerland when our marriage collapses. After eighteen years, I can no longer see a future for us, but it's our financial debt that does us in. He's maxed out our credit cards for the last time. The night I close our joint bank accounts, he walks out.

Two decades of marriage down the tubes, but I could turn cartwheels.

He returns two hours later.

Mid-January, I file for divorce.

In March, the house is supposed to go on the market. I can't wait to see the last of it. Seven A.M., painting day, Frau Anna Helga Amelia Holstein and her crew arrive to peel, pare, prune, plant, pumice, prepare, and paint all thirty-two hundred square feet. At seven-fifteen, Anna peeks around the kitchen door and beckons me with her finger. I follow her up the stairs. At the bedroom door, she puts her finger to her lips and points. There, in a snapshot, is the problem. Amid the painters and all their paraphernalia, Albert squats, cross-legged, smack in the center of the bed like a Buddha, obdurate, obstinate, oblivious.

He's *not* moving.

When I call Pammy later that day, she sounds perfectly sane. "He's trying to drive you crazy, don't you see?"

She's right. All these years I've doubted my own sanity. It's been brainwashing and doublespeak. Is this how she feels when the voices start in on her?

The house goes on sale April 1. A week later the stock market plummets. Now what? By June I've become a landlord, but on the day the kids and I move into our condo, I uncork a bottle of champagne.

Over the next twelve months, Pammy is hospitalized so many times she doesn't remember what year it is.

One spectacular day in September 2001, she calls me at the office. "Lynnie, they're bombing the World Trade Center!"

Oh, no, she's stopped taking her medication again. A glance at the clock, eight-fifty, I've got a full day ahead.

"Pammy," I say with a sigh, "take your Zyprexa. I'll call you around noon."

Then I turn on the radio.

SPRING 2003

Carolyn

"Well, Jaysus, Mary, and Joseph—is it here you are?" Pammy's Irish accent tells me that she's in a good mood. I smile. Then I hear clunking as heavy objects are moved away from the door, clanging of pots and pans, and more thumping followed by crackling of paper or plastic. "Just moving the kitty litter," she calls. *And her nightly fortification against intruders.* Finally, the door budges inward and Pammy's face appears around the frame. "Sorry," she says sheepishly. "You gotta push by. Don't look around. I know it's a mess, but I haven't been able get things cleaned up."

I'm lugging my PowerBook and computer paraphernalia, but I manage to squeeze between the half-opened apartment door, the recycling bin overflowing with plastic. Her kitchen is so tiny there's just about room to take a breath. And filthy. *Why don't I get used to this?* I think. *Pammy's been sick for years, you idiot, get real!* But I want to shake her with the same embarrassed helplessness and rage I felt back in seventh grade. Hopefully, stupidly, I glance through the kitchen to the living room where, as usual, there is not a free surface in sight. *She knew I was coming to see her, couldn't she at least have made an effort?*

But I hate myself for being so petty, so mean.

What did I expect—her new swank surroundings at Corporate

Circle would cure her schizophrenia? In the living room, I deposit my bags on the floor and start clearing a space to sit down.

"Here, I'll take those," she says quickly. She points to a pile of books occupying the canvas sling chair. I hand the stack to her and she carries them to her bedroom. The last time I visited, she and her friend Kevin had cleaned and organized the night before, and the place looked quite respectable.

Still, the apartment is distinctly Pammy. Books blanket the living room, filling shelves and tabletops, spilling onto the floor, insulating her from the world and yet at the same time connecting her with a life she can't otherwise experience. Volumes of poetry and literature are wedged into used barrister bookcases; history books, novels, texts on botany, neurophysiology, China, are stacked haphazardly. More book piles sway in the bedroom. They creep out from under the bed and spread from there. Deep in the closet are books on subjects she's exhausted or lost interest in. Pammy's paperbacks, magazines, poetry volumes, her own writing journals caulk the remaining crevices the way esoteric information fills the deep meandering furrows of her brain.

Many of these books are clearly old. I recognize some I gave her and others she "lifted" from the shelves of my condo—between us is an ongoing banter that how can a book be mine if it is hers? Then her art books catch my eye. I would never spend so much money on so few books, and I earn my living. *It isn't fair that she gets to buy and also has time to read them.* They are beautiful tomes; they look brand-new and absurdly expensive, with gorgeous photographic reproductions. I open the nearest volume and flip the glossy pages wishing I had time to read it. I could take it—she'd never know. I want it so badly my mouth waters, envy knowing no propriety.

"You know, you can have that if you want." Her offer is real and I'm ashamed.

Her walls also bear evidence of eclectic interests. Above her forest-green recliner is one of my favorite pictures of Baryshnikov. Loneliness emanates from his face; it makes me think of Pammy.

On another wall, in a casual arrangement of sepia photographs, I recognize Grandma Wagner, Mommy's mother, as a young girl. I find her rigid posture and unsmiling face unsettling. On the opposite wall are fading black-and-white photographs of me and Pammy as toddlers, adorable twins in matching ruffled pinafores, with bows taped into our wisps of golden hair. In another picture we are around five and our hair is identically braided. In this picture we both smile naturally, with no hint of madness, no warning of what lies ahead.

"*The reporter* is coming over at three, y'know?"

"Reporter" means Ada, who has been interviewing us and the rest of our family for almost a year. She's writing an article for the Sunday magazine in a Hartford newspaper, inspired by Pammy's taking first place in the BBC World Service International Poetry competition and the memoir we are writing about twins and schizophrenia.

"I think she said the photographer will be with her this time." I say this carefully, knowing what will happen next.

"Oh, shit! I hate it when Mark comes. I look like a fucking blimp. He doesn't know I used to look like you until I started this fucking drug." She pulls out her shirt and says, "Look at this, size 1X. Women's. Which means *fat girl.*"

"Pammy, don't. You'll only make it worse. Someday there'll be a medication that doesn't cause weight gain. Try to put up with it for now."

"You would say that. You don't have to deal with people in the elevator making comments about how much you must like hot fudge sundaes and potato chips. D'you have any fucking idea what it's like to tell people that you and I are twins and have them laugh. They think it's a joke—that we're fraternal twins and I'm naturally obese. And these hooters—" She makes a cupping gesture with her hands as if weighing melons. I'd laugh if I dared. "Where the hell did these come from?"

"Pammy—"

"Oh, shut up. Of course they admire you—they love that you're so skinny and pretty. Sometimes I hate you for it." She looks at me and her scowl lifts for a moment. "You know what I mean. It's not really you I hate but the constant comparison."

"I know."

"So fuck Mark and his fucking camera. I don't want him taking any pictures where he can make me look like an elephant."

Pammy wades awkwardly through her stuff, falls heavily into her chair, and closes her eyes. Then she appears to change her mind. She opens her eyes but seems dazed and absent like a sleepwalker. She fumbles for a cigarette and quickly lights up. As if reading my mind, she blurts out, "Oh, shit, I forgot!" and begins to snuff it out. "You'll get a headache!"

I know this is sincere, but I point to the fan blowing behind me. "No, it is okay—you've got this set up to help, haven't you?"

She nods. "I'll just turn it up higher."

She just took her medication, and I know she needs to smoke while waiting for the pills to work. The truth is, I'll probably get a headache no matter what, given the stress of the day. "I'll make us some coffee," I offer. Pammy's eyes are closed again, but she nods.

I busy myself for the next fifteen minutes while she takes a nap. There's no food in the fridge except the light cream I brought with me at her request. At forty milligrams, Zyprexa has attenuated her psychotic symptoms at the expense of a deranged metabolism and inexorable weight gain. She hates it so much that every few months she stops taking the medication. I hate seeing what I'd look like if I gained so much weight. It's like seeing myself in one of those "fattening" mirrors in a carnival.

I'd tell her to exercise more, but I know it won't make much difference. Most of my patients on Zyprexa gain weight. Even Pammy's Ritalin, doubled to combat medication-induced lethargy, has no effect.

By the time the coffee is ready, Pammy looks awake again. We've just settled in when the doorbell rings—Ada and Mark. I'm disappointed because, in spite of their efforts not to interfere, they do and, being watched by them, we won't get much writing done.

"Hi, guys," Ada says brightly. Ada is always bright, always cheerful, easy to be around, but the kind of person I would have hated when I was a teenager. Mark, the movie-star-handsome photographer who lumbers in under the weight of several enormous cameras, follows her.

Mark deposits the cameras discreetly out of sight. Ada takes the chair Pammy has cleared off. What a pair; Ada is endlessly curious, chatty, chipper, where Mark is silent, impenetrable, a camera himself. He makes me nervous.

Today Ada seems extra eager to please. She says she was up to see our sister Martha yesterday. Martha told her what it was like to live at home when Pammy and I would eat a single graham cracker for dinner.

I feel betrayed, stripped naked. Why did she tell Ada about that awful time in high school? Who gave her permission? Who the fuck had the nerve?

I glance at Pammy, who is quiet, staring at the floor, her fingers tapping angrily. She doesn't look at me or at anyone.

Don't they realize that it is hard enough to write a memoir? Do they have any idea how painful and embarrassing it is to go back and remember—and then expose it to the world? I glance over at Ada, who continues to chatter about Chip and Martha visiting Pammy in the hospital. Finally she interrupts herself and says, "I know you guys want to work on the book. So go ahead, do what you would be doing anyway. We'll be flies on the wall."

But how the hell do you act normal when two strangers are watching, recording, writing notes, and taking pictures?

"Hey, Pammy, they're flies," I remark in heavy New Jersey, thinking to humor her away from an impending explosion. "Do youse have a really big flyswatter?" I glance their way, but neither Ada nor Mark reacts.

Pammy doesn't answer either. I can tell she's pissed off because she lights another cigarette, jams it in her mouth this time without apology, and mutters something inaudible. She shifts positions several times, stabs out the cigarette in the Altoids box she uses as an ashtray, and immediately lights another. Ada realizes something is up. She stops talking. I can feel her look my way.

Finally, in a voice tense with sarcasm, Pammy breaks the silence. "Of course, neither Chipper or Martha go out of their way to come see me. Chipper always protects himself, says his *wife and kids* want to visit, but I know it's just so he doesn't have to be alone with me. Martha only comes when I need help cleaning."

Then, without warning, she turns on me. "And Lynnie hates me, she wishes I'd never been born!" Her eyes narrow to slits, and I realize she is in a place I don't understand, tortured by memories that belong only to her.

Ada shakes her head, her mouth open. "Pammy, I don't think that's true. Why do you think that?" Mark just listens.

"Oh, you think you know her, but you don't. You've heard her tell you about being afraid of me when we were kids? Well, she wasn't afraid of me, she wanted to kill me then. She wants to kill me now." Pammy's voice carries like a megaphone through the tiny apartment.

Ada's eyes dart back and forth between the two of us. She's opened Pandora's box. She looks at me. I lift my eyebrows. I don't know what blew up either, but I've been here before. She turns back to Pam.

Pammy levers herself out of her chair and aims an accusing finger at Ada. "Look, you want honesty? I'll give you honesty. I am sick to death of Lynnie being threatened by me, copying me, trying to take me over! If she can't develop a personality and some confidence of her own, she can't come stealing it from me. I'm tired of feeling blamed for her inferiority. It's her problem!"

"Oh, stop it, Pammy—where did that come from?" I sound weak, unconvincing, and oddly I want to laugh. Mostly I feel detached. "I came up here to work on the book and now out of the blue you're attacking me."

"It's in your writing!" Pammy shouts. "You said so yourself. You hate me for always winning!"

"That's not true! I'm writing about *old* feelings!"

"Yeah, old feelings you still have! Old feelings you blame me for. Old feelings that I destroyed your life!"

"Stop it, Pammy! You don't know anything. I've never felt you destroyed—"

"Yes, you do. You've always hated me. You want to kill me. I hate you for hating me, and I'm not going to be responsible for you anymore!" she screams.

This last accusation pushes me too far. I rocket out of my chair, shouting back, "Oh, fuck you, Pammy, fuck you, fuck you, FUCK YOU! You should talk about who has to take care of whom. Just fuck you!" I stomp my way over the minefield of magazines and books and hurl myself into the kitchen, out of her line of fire. I continue yelling. "We've talked about this! You said you understood. This is about feelings I had when we were growing up. Not now!"

"It is still now! You even said so!"

"Oh, I don't even want to be here anymore if this is what you are going to do to our time." I want to walk out and slam the door. I stay in the kitchen out of her sight. No one speaks. Not Even Ada. Finally I peer around the doorway. I can see Pammy from where I stand.

She looks up, sees me, and shrieks again. "You didn't come up here to see me, you came up here to make sure I didn't claim the book was MINE!"

This is our story, our lives, I am only a supporting actor. She's the main subject, the leading lady. *Ha! The story of my life, being number two.* Hot tears well up.

She seizes my tears as target. "Oh, there you go," she yells, mocking me. "Feeling sorry for yourself again? I'm sick of you making me out to be the evil sister who hurts poor little Lynnie."

"Oh, go to hell! You think I drove all the way up here for this? I came up here to work on our book—"

"*My* book!" She hurls the next verbal barrage at Ada and Mark. "See?" She jabs her finger at me. "*This* is the problem! She can't stand the fact that *I* already wrote this book. *I did.* That's a simple fact she can't accept. She wants to get credit for what I've done."

"But, Pammy, that was another book," Ada says. "I thought you and your sister were writing this together."

It's true. I don't want to say what I'm thinking out loud. She'll never understand how much I have felt I don't matter.

"Well, okay, be that way," Pammy says. "It is true. I was born first and I did just about everything first. You just have to stop comparing yourself. Get on with your life!"

"Pammy, what are you talking about?" I really have no idea what she's harping about.

"Oh, come on—it's still about the crowns. You think I didn't know you were gloating? You loved it. You got to be the girl, I had to be the boy." Her voice is softer now.

I step out from the safety of the kitchen. "Pammy, I didn't know. I didn't try to hurt you. Not on purpose."

"But it was my class. My turn to wear the crown."

"I know." I start to cry. "I'm sorry."

"I know." Pammy starts to cry.

$\mathcal{E}$ARLY $\mathcal{S}$UMMER 2003

Carolyn

In August I go down to Maryland to spend some time with my friend Johan. When we met at a ballroom dance in August 2001, he was living in New York and teaching college physics. I think we were both surprised by how well matched we seemed, and after a few try-out lessons in September we became dance partners, agreeing to share the costs of hours of coaching and practice sessions preparing for competition. By November we were lovers, and I thought we might have a future together. Then, in June 2002, he was offered a research lab job in Maryland, and for reasons I didn't understand, promptly resigned his academic position and moved to Silver Spring. For the past year we've been alternating weekends, commuting five hours to see each other, our relationship squeezed in between dance lessons and practices.

One morning the phone rings. Johan answers. He's downstairs putting a final coat of forest-green paint below the chair rail he installed in the dining room. I hear him clamber off the ladder and stumble for the phone. There's a pause after he answers, and when I hear him on the stairs I realize the call is for me. I meet him at the landing.

With a grim expression he points to the phone. "It's a doctor from University Hospital," he whispers. He hands me the receiver.

"University Hospital?"

He nods.

Okay, something's wrong with Pammy.

I sink to the top stair. Johan sits down close to me, his tattered jeans pulling tight over thighs muscled hard from bike riding. His paint-flecked hand rests on my knee, and the aroma of his aftershave stirs a wave of unexpected desire. For a moment I press against him as if he could screen out the bad news. Then I put the phone to my ear and feel his eyes scan my face for a clue to how bad things are. I don't meet his gaze but pick at the bits of adherent color on his knuckles. I am grateful that he isn't scared away, that he waits with me, offering comfort if I need it. He knows that my sister has schizophrenia, but he doesn't really understand what that means or the degree to which her illness invades my life.

"Hello . . . hello?" I say.

There is a click at the other end as if the person has switched on a speakerphone.

"Yes?"

"This is Dr. Spiro. You wanted me?"

The voice at the other end is garbled and barely audible.

"I'm sorry," I interrupt in a loud voice to get her attention. "I didn't hear what you said. Would you repeat it?"

All I get are the continued cracklings of a bad connection. The phone goes dead. I shake my head and swear under my breath. Johan looks perplexed. Johan, like my ex, is a physicist, and recently I have noticed other similarities that worry me. I think my job and situation with Pammy make him more anxious than he admits. When we first met, Johan admitted to a slick Hollywood-nurtured image of psychiatrists as highly intellectual, inscrutable males, cigar smokers with heavy Viennese accents, favoring free association and dream analysis. I blew the Hollywood image fast. On one of our first dates my phone rang, and after a terse conversation with a patient, I hung up and let fly a string of four-letter words. Johan looked horrified and remarked that he wouldn't stay around if someone made him that angry. Since then I've tried to talk to him about our own conflicts, but it doesn't get anywhere. If I display any anger, particularly at him, he walks out.

For now I try to keep the lid on our own conflict and take patient telephone calls in another room. Inside, I worry about the future of our relationship. The handset sounds again. I catch Johan's eye and point to the phone. "I'll tell you later." We both know I won't. He nods, brushes a kiss on his index finger, touches it gently to my cheek, and makes his escape. When he leaves, I click on Talk.

"Carolyn Spiro? Are you Dr. Spiro?" It's a female voice. Very young. She pronounces my name Speero.

Reflexively, I respond, "It's Dr. Spiro with a long *i*, like spine or spirochete. Why are you calling me?"

"Pamela Wagner, she's your sister, right? She's here with her friend Kevin, who brought her. She's completely unresponsive. We had to sign her in on a fifteen-day paper."

"I don't understand. She was fine when I talked with her a few days ago. What do you mean unresponsive?" Unease creeps into my own voice.

"She's catatonic. Won't speak. Won't move. Has she been like this before?"

"Well, twenty years ago, yes, but never since then!" Immediately, all the worst possibilities come to mind. *A stroke, an overdose, a brain tumor? God only knows what.* I blurt out, "What have you done with her so far?" I know my tone is too sharp, even accusatory, but I'm scared.

"So far, her vitals, electrolytes, and CBC are normal. We're waiting for the final results of a tox screen. She have any drug history?"

"Of course not! An illegal drug is the last thing she'd take." I'm thinking, *How the hell did Pammy get stuck at University Hospital with a resident who doesn't know squat? She's already got a good psychiatrist.*

"You'd be surprised how many families say that—"

I cut her off. "Well, I'm not just any family and I don't like what you're hinting at."

"Look, I'm not trying to be offensive, but with an unresponsive patient, you always have to consider the possibility—"

"Okay, okay, do what you need to, but the drug screen will be negative." In all the years of Pammy's illness, substance abuse has never been a problem. Thank God. However, the resident is correct to include it in her differential. "What else can I tell you?"

"She's been here two days and we need to get some information—"

"She's been in your hospital over *two* days and you're only calling me *now?* What on earth is going on?" I'm not quite shouting. Johan peeks around the door to make sure everything is all right. Maybe I should page Dr. Haas and get Pammy transferred to Newton where they know what they're doing.

"I'm trying to tell you." The resident sounds tired, as if she's been up all night. "But you're not listening."

Now I'm silent. The doctor is right; I'm not letting her get a word in edgewise.

"I'm sorry," I murmur.

There is a sigh and a pause at the other end of the line before she speaks. "We should schedule a meeting next week and get all your questions answered. But there are a few things we need to discuss right now."

My silence tells her to go ahead.

"What I need to know now is, do you have any idea why she's like this?"

"No." *That's the sixty-four-thousand-dollar question we all want answered.*

"But she has been catatonic in the past, you say."

"Yes, a long time ago."

"Does she have a conservator? She'll need one for ECT if she can't sign for herself."

"What?"

"Electroshock—"

"I *know* what electroconvulsive therapy is. It's the question of a conservator . . ."

"Right. We can't tell if she understands. We'll need someone to agree to ECT."

"No!" Again, too abrupt. "I mean, no, she does not have a conservator. But if you want my opinion, try everything else first. I *know* she doesn't want ECT."

The problem is, do I really know what Pammy wants anymore? Do I even have a right to presume to know? Have I ever known?

"Kevin says she won't take her Zyprexa," says the doctor.

"That's true. After gaining eighty pounds."

For a while there is silence at the other end. Then with a sigh she adds, "Well, we'll see how she does."

If it weren't for side effects, there's no question that for Pammy Zyprexa is a miracle drug. Here's a medication that works better than any other she's taken since the day her psychotic symptoms began. She started taking it shortly after it came on the market and had several years of relative relief from psychosis. For a while, like the mathematician John Nash, subject of the movie *A Beautiful Mind,* she was able to keep the voices, the delusional beliefs, the terror, and the hopelessness in the background.

But the weight gain has resisted everything. When the scale hit a number she refused to tell me, that was it.

I can't say I blame her. But I dread what's to come.

Pamela

Annie, the weekend nurse, peers at me, her voice pressing on me like a wad of thick bandages, "Pam? Pam?"

But I am in nowhere land, no feelings, no thoughts, nothing but a blank empty space where Pam used to be. I am a broken bowl of nothing, still breathing and alive, but little else. No needs, no desires, no wants or urges, an involuntary Buddhist dissolving into the void. Annie and my friend Kevin and my rooms and my body in the chair are as far away as the Hubble telescope and no more important than stardust. From a distance or as if muffled by a pillow, I hear Kevin explain that I started slowing down the night before. But now I am worse than ever.

I wish they'd go away, leave me to my nothingness in peace.

It is quickly a peace that is passing. I am Buddhist no longer, but merely petrified, a wooden doll, stuck, immobilized in air as viscous as tar, my brain stuttering and failing to connect. It isn't that I don't want to move; it is that I can't move, can't get up the *will* to move, to want to *want* to move and talk and interact. I am lost, and I am scared. Yet I don't quite care.

Caring takes too much effort. It's too hard to respond or speak or move, and the air is too padded and heavy to let me. I feel as if my brain has sunk down around my feet and can't think any higher. So

I stay as I am, sitting motionless in the chair under the mattress of air pressing down on me. Annie asks again, her voice brimming with worry that should worry *me* but fails to, "Pam, can you answer me? Pam? Pam?"

I don't know how I got to University Hospital. All I recall of the next several days is lying in a bed, neither eating nor drinking, motionless as a board, silent except for occasional involuntary moans when I need to go to the bathroom. Kevin visits, I know that much, because once I hear him explaining to the doctors I've been catatonic before and when I come to I "go wild." They should be prepared for that, he warns. I think Lynnie comes at least once; later she tells me she refused to sign papers consenting to ECT because she knows how much I fear such an assault on my brain, though they tell her it is the best way to get me out of what they term a "desperate situation."

The fog that settled over me at home, the weight of unbearable reality, continues in the hospital. Time drifts and slips. Because I can't drink—not even when one nurse, unaccountably furious with me, pinches my nose closed and tries to pour water down my throat— they insert an IV. Finally, the mustachioed man I think of as Big Doc appears in my room one evening with the resident and several nurses. Big Doc is holding a syringe and explains that it has been shown that three milligrams of IV Ativan can bring a person out of catatonia. He says this within my hearing, but I don't think it is for my benefit. He doesn't act as if I'm not there, can't hear him. He's simply instructing the others in a technique they don't get to use very often. He is using two milligrams at first, he says. Then he inserts the syringe into the IV catheter and pushes the plunger.

But I *have* heard. I want desperately to be able to "come to" as they do in the movies, sit up and smile. I no longer like the fog and would even accept ECT to get out of it.

Big Doc watches me intently, as do all the spectators. "It takes some time," he assures them, none too confidently, I think. He re-inserts the syringe and gives me more Ativan. Then they all stand back in a semicircle around my bed, waiting and watching.

Again, nothing.

Someone coughs nervously. One of the nurses leaves the room. She has more important things to do. Then Big Doc does something unexpected: He leans over me and brushes the hair off my forehead. "Pam? Can you hear me? Can you respond?" he asks, his booming instructor's voice gentled by concern. Still I can't move, can't speak.

He takes my fingers. "Pam, squeeze my hand. Try." I try, but it's no use. Then suddenly, a movement, like flowers pushing up as if they are growing right out of my hand and reaching out to squeeze his. "Yes, that's right, you're doing great," Big Doc encourages me. "How about blinking your eyes, can you do that for me?" And suddenly, haltingly, I can. My words sound like my whole mouth has been Novocained, but I can grunt a recognizable yes or no. I am back, and I can tell from the way he tries to conceal his beaming that he is both glad for me and proud of his skill.

It takes me a good two days before the fog lifts entirely and my brain inches back up into my skull. I need at least one more dose of Ativan when the mattress threatens to descend again and resume its hold. But within a day I can talk again and go to the bathroom by myself. And I can eat and drink.

Then, as Kevin has warned, the frenzy hits. It starts with simple irritability but quickly escalates until I am screaming and swearing like a harridan and they move me into a seclusion room. I get so out of control they put me in restraints and I'm told that at one point I take off all my clothes and race around the unit stark naked. More than once, enraged that my bathroom door is locked, I take a dump right on the floor of my room. I use markers to scribble four-letter words and graffiti quoting whatever the voices tell me. *FUCK THIS SHIT, YOU COCKSUCKERS! I AM THE OGRE THAT ATE MANHATTAN! KILL ME! I DON'T CARE!*

I don't care that Zyprexa would help. I hate it more than anything, even more than being insane.

Carolyn

It's been many weeks and Pam's still in University Hospital. Once the catatonia resolves, she goes wild, terrorizing the staff and me with her ranting. On the phone she snaps at something I say and launches into a tirade of accusations, often hanging up on me in a fury. Farmington is a long drive for me and I can't visit her as often as she thinks I should. Sometimes I need my own time. I'm tired of this illness. I hate schizophrenia. I hate the uncertainty and the feeling that we're always stumbling from one crisis to another. I hate the false hope, the longing for a cure when only a temporary remission is likely. I don't want to care about Pammy anymore. I want to feel nothing. During a couple of phone calls this week she's hinted that she's not safe on the unit and I know she's waiting for me to ask why. I don't. Phone call after phone call, we circle each other like wary bitches, her hopelessness, my helplessness. It's a deadlock. Around and around we go as a murky silence fills in around her words until I hang up the phone.

But this afternoon I got a call from the social worker telling me that for Pammy's safety, she's been moved back to the bare mattress on the floor of a seclusion room, a twenty-four-hour sitter watching her around the clock. You don't have to be Einstein to figure out that something is wrong. They still want to give her shock treatments, but she is "non compos mentis," not sane enough to consent.

It's around nine P.M. when I call the patient phone.

I'm sitting on my bed when I punch the numbers of the long-distance service, the thirteen-digit PIN code, and finally the number of the patient phone on the psych unit. It's busy. Sometimes the situation with Pammy feels surreal—I work as a psychiatrist by day, and here I am still dealing with my most difficult case, my sister, at night. I wonder what some of my patients would think if they knew. I dial a few more times. Finally the phone connects.

After close to a dozen rings, a man answers and I identify myself and ask for Pam. The man wants to know who I am, and I'm tempted to tell him it's none of his business.

"Oh, Lynnie, her sister—you were here on Saturday . . ." He trails off as if he's forgotten already.

"Frank?"

"Yeah."

"Can Pammy come to the phone? Can you get her?"

"I don't know if she wants to talk. It's been—" He covers the mouthpiece and I hear him whisper at someone standing close by. "She's been having a hard time. No one got much sleep here last night—"

Suddenly, a fast-talking young female voice comes on the line. "Hi, Lynnie. It's Maylinda. Remember?"

"Of course I do—"

Maylinda cuts me off and it is clear she's in "talk-only mode."

"You know, Pammy really thinks the world of you. She's always saying stuff about Lynnie this and Lynnie that. Don't take it to heart, what she said on Saturday—she don't mean it. I felt bad for you after drivin' all that way. I didn't want her to hurt your feelings and have you up and leave. Sure you ain't mad?"

I try to answer, but Maylinda rushes on.

"Well, as I said, I could tell you was getting uncomfortable."

"Is Pammy—?"

"Pammy is really a wonderful lady, wonderful person, y'know!" The words careen out of her, rushing on like a freight train with no one at the controls. Once again I have that old feeling, odd as it is given the circumstances, of being relegated to the Pammy Fan Club, of being just one of her many fawning admirers.

"She's real sick, I know," Maylinda hurries to add. "But y' remember Lana, she was the skinny lady here on Saturday, well, if you know Lana you know she don't smile for no one, but there she was lit up like the biggest Christmas tree when your sister made her show off them watercolors she painted. Well, I gotta go." Before I know it, Frank is back on the line.

"Well, anyway . . ." Frank says. I'm beginning to feel like a Ping-Pong ball.

"But is she coming to the phone?"

"Who?"

"Pammy—"

"Oh, yeah—" Pause. "I don't think she wants to talk—"

I have an odd, momentary sense that Frank's trying to protect me. I hear him talking to someone and I make a mental note to thank him the next time I visit the unit. A few minutes later Pammy's angry voice stabs the background, something having to do with an infected toe. She's still swearing when she picks up the receiver.

"Goddamn fucking doctors here are incompetent!" She shouts in a voice hoarse from yelling. "My toe is killing me! They can't figure out the right antibiotic."

During my visit last week a nurse brought in a foot tub of warm water and for ten minutes of soaking Pammy subjected her to a barrage of complaints. As if the curses didn't register, the nurse took her painful foot into her bare hands, dried it with terry cloth, and gently examined the affected digit. When a slight movement of the toe caused my sister to pull back in pain, I saw a sympathetic wince cross the nurse's face. It was lost on Pammy.

"And, except for one or two, the nurses here are useless."

"What about the sitters?"

"Sitters are paid to do nothing. Sitters are expected to sit and eavesdrop. There's one here right now listening in."

Someone protests in the background. Pammy retorts, "You are so. If you weren't listening in you wouldn't be able to argue with me. I'll bet you're hoping for something hot." She turns her attention back to me. "Besides, everyone knows they got bugs all over this place. You can't even go take a shit without somebody watching."

"I guess not . . ."

"Yeah, well, so I gave them something to watch. What was I supposed to do? They wouldn't unlock the bathroom, so I took a shit on the floor. Of course I was punished for it. Why else do you think they got me put away in solitary confinement? It's to fucking show me who's who. Fucking sadists. Last night they tied me up and ignored me. I kept trying to tell them the akathisia was driving me mad, but they wouldn't listen, just told me to shut up. They have no idea what it's like to have this horrible squirrelly feeling. I told them to give me Inderal, but did they listen? Who am I but a stupid patient? I couldn't possibly know what is wrong. They finally got me the Inderal but they had to make sure I didn't think they gave it to me because I asked for it. Fucking liars. They hate me. It'll make their life a lot easier when I go away."

"What do you mean?"

"They hate me."

"But what do you mean, go away?"

"Oh, come off it, Lynnie. Don't act like you're so innocent." Her voice is cold steel. "You wish I'd get it over with so you wouldn't have to bother—"

A thought flashes, *Don't you dare!* Followed by, *I hate you!* I want to shriek at her to be grateful for once in her life, to stop despising everyone who tries to help. I want to hurl terrible, hateful words at her, call her a selfish pig, worse, a fucking manipulative borderline who threatens suicide whenever she doesn't get her way. No wonder Mom has such a hard time staying objective or neutral with her. Sometimes Pammy's rage doesn't feel psychotic, it feels real.

I want to dare her to kill herself, tell her she *should* kill herself instead of torturing me like this. *I'll show her—it doesn't bother me at all.* I want to slam the phone, break it to bits, and never have to talk to her again.

Instead, I offer my usual anodyne. "You know you aren't a bother to me."

"Fuck you. Don't lie to me. You hate just doing errands, so don't try to convince me you don't mind driving an hour and a half to visit me in the hospital."

"It's worth it to me," I say, knowing I sound utterly unconvincing. I can barely muster the energy to convince myself anything is worth doing for her, let alone remember I really do care and would be devastated if she died.

"It's a good thing for you, isn't it?" She says this in such a nasty tone.

"What do you mean?"

"It's good for you. You get to swoop in to save the day like Superwoman. You get to pick when you have to put up with me,"

"What would you have me do?"

"You wouldn't believe what they do to me here. You could be here when I need you instead of just when it's convenient."

"Goddamn it, Pammy, I come to visit because I want to. So shut up right now or I'm going to get off the phone!" She lapses into silence, but I know she hasn't hung up because I can hear her ragged breathing. I grit my teeth so hard I could crack a filling.

Over the next week things do not improve significantly. Pammy continues to be unpredictable, moody, and violent, and refuses to take any medication, let alone Zyprexa. When the hospital applies for and receives a court order permitting them to medicate her against her will, Pammy swallows the Zyprexa only to avoid a forced injection of something worse. I'm relieved, though I know her cooperation will be short-lived. Pammy improves dramatically on Zyprexa and, as expected, the moment she is discharged from the hospital she stops taking it.

She has been in her apartment only a day or two when symptoms of psychotic mania emerge. Sleep is the first thing to go, but quickly the drive to talk takes over her days and nights. The phone acts as a one-way valve governing her connection to the rest of the world. Through the night she phones one person after another and jabbers urgently until the person at the other end pleads exhaustion and hangs up on her. When she can't reach me or Mom or Kevin or her doctor, she becomes frenzied, as if she's hurtling into the dark and still gaining speed. The increasing pressure to talk possesses her. Finally, she goes online, not just to chat, but with a credit card. Mine.

After five days, unable to sleep, she calls me in a torrent of weeping. Through the tears, an unintelligible stream of words pours out of her. I realize what has happened. Command hallucinations have made her push burning cigarettes again and again into her forehead, calling it the mark of Cain, a warning to the rest of us. When I tell her quietly I'm going to call 911, she doesn't argue, just sobs in relief and begs me to forgive her. I stay on the phone until the police arrive.

Weeks later she's not nearly so difficult in the hospital, but there's no discussion of a discharge date. This time even Pam isn't badgering to leave. Something is wrong. A nurse urges me to call her. Nine-thirty at night I reach her. Not sure how to begin, I chat about the kids, my dancing—just stuff.

"So why did you call?" she interrupts. "You usually are asleep by now."

"They told me something about a plan."

"Damn it! I told them not to." She sounds more worn out than angry now. "I knew you'd only worry."

"You were right. So?"

"What'd they tell you?"

"Not much. Confidentiality. They said I needed to ask you."

"It wouldn't help if you knew. You'd only get upset, and there's nothing you can do to stop it." She pauses and then adds, "It's *his* plan, really. He's worked out everything."

"He?"

"You know, the hazmat man. He's mad that I told the staff, because now they're watching me twenty-four/seven."

"He's telling you to kill yourself? That's the plan?"

"No, it's not suicidal." She stops. I wait. She goes on carefully, "I know what you're thinking, but the plan *isn't* lethal. He's assured me of that—"

I interrupt her. "That's supposed to make me feel better? It won't kill you—"

"There are safeguards . . ."

"So what? I should be happy it'd only maim or disfigure you? And that's okay? I'm sick of it. How can you do this to me?"

"Lynnie, I don't *want* to do it." There is something eerily genuine in this offering. Cold, I pull the blankets over me. Pammy's quiet now. Finally, she continues. "I called Dr. Haas, and she phoned the unit to make sure I don't get out."

"Why?"

"Because I'll have to do what he tells me. Every day he reminds me of the plan. He has given me specific instructions. He won't let it kill me, but it would set things back for a while—"

"Set things back?" I say numbly, voicing an obligatory question I don't want answered. She's right; I don't want to know the details of her plan if there is nothing I can do but wait. I don't like suspense in any form. At movies, I close my eyes at scary scenes to avoid any visual memory able to roam around in my brain at night. I don't like to watch reruns of the Olympic skating events even when I already know the outcome.

But of course she tells me anyway, delusions about the man, the little red dancing hazmat man, his orders, his demands. He matters. I don't. She has no idea of the agony of insomnia this causes me, with nightmares destroying what little sleep I can steal.

Pammy, night after sleepless night, here's how the scene plays out in my head: with a single-mindedness that astounds me, you've methodically designed every step in painstaking detail. To ensure that nothing interferes with achieving the desired outcome, you and the hazmat man have anticipated most complications. You've had weeks to observe in detail the nurses' shift schedule and learn their idiosyncrasies. Several doctors and nurses take your symptoms seriously and recognize the plan as psychotic, compulsive, ominous. However, the attending physician and some nursing staff see your plan as manipulative, designed for attention-getting and drumming up sympathy. They may be perilously casual with your supervision, letting fifteen-minute checks expand into twenty, flouting the suicide watch regulations by socializing or ignoring increasingly obvious warning signs. Accordingly, you have timed your actions for change of shift when supervision is more likely to be lax.

The day has come. Hours of covert observation have paid off. With barely an effort you've slipped out of the hospital—the sitter thinks you are in the bathroom with cramps and it hasn't occurred to him or the nursing staff that you've gone AWOL. By the time someone realizes you've been on the toilet too long, it's too late.

Blending in with other families, you've made it down the corridor and reached the top of the escalator. You even have time to slip out of sight into a restroom when you spot a psych nurse sprinting up the stairs. When the coast is clear, you make it down to the lobby and out the front door in full view of the security guards and cameras. Your hospital bracelet is clearly visible, but no one is looking and your behavior doesn't flag attention.

For once in your life you've a reason to look neat enough to fit in. You've tried to comb your hair and have managed to pull it into a semblance of a bun at the nape of your neck where it is wrapped and held in place by one of the scrunchies given to you by Ada. You wear an outfit, loose slacks of light blue and a matching T-shirt, clothes I bought you when you were hospitalized in Newton last spring. You look like any other fortyish Farmington woman, someone's cleaning lady perhaps, or an off-duty LPN or waitress. I suppose you could pass for a housewife, but you are clearly less well-off than many in this area, you sport no diamond or gold jewelry, wear simple flat sneakers. Like most people you could afford to lose a few pounds, but in spite of the weight you look easily five, maybe ten years younger than your age.

It's the first time in months you've been outside. You stride down the long hospital drive in a heavy loping rhythm, merging with a group of early morning walkers. You jog across the street and duck into the mini-mart at the gas station. You call for a taxi. A few minutes later a cab pulls up to the curb. You open the door and peer in, trying not to let on that you are checking for listening devices. The vinyl seats are worn and even ripped in places, but seat belts are accessible and the passenger compartment is spotless.

The driver, wondering why you hesitate, twists slightly in his seat and says, "Well, are you going to get in?"

You don't have time to waste. You scan the passenger compartment once more and reassure yourself that there is nothing to foil your plans. You haul yourself into the cab, issue directions to Wal-Mart and sit back. At every stoplight, you see the little red man with the mustache watching and making sure you are following the instructions. . . . It doesn't occur to you how he can be at every intersection ahead of you with no visible means of transportation. No matter.

*Time passes. The cab stops. You look up. Wal-Mart. Already? For a moment you experience a brief ripple of doubt; maybe you should go back to University Hospital. Then you look out the window square into the eyes of the dancing red man with the mustache. The biohazmat symbol in satanic red and black pulsates around him, over him, through him, calling you. Other words pass briefly through your head—*Through him, with him, in him, *words of another sacrifice . . .*

You don't bother reading the meter, a few twenty-dollar bills should do. You slam the door behind you and disappear into the store. Do you wonder if the driver will read about you in the papers tomorrow morning? Do you care?

A rush of warm air hits your face. A cacophony of sound assaults you, the buzzers, bells, and clangs of modern cash registers, the squawk-

ing PA announcements, the clatter of carts and the screeching of metal wheels, the squealing and chatter of children. It has been ages since you were in a store alone. You've forgotten the overwhelming noise and how the bright lights and vivid colors flood your senses, confuse you. Like New York City at Christmas—so many people rushing around. You almost turn back. But the hazmat man is behind you, blocking the exit.

In that instant, the noise from the cash registers, the howling children, the bells all merge to dim background roar. The glaring lights and flashing colors slowly blend and fade to gray. Everything becomes a confusing blur except what lies directly in front of you; that path is crystal clear. It is as if you peer through a microscope and see details we human beings are not meant to see. You understand there is no escape, no way out, but forward.

Oblivious now and almost ecstatic, you push the gray plastic cart ahead of you up and down the aisles. You pick up a small jar of Crisco and toss it in the cart. "Not the little one, stupid! The biggest one!" You put it back and lug the biggest tub off the shelf and into the cart. Cooking oil is nearby and you look for the largest bottle. Lighters are easy; you will throw in a half dozen at the checkout kiosk.

The nightgown is more of a problem than you realized. You pick up a pink nightie that looks like something our mother would have worn twenty years ago. You glance at the size tag where in bold print it says, NON-FLAMMABLE. You pick up another—the same tag, the same print. Another and another. You look around for the hazmat man but you don't see him anywhere. Now what?

Then suddenly, thwamp, like the Concorde breaking the sound barrier, the real Wal-Mart world is sucked back to life like air into a vacuum. Suddenly all the fluorescent lights glare at you, flashing white hot on your retinas. You groan and press your head between your palms. The pain is unbearable. The nightgown will have to do. You throw one into the cart and race through checkout without bothering to take your change.

You don't know how you drag yourself home, but in the elevator at your apartment you have a momentary respite from light and sound.

Finally, the twelfth floor, the eleventh hour. In your apartment do you hesitate? Do you wonder even for an instant if you should go through with this? Do you question if you can stand the pain? Do you think about me and wonder what I will do? Do you think about how this one terrible act will scar me for life? Do you stop and ask God if he really wants you to do something so horrific?

Or do you methodically put the grocery bag on the table as if you were going to prepare dinner, take the gargantuan tub of Crisco out, banging it heavily on the counter, followed by the gown, the oil, the lighters.

Then do you strip quickly and throw your useless clothes in a clump on the floor? Do you get totally naked, or only uncover skin bit by bit, body part by part? Or knowing it may be your last, do you slip off each article, take off each piece one at a time, folding it carefully before placing it in a neat pile. Do you want me to know how deliberately this was planned? Do you wonder what I will think or feel?

How do you start? Do you look at yourself in the mirror? For all that you hate the expanse of flesh under the skin, do you wonder even for an instant if you will hate it still more if you survive? Do you have any tender good-byes for the skin that has faithfully clothed you, kept you warm for fifty years, grown with you as needed, protected you from microscopic assaults, warned you when danger was near, and allowed you to feel the difference between silk and steel? Do you whisper a halfhearted apology to the devalued flesh you are about to destroy, flesh which has been unfailingly loyal and without which you cannot live? Do you stop and ask yourself the question: do I have a right to do this? What will it do to Lynnie? What will it do to our family?

The details: How do you open the can? I haven't used Crisco in decades. Do you need a can opener or is it equipped with a pull-top lid these days? What does it look like? Is it white or does it have the sickening cast of jaundice? Does it smell? Do you grimace at the feel of the smeary stuff on your fingers? Do you think of the pies and pastries surely pictured on the glossy label? Does the Crisco feel squishy and slippery on your skin, coating like mud? Does it disgust you and make you want to throw up, so gross you hurry to get it done?

If you think at all, do you think of us, of me, your twin, as you make these final awful preparations? Do you remember Round Hill Road and our first bicycles, England and creamy rice pudding and Hampstead Heath and our best friend? Do wonder what I am doing at that very minute and what I will do afterward? Do you stop and consider writing a note or are you numb with fear, or dead to feeling anything at all except the inexorable march of time toward the final moment?

When you start the water in the tub do you wonder why bother with water at all? Do you turn on the warm faucet as well as the cold or do you figure it won't matter in the end? Will you stop and look around at your apartment, the pictures of us as children, the little girls who once mirrored each other, the books and videos you've shared, the poems and stories you've written, the book we are writing that you will abandon me to alone, adrift, bereft of the sister who made it make any sense at all?

When all is prepared will you wait, hoping for a knock to come at the door before you can act? Do you think to call me first or hope that I will intuit something through the air and call—that I will keep you on the phone and away from the lighter until EMS can rescue you? Does it occur to you to ignore the voices and demands of your demons and ask God to help you?

Or do you just pick up the lighter?

I don't want to imagine the rest of the gruesome scene. I never wanted to hear it. Can't I be protected from something? Must I always be the one to know, to help, to suffer, to bear? I hate you for doing this to me, infecting me, disturbing my sleep with the horrific details of your immolation.

And yet I would feel betrayed if you didn't tell me. I am trapped between wanting freedom from you and wanting you.

"Hail Mary, full of Grace, the Lord is with you. Blessed are you among women. Blessed is the fruit of your womb, Jesus. Holy Mary, Mother of God, pray for us sinners, now and at the hour of our death."

Carolyn

As I pull off Route 84 at Exit 39A, the buzzer tells me I have only a
few miles before I run out of gas. As luck would have it, the gas station across the street from the hospital is open and I swing my VW
up to the pump.

At least the hospital will be quiet at this hour on a Saturday. As I
wait for the tank to fill, anxiety thrums in my chest. When the command hallucinations and the pressure from the hazmat man to set
herself on fire became unbearable, Pammy herself begged for ECT.
She had her first treatment yesterday and I worry about her memory.
Will she remember that she consented to the treatment or will she
think I forced her?

Tank full, I return to the car. I've killed as much time as I can.
Pammy has been in University Hospital most of the summer and the
seventy-five minutes to Farmington has become routine. At the medical center I creep up the now familiar serpentine drive. As I round
the final bend at the crest of the hill, I spy the metal stick-figure
sculpture of a family looking out over the valley. I feel oddly tranquil.
Pammy and I, separate, have become individuals, our lives diverging
more than ever imagined. Schizophrenia or not, we are still twins,
still in some indefinable way part of each other, still one, connected
in some mystical way, bonded through genetics no matter what.

Though I do not live in schizophrenia as she does, I live under its shadow and am rocked by its unpredictable course. Though I try not to think of it too much, I know the statistics: I am likely to out-live her. Even though I still believe her illness opened a door for me many years ago, I no longer feel guilty about it. Life has a way of as-serting itself, and just when we think we've got it figured out, some-thing changes. For now, I am at peace with Pammy's schizophrenia. For now, hope is enough.

I park, gather my things, and lock the car. Fat cumulus clouds swell and merge on the distant horizon and seem to pummel each other like lovers, while above me the flawless sky is stained a virgin blue. On the sidewalk to the hospital lobby I pause and take in the view. I am grateful for the end-of-summer warmth and though I am alone, I am not lonely. In a deep breath, I smell the spicy notes of fall and a pang of sadness catches me by surprise.

$\mathcal{E}$PILOGUE

OCTOBER 2004

$\mathcal{P}amela$

As I read Lynnie's description of my hospitalizations in the fall of 2003, which ECT has largely erased from my memory, I am by turns horrified and ashamed. I cannot believe I've caused her so much anguish. It is a terrible thing to be psychotic; it is a horrible, frightening, and debilitating condition, the aftereffects of which can last for years. But I never understood quite so viscerally how difficult it is to be the helpless sister of someone who is psychotic. I can't even imagine how it is for the rest of the family. Ignorant of my effect on others—nursing staff, friends—I've lived inside the nightmarish fragments of a time and country beyond understanding, an everlasting present that has no connection to anything or anyone. I've been literally in a world of my own. Small, terrifying, and constricted as this world is, it's been all I know.

I don't remember the whys and wherefores of my raging and outrageous behavior in September; after ECT, I recall even less. Perhaps this is for the best: I did not behave like the kind of person I am when not in the throes of madness.

But madness it was, as anachronistic and moodily romantic as that term is. What else would you call it? I had no idea what I was doing or why. I acted solely upon impulse, delusion, and hallucination. That was my reality.

In catatonia, I abdicate living—not by choice, it's true, but nevertheless I am for that time effectively lifeless. And I come close to relinquishing life altogether in my compulsion—governed by the command hallucinations of the hazmat man—to burn myself alive to atone for imaginary crimes. My sin is in being, and I have to unbe, to burn in hell, literally to give myself over to the flames. I am dangerous, I am Satan, the ogre that ate Manhattan, and if I burn the mark of Cain onto my brow, I care little about scarring. All I want is to protect people from my essential evil, from me; my mere presence could poison them beyond remedy. Even in my most evil moments, moments when I feel that I need to destroy myself to save the world, I am still trying to preserve others.

Carolyn

I can never really know the hell in which Pammy lives. When I hang up the phone, hell disappears. But she knows nothing else. Hell is her life. When I look back over the past decades, I weep for her.

I weep for our mother and father, too. In the 1970s, psychiatry had few tools with which to treat schizophrenia and the diagnosis was feared perhaps more than cancer. The common misunderstanding then was that parents were somehow to blame for their child's schizophrenia—that something they did or failed to do was the cause. Now, it is understood that this is not so. But, even today, a diagnosis of schizophrenia brings horror, stigma, and denial. No parents should be blamed as our parents were, at least implicitly, for such a devastating disease. By operating as though unproven (and eventually disproved) psychodynamic theories were fact, my profession caused untold pain to our family and surely many other families already torn apart by an illness no one really understands.

Today, though supportive from a distance, our parents, siblings, and extended family are uneasy around Pammy. They fear that a wrong look or word will undo her fragile hold on reality. With good reason. At one time or another, each one of us has been the subject of her psychotic tempest. Dad, at first mistaking Pam's psychosis for willfulness, chose to withdraw rather than risk his feelings. But I believe that he never stopped loving Pammy, his firstborn. When he would say "she's dead to me," there were tears in his eyes. The earliest decade of her illness for him was a head-on collision with disappointment and shame. Pammy, the embodiment of his dreams, smothered by something he didn't recognize or understand. None of us did. Over the decades, Mom, worn down by years of bridging the gulf between daughter and husband, seemed to acknowledge defeat.

But in recent years, she joined me, Chip, and Martha when we began to stop accommodating Dad's attempt to wipe the pain of Pammy's life from his conversation, his life, his memory. We started talking in front of him about Pammy, her symptoms, her hospitalizations, her treatment. In early 2000, Mom went to see her at Newton Hospital, a difficult task made more excruciating, I'm sure, by her memories of Pammy's early hospital treatment. Soon after, Chipper and Martha and their families also visited the hospital. And, as they rallied to help me support Pammy, Dad's façade began to crumble.

Then, one day last spring, he walked back into her life as if he had never left.

Pamela

Thanks largely to Ada's long article in the Hartford paper the previous year, Daddy was finally able to take a brave step toward reconciliation. One miraculous day in 2004, during another hospitalization, he came, alone, to visit me for the first time since my college breakdown, accepting me just as I was at the time and just as I am today, without judgment, without rancor, without visible disappointment. I admire that immensely. It has meant the world to me.

Unlike Lynnie, who converted to Catholicism in 2003, I do not have the church to moor me, to harbor me, to keep my head above water during periods of crisis. To me, human history is forever marred by greed, evil, and injustice. If the universe is good or at least blameless, I can only believe that it must run on its own devices. Governed by its own laws, with its own forces that we know little of, it is a universe of paradox and inconsistency. We can but marvel at and accept it, with a Buddhist-like detachment making life bearable.

Life has a will of its own, I've come to understand, and it is not easy to let it go. I can live only in the now, happy to be well for the time being, and alive—but not overly attached to the possibilities of tomorrow.

$\mathcal{A}$CKNOWLEDGMENTS

There have been numerous people who have helped us in our writing, but in particular we'd like to thank E. Fuller Torrey, M.D., without whose helpful advice, this book, written in two voices, would not have been attempted. In addition, Sue Horton, who was at the *LA Weekly*, was the first person to encourage us to write in the memoir form.

These people, directly and indirectly, contributed: Joe and Lynda Balocca, Phil Becker, Roger Boshes, Ellen Brotherton, Maria Byron, Brian Chiko, Jan Choiniere, Joe Cornelio, Holly Gibson, Carol Goldberg, Mizzy Hanley, Paula Kirkpatrick, Mel Lewis, Tim Pritchett, Joyce Marcotte, Uncle Cy and Aunt Lynn Levine, Kenneth Liegner, Michael McAndrews, Kathy Megan, Lois Morton, Randy Ozar, Elissa Rosen, Ana Velasquez, and all the nurses at New England Home Care, Leila Raim, Linda Rost, Bob Sandine, Barbara Sax, Chickie Smith, George Vaillant, Dan Weisburd, Bill Williams, Penny Wolfson, all the staff at the hospitals that treated Pam after Y2K who supported us through the worst of times, St. Philip Church, and especially the RCIA, which transformed both of our lives in ways we are only just beginning to learn.

Thanks to Diane Higgins, acquisitions editor at St. Martin's Press, and associate editor Nichole Argyres, for ushering our book into the world. Most important of all we wish to thank Elizabeth

Frost Knappman, our agent/editor par excellence, whose expertise guided this book from start to finish.

Irene Kitzman has been like a sister to Carolyn, and extraordinarily generous with her time, her intellect, and her wisdom. She continues to be an unfailing champion for Pamela and an unflagging inspiration to both of us. We owe gratitude more than we can say.

We also wish to thank Mary B. O'Malley for getting Pamela through the many bad times as well as the good, and for knowing that we were capable of writing this book even when we did not.

We both thank Allie and Jeremy, Carolyn's children, for putting up with our moods, our feuds, and our panics, and for making it all worthwhile.

1. Before reading this book what did you think schizophrenia was? What do you think it is now?

2. The "crowns incident" was significant for both twins. How did this theme play out in the rest of the book? Talk about how childhood events, seemingly meaningless, can form and change you for the rest of your life.

3. It seems that Pam first experienced symptoms in 1963 when JFK was killed. If she had told her parents, teachers or Lynnie, how do you think they would have handled it at that time?

4. Carolyn reacted very differently, both to JFK's death and to adolescence in general. Do you think her response was "normal"?

A Reading Group Guide

5. How would you interpret the twins' experience of Gray Crinkled Paper? Is it only another one of Pam's delusions, or could it have a greater spiritual or metaphorical significance?

6. Treatment of schizophrenia has changed a great deal since the 60s although there is still a terrible stigma attached to having this illness. What do you think should be done to reduce the stigma surrounding mental illness?

7. This book was written in part to help others understand the experience of schizophrenia both from the viewpoint of the sufferer and the sibling. Has it succeeded? Why?

8. Carolyn becomes a psychiatrist while Pam gets sicker. Why doesn't she treat Pam herself? Do you think family members should treat their own siblings or children? Why or why not?

9. What role does writing play in Pam's life? Do you think it is true that madness and creativity go hand in hand?

10. From your own experience, what do you think of the current state of mental health care? Is it adequate? What changes would you make?

For more reading group suggestions, visit
www.readinggroupgold.com

St. Martin's
Griffin